THE
MONTESSORI
BABY

THE
MONTESSORI
BABY

A PARENT'S GUIDE TO NURTURING YOUR BABY WITH
LOVE, RESPECT, AND UNDERSTANDING

SIMONE DAVIES AND **JUNNIFA UZODIKE**

WORKMAN PUBLISHING | NEW YORK

Workman
Workman Publishing
Hachette Book Group, Inc.
1290 Avenue of the Americas
New York, NY 10104
workman.com

Workman is an imprint of Workman Publishing, a division of Hachette Book Group, Inc. The Workman name and logo are registered trademarks of Hachette Book Group, Inc.

Design by Galen Smith and Hiyoko Imai

The publisher is not responsible for websites (or their content) that are not owned by the publisher.

Workman books may be purchased in bulk for business, educational, or promotional use. For information, please contact your local bookseller or the Hachette Book Group Special Markets Department at special.markets@hbgusa.com.

Library of Congress Cataloging-in-Publication Data is available.

ISBN 978-1-5235-1240-9

First Edition March 2021

Printed in China on responsibly sourced paper.

10 9 8 7 6 5 4

To every baby,
may you be guided to develop your unique potential.
You are a gift.
—Simone

For Solu, Metu, and Biendu, my Montessori babies:
Thank you for teaching and inspiring me daily.
You are my greatest blessings.
—Junnifa

CONTENTS

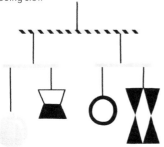

ONLINE RESOURCES

GO TO WORKMAN.COM/MONTESSORI FOR:

Junnifa's observations of Solu—birth to 15 weeks

Psychomotor development timeline

How to make a topponcino

How to make Montessori mobiles

How to make a patchwork ball

How to make rings on a peg or dowel

How to make rattles

How to make an object permanence box

How to make a ball tracker

INTRODUCTION

1

IT'S TIME TO CHANGE
THE WAY WE SEE BABIES

For a long time, people believed that babies were unable to understand what was going on around them. They thought babies couldn't "do much." "They just eat and sleep and cry a lot," people would say. Babies were treated as fragile. We were told we needed to wrap them up to protect them.

Then we discovered that babies are in fact learning so much in the early months, and we began to overparent them. We pushed them to learn faster and earlier. We compared our new baby to other babies, afraid that our baby wasn't developing fast enough.

We were told that we needed to buy the best gadgets for our baby: the best educational toys, the best clothing to cover every part of their body, a support for while they sleep, a device to help them sit up sooner, a bed that rocks them to sleep, monitors of every kind, and apps to track everything.

Let's stop.

Let's bring into focus this new life we have brought into the world. Let's look to our baby to see what their unique needs are; what they want to learn; and how we can support them in a more mindful, slower way.

> *What if we handled babies with respect and learned to ask their permission before handling them?*

> *What if we observed our baby first, rather than rushing to fix things?*

> *What if we saw babies as strong and capable, discovering the world around them like explorers, seeing everything for the first time?*

> *What if we realized that babies are already taking in everything from birth (even from in utero) with all their senses?*

What if changing diapers, feeding, and bedtime became moments of connection instead of chores to be rushed through?

What if we slowed down to make time for language and for conversation, even with a newborn baby?

What if we made time for babies to lie on a simple mat to stretch and learn about their bodies?

What if we didn't prop them up into positions that they are not yet ready for, like putting them up to sit or holding their hands to allow them to walk before their muscles are ready?

What if we recognized that a baby has points of reference—their hands, our voices, the places we feed them, and the rhythm of our days—that help orient them?

What if we let go of everything we are told we need to buy, and instead provide a simple, beautiful space for our baby?

What if we learned to see that every baby is a unique soul, and that we are here to be their guide on this planet, to support them to grow into the best version of themselves, without pressure from us, and without feeling abandoned?

What if we lie in the woods, on the beach, in the park, and in the mountains, and exposed them to the awe and wonder of nature?

OUR MONTESSORI STORIES

When Simone's first baby was born, she remembers feeling deeply moved by the ability to create new life. She did the best she could with the information she had, but all became a lot clearer when she found the Montessori approach when her son was around 18 months old. And, like many parents, she wished she had learned these principles earlier.

With her second baby, Simone applied everything she had learned about Montessori as best she could. Since then she completed her Montessori training (over 15 years ago); her little babies are now young adults, and she's been helping families apply the Montessori principles with their own babies through her parent–baby Montessori classes at Jacaranda Tree Montessori in Amsterdam.

Junnifa was working as a strategy manager for an automotive company in Kentucky, when she serendipitously discovered Montessori. She had accompanied her mother, a teacher, on a visit to a Montessori school and was so moved by what she observed that she decided to take a 6-week introduction to Montessori course to learn more.

Junnifa completed the AMI 0–3 diploma training one week before the birth of her first child. She implemented what she learned and was amazed by the positive effects it had on her parenting and on her child. She started her blog, nduoma.com, to share her experiences. Hungry for more, she continued to expand her knowledge of child development. She completed the AMI diploma courses for the 3–6 and 6–12 age groups as well as the Resources for Infant Educarers (RIE) training.

Junnifa now runs her own Montessori school called Fruitful Orchard Montessori School in Abuja, Nigeria, where she lives with her husband and three young children. Junnifa sits on the executive board for the Association Montessori International (AMI), the organization founded by Dr. Montessori to preserve and propagate her work.

The birth of this book came about effortlessly. Junnifa was visiting Amsterdam from Nigeria for some AMI board meetings and came over to Simone's for some home-cooked food. We were just planning to catch up but within an hour we realized we both wanted to write a book about Montessori for babies. By the time Junnifa departed just a few hours later, we had eaten some tasty food and drafted the outline for the book you are holding today.

Every parent and child can benefit from the Montessori approach from the first weeks, the first days, the first hours—and even while our baby is in utero.

Babies are natural learners from birth, not empty vessels to be filled. They are observing everything. They communicate with gurgles and different cries. They never stop moving.

As Dr. Maria Montessori wrote in her book *The Absorbent Mind*:

> "[A baby] is by no means passive. While undoubtedly receiving impressions, he is an active seeker in his world. He himself is looking for impressions."

May we all learn from this book how to apply Montessori in our homes from birth, how to respond to our babies' cries, how to know which activities they are looking for, how to set up our homes—and how to do the work we need to do as parents to raise secure babies who are ready to explore the world around them with confidence and respect for themselves, others, and the Earth.

WHY WE LOVE BABIES

It's true that babies demand a lot of time, they wake us during the night, they leave us exhausted, and sometimes they cry inconsolably for hours. So why do we love babies?

Babies remind us of how innocent we are when we come into this world. When we see a newborn baby, we can't help but see how every person started life in this way, without any judgment, without any fears, without any baggage. Just as themselves.

Babies give us hope for the future. The birth of a new child and our hope for their new life lead us to hope for a better world for them. That they will love learning, that they will learn to care for humanity and the Earth, and that there will be no violence or war.

Babies are seeing the world for the first time. We love observing a baby take in the world around them. The way they look and explore everything for the first time. Our faces, a leaf, the sun peeking through a branch. It reminds us to look again with fresh eyes at the world around us with wonder.

Babies don't give up easily. We can sit and watch a baby stretch for their toes and try to bring them to their mouth again and again until they finally reach them. A baby will bat at a ball on a string until they master accurate movements. Babies learn to persevere if we give them the chance.

Babies say what they need. A baby doesn't think, "Is this a good time to ask?" They use their cries to tell us that they have a dirty diaper, that they are hungry or tired, or that they are all done with whatever they are playing with. We might be able to distract them for some time, but they will keep insisting until their needs are met. This directness is a handy skill to have.

Babies smell so good. Ha! But it's so true. Why do babies smell so good? There is nothing better than the smell of a freshly bathed baby.

Babies are new human life. It is a powerful experience to create another human life, and research shows that we are wired to look after babies. And we ask ourselves, "How can something so small be so perfectly created?"

WHAT WE NEED TO KNOW ABOUT BABIES

In past generations, most people grew up with a lot of babies around. We shared homes with parents and grandparents, and cousins, nieces, and nephews would be in and out of each other's homes, with older children looking after the babies of the extended family.

Simone was the youngest child in her family. The first baby she spent a lot of time with, other than while babysitting, was her son.

She read some books, attended some birth and prenatal yoga classes, but she felt largely unprepared for looking after her son. It was trial and error. Getting him to sleep was not easy (a complicated sequence of rocking him and singing), but luckily feeding went well. Simone prided herself on taking him wherever she went, even in the very early days. She cooked food while he napped and played with him nonstop when he was awake. She didn't want him to cry, so if nothing else would work, she would feed him again.

Looking back she understands that she made a lot of extra work for herself. She hadn't yet learned to observe her son's natural rhythm, let him explore on his own, and trust that he didn't need an adult to entertain him full-time.

Here's what she wished she had known.

Babies are absorbing everything. Babies are exhibiting what Dr. Montessori identified as *the absorbent mind*. Babies may not be able to focus more than 12 inches (30 cm) in front of their face, but they are already taking in as much visual information as they can. They also absorb the smells, the space around them (for example, if it is light/dark, cluttered/calm, warm/cold), and the feeling of touch on their bodies. They hear the sounds of our daily life, our voices, music, and moments of silence. They taste their fingers, the milk, and anything that goes into their mouths.

We can have conversations with babies. Here we don't mean just speaking to a baby. We mean speaking *with* a baby and waiting for their response—even with newborns. The conversation needn't be verbal. We can lay our baby on our forearms with their head cradled in our hands, face-to-face. We can poke out our tongue. Wait. Watch. They try to open their mouth. Their tongue comes out. We respond by poking out our tongue. And so it continues.

Babies need time to move and explore. A baby needs time to lie on a mat on the ground and stretch their whole body. Even newborns can lie on a mat, a mirror beside them, as they start to see what it's like to move their limbs and interact with the world around them, and notice how things respond to their efforts. We can support them by giving them as little help as possible and as much as necessary.

Babies need to be treated gently, but they are not fragile. We need to be sensitive to their transition from the womb to the outside world (a period of symbiosis) and handle them gently with a respectful touch. And at the same time, we don't need to wrap them up and over-coddle them. They can have their hands, feet, and head uncovered (if the home is warm enough), so they can have free movement. Their neck and head will get stronger in the first weeks and won't need extra support after too long.

Babies are building trust in their environment, their caregivers, and themselves. During the first 9 months—sometimes referred to as extero-gestation or the external pregnancy—the baby is still adjusting to being in their new environment. They are working on building trust in their environment and in themselves and learning to rely on their parents (and any other caregivers).

In the first year, babies move from dependence, to collaboration, to independence. At birth a baby relies on the adults for their food, shelter, clothing, diapering, and to transport them from place to place (dependence). As they grow, we invite the baby to take part in the process—asking them to raise their arms while dressing, explaining what we are doing as we prepare meals, giving them time to touch and explore the things around them (collaboration). Before the end of the first year, a baby is taking steps toward independence—sometimes actual physical steps, as well as voluntarily choosing a toy and making it work, calling out or making a sign to express themselves, bringing food to their own mouth to eat, confident of their place in the world (independence).

Babies thrive from a secure attachment. When we lay the foundation of a strong and secure attachment, the baby feels safe to explore, to move toward independence over time. They learn to rely on us, to trust us, that we will respond to them and give any help or support (if needed). "Secure attachment" in attachment theory is where one's needs for closeness and food are usually consistently met as a baby. Attachment creates the deep emotional connection between baby and primary caregiver(s), a bond that endures over time.

Babies will cry to communicate their needs. Some people are able to tell why their baby is crying. Sometimes the cries will all sound the same. We can become a detective. We ask them, "What are you telling me?" as we observe them. We respond, rather than react. We don't simply pick them up and start bouncing them to stop them crying. Because first we need to see *what they are telling us.*

Babies don't need so much stuff. The principle of *less is more* applies to babies. Some loving arms, a place to stretch, a place to sleep, adequate nutrition for their belly, and a warm and cozy home to explore. These are the things a baby needs. We do suggest some Montessori activities in this book, but we could buy nothing at all and still practice Montessori at home. Montessori is less about the stuff and more about looking at our baby, accepting them for who they are, seeing how we can meet their needs, and supporting them to independence, which will continue throughout toddlerhood, childhood, and adolescence.

Babies gain security from points of reference. As they discover the world around them, they will come to look to *points of reference*. These are things in their daily life that help them to orient themselves. These can be their hands, our voices, the space where they lie to sleep, where they feed, and the daily rhythm (doing things in the same way each and every day). Such predictability provides reassurance to the baby.

Babies know a lot that we don't know. When we look into a baby's eyes, there is a lot of mystery waiting to be discovered. They are saying to us, "If you want to learn about me, watch me." Observation becomes a form of respect—we observe our baby before responding and learn to understand them better.

HOW TO READ THIS BOOK

This book has answers to the questions we get asked every day about raising babies in a Montessori way. It can be read from cover to cover. Or picked up and opened to any page for some inspiration.

The book covers what we need to know about babies, how we can set up our homes for them to feel secure and welcome (we don't need much), how to observe our baby to see what they are practicing in the moment, and how we can support their development. It addresses all the practical questions about eating and sleeping (and the Montessori floor bed) and explores all the ways to build a respectful bond with our baby.

Don't overlook the chapters on the work we adults can do to prepare ourselves for parenting in a Montessori way (like letting go of our own desires for who our children will become) and how we will work with others in our baby's lives (from grandparents to caregivers to partners) who are so important in parenting our babies. And we won't leave you hanging—we'll also cover what is coming next as our babies become young toddlers, and a little about what to expect from Dr. Montessori's observation of children from right at birth through 24 years old.

There are handy checklists throughout the book for easy reference, observation exercises, and at the end of each chapter there are practical suggestions on how to get started. In the appendices, there is also a comprehensive list of activities by age and a month-by-month guide to refer back to often. (We've also provided some DIY instructions for some Montessori mobiles and activities, which can be found online at workman.com/montessori.) And in chapter 9 (page 236), there is one of our favorite pages in the book—a note from our baby to visiting grandparents, friends, and caregivers, which can be copied and hung somewhere visible.

The principles in this book are based on our Montessori training with the Association Montessori Internationale and on our experience working with families and raising our own children. All of this is derived from what Dr. Montessori has written about infancy, as well as her collaborations with her students Adele Costa Gnocchi and Grazia Honegger Fresco, who have been largely responsible for developing Montessori's vision of the youngest children—this includes creating the Assistants to Infancy training (by Costa Gnocchi) and the Montessori Birth Center in Rome (where Honegger Fresco was honorary president up to her passing in 2020). Dr. Silvana Montanaro was also a contributor to this work, and we draw on many supportive principles from Emmi Pikler's work, the RIE approach, and the principles of respectful parenting.

We wrote this book to speak for the babies in utero, those just born, or rolling, or sitting, or crawling, or taking their first steps. They want us to know that they are all unique souls, born into our homes for us to care for them in a way that they will feel secure, respected, and loved. That we will help them grow from a baby dependent on us for all their needs, to a baby who is able to collaborate and communicate with us, and by the end of the first year, moving toward increasing independence as a curious child ready to explore the world even more.

We can give our baby the message: "You are capable and respected. We want to be present for you, we seek to understand you and your needs, and we will do our best to be patient." We can learn how to handle our babies with love and respect and to support them to build their trust in themselves and their surroundings (including us).

Every baby is unique. No baby has walked or talked in the same way, fallen asleep in exactly the same way, or fed at the same time as every other baby.

May this book allow you to observe the joy of your growing baby. Observe the smallest ways in which they are developing and changing every day, hour, and minute. May they never lose that joy and wonder.

Here's to learning more about our Montessori babies.

WHAT BABIES ARE REALLY TELLING US

Instead of thinking they don't understand

They want us to tell them what is going on and treat them with respect

Instead of nonsense baby talk

They want real connection and conversation where we take turns

Instead of the latest gadgets

They want a simple, beautiful, inviting space to explore

Instead of being picked up quickly from behind to have a diaper changed (or hearing that it stinks)

They want to be able to see us, be asked if they are ready to be picked up, and have time to respond

Instead of distracting them when they are crying

They want us to pause, observe, ask what they need, then respond

Instead of allowing anyone to touch or kiss them

They want us to ask them first

Instead of being overstimulated

They want to have one or two things to interact with

Instead of interrupting them when they are playing

They want us to wait until they are finished concentrating

Instead of putting them into a sitting or standing position before they are ready

They want us to follow their unique development and let them master this for themselves

Instead of rushing through eating, bathing, and changing diapers

They want to use these activities as moments for connection with us

Instead of sitting in front of a screen

They want to interact with the real world

Instead of rushing through our busy days

They want us to handle them gently, mindfully, and slowly

MONTESSORI PRINCIPLES FOR BABIES

2

WHAT?

MONTESSORI EDUCATION FOR BABIES?

You may be encountering Montessori for the first time, you may know of Montessori but perhaps did not know it could be applied at home or specifically to babies, or you may already know about Montessori and babies. This section can be an introduction for beginners or a refresher for those already familiar, as it will provide an overview of Montessori education and how it applies specifically to babies.

This education that we speak about in Montessori does not just happen in a classroom and is not limited to the traditional notion of an instructor teaching a child. Instead, it involves everything that we do with children and everything that they experience from the very beginning.

Montessori is a philosophy that looks to support the natural development of each child to their maximum potential. It views education as a tool to aid this process and believes such learning can start from birth. This means that it can be applied to babies, too.

> "The first hour of education is the hour after birth. From the moment the senses of the newborn child begin to receive impressions from nature, nature educates them. It takes great strength to be able to wait patiently for them to mature."
>
> —Johann Heinrich Pestalozzi

A BRIEF HISTORY OF MONTESSORI

Dr. Maria Montessori was an Italian medical doctor and scientist with a background in anthropology. Montessori education grew out of her work with children with learning differences. Dr. Montessori believed that the children needed to nourish their minds in addition to their bodies. She recognized that they needed more stimulation, so she incorporated materials and techniques developed by French physicians Jean-Marc-Gaspard Itard and Edouard Seguin. After working with the children for a while, she registered them for a statewide exam. The results were inspiring. The children did very well, exceeding expectations, and she began to wonder if her newfound method could work for other children.

An opportunity came for her to try out her ideas on children without learning differences, when the developers of a housing project in San Lorenzo invited Dr. Montessori to build classrooms for the children who would be living there. She called these classrooms *Casa dei Bambini*, meaning "children's house."

Dr. Montessori observed the children in the children's house much like a scientist conducting an experiment. She made modifications based on her observations and was astonished by her findings. She discovered that there were many misconceptions about children and that, given the right environment, they flourished in ways that had not been previously thought possible. They were capable, careful, kind, unselfish, and able to teach themselves if there was a rich learning environment to explore. People visited the San Lorenzo children's house from around the world to study her program and take her training. They then went home to start their own schools and programs.

Her trainings were often taken by young mothers who would come with their babies. Dr. Montessori observed these babies and noticed that they were more conscious and capable than most people believed them to be. This piqued her interest. She continued to observe these babies and wrote about her ideas. She later collaborated with prenatal clinic workers and went on to start a birth center, an infant school, and training programs for "Assistants to Infancy" in Rome.

Dr. Montessori came to believe that education should begin from the moment of birth.

WHAT IS MONTESSORI?

Montessori is different from the top-down learning of traditional education, where the teacher stands at the front of the classroom and tells children what they need to learn. Instead, Montessori sees every child (and baby) as unique, with their unique way of learning, unique interests, and unique timeline.

The Montessori educator sets up the classroom as a rich learning environment. The child has the freedom to choose an activity they wish to work on (either by themselves or with another child or in groups), and the teacher will observe to see who needs help or who needs a new lesson. With mixed ages, the older children will be modeling for the younger children and are able to help them. In doing so, the older children reinforce their own learning. And the younger children naturally learn so much by observing the older children.

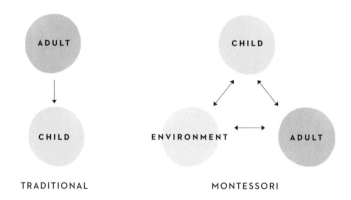

Observing a Montessori classroom for the first time, it's hard to believe that no one is telling the children what to do and that they are self-motivated to master new skills and acquire new knowledge.

Similarly, in our homes and with our babies, we can set up beautiful spaces with inviting objects and activities for our babies to explore, we can observe when they need help, and we can allow them to make discoveries for themselves.

SOME IMPORTANT MONTESSORI PRINCIPLES

The Montessori philosophy is based on some foundational principles, which include an understanding of our child's nature, characteristics, and needs. Understanding these principles is key in applying Montessori to our babies.

1. Absorbent mind

The absorbent mind is a special state of mind that children possess from birth until around the age of 6. It allows them to learn easily and pick up the characteristics and cultural elements of their immediate environment. They do this unconsciously and without effort. They see and hear things around them, they take them in, and then one day, without having made any effort, they replicate what they have taken in. It is the absorbent mind that makes it easy for children to learn language spoken in their environment. It is why children pick up the same gestures as the people they spend time with, or easily learn to dance when surrounded by dancers. Every aspect of the environment—tangible (like language) or intangible (like our attitudes)—is absorbed by our youngest children.

There is a common experiment in elementary school where children place a plant or celery stalk in a cup of water with some food coloring in it. The children observe the leaves and petals as they change color. This is exactly how the absorbent mind of the child works—it absorbs the characteristics of the environment, and these characteristics then become an inseparable part of the child.

The absorbent mind is a great tool, but like most great tools, its benefits depend on its use. It is an enormous opportunity, as well as an enormous responsibility.

> "He absorbs the life going on about him and becomes one with it."
>
> —Dr. Maria Montessori, *The Absorbent Mind*

Knowing this is a great gift to us as parents. We can model the behaviors and attitudes we want our child to adopt, surround our child with beauty and nature, speak to them using rich language, and give them rich experiences, knowing that even from birth, they are absorbing all of these things, which become an indelible part of them.

2. Human tendencies

Humans are born with natural instincts or inclinations. These human tendencies guide our behaviors, perceptions, and reactions to our experiences.

When we understand what might be driving our babies' behavior—their standard human tendencies—we are better able to perceive and interpret their needs and respond appropriately.

Some human tendencies that are evident in infancy are:

Orientation

This is the desire to know where we are, to familiarize ourselves with our surroundings, and to have an idea of what is happening around us. As adults, when we go to a new place, we often try to orient ourselves with familiar landmarks. We might also find a person familiar with the place who can guide or direct us. This need is also present in babies. They too have a need to be familiar with their surroundings and what is happening around them. We can help them by providing familiar markers or connections.

When the baby is first born, the earth is a brand-new environment without "points of reference." But the mother's voice and heartbeat—both of which the baby would have heard in the womb—are familiar landmarks, or points of reference, that can help them orient to their new surroundings. The baby's hands are another familiar landmark. They have touched their face and moved their limbs while in utero, so they can find comfort in these familiar friends. We often unknowingly take away these references when we put gloves on the baby's hands or dress or wrap our baby in a way that restricts access to their hands or to free movement.

Soon, a hanging mobile, a picture in the baby's room, furniture, or designated places for different activities can all serve as points of reference for the baby. The baby will continue to add new ones as they grow, but a caregiver's presence and voice will continue to serve as landmarks for the baby through infancy.

Order

As human beings, we desire consistency. It is the same for babies. Order and consistency are what help them to orient themselves and to feel secure. In our baby's surroundings, there needs to be a place for everything, and things needs to be in their place. The baby's days and activities need to be predictable. We can help them by creating orderly environments and developing routines and cues that will help them anticipate where they are or what comes next. We can make a place for everything— starting with a place for feeding, a place for sleeping, a place for physical care, and a place for movement and playing. We can go further and have a fixed place for objects in the environment.

Communication

Communication is how we share our feelings, experiences, thoughts, and needs. Humans are able to communicate from birth. Babies communicate with their gestures, body language, cries (yes, they are letting us know they need something), babbles, and, eventually, with their words. In the same way, they pay attention to, absorb, and gradually begin to understand our communication with them. From the very beginning, we are programmed for two-way communication.

Therefore, we can communicate with our baby by talking to them, smiling, gesturing appropriately, and also being conscious of our body language. Even the way we touch the baby is a form of communication and a message to them. We can also pay attention, listen, and look to understand the baby's communication to us, and in so doing we can meet their needs.

Exploration and Activity

Humans are explorers. We interact with our surroundings to understand and master them. Babies look at things, taste them, smell them, touch them, move them around, bang them, throw them, and generally explore. This is how they come to understand how things work. We need to allow opportunities for this exploration. We can provide the baby with things to explore, give them time to explore, and make the environment safe for exploration.

Solving Problems

We humans are problem solvers who need to use our mathematical mind. We often unknowingly rob babies of the opportunities to meet this need. You might wonder how a baby could solve problems. It can be as simple as reaching out for a toy rather than having it placed in their hand. Or using their senses of smell and sight to find the nipple of their mother or bottle instead of having it put in their mouth for them. Or crawling the distance to get a ball versus having the ball brought to them. Or figuring out how to free their hand when it is stuck under them. These little opportunities allow the baby to figure out distance, consider options, and solve problems, thus meeting the human tendency of a mathematical mind. We can support this tendency in the baby by allowing opportunities for free play and exploration.

Repetition

Watch a baby who is learning to sit, stand, or walk. Often, the baby pulls up to a stand, sits or kneels, and then stands right back up. They do this repeatedly if they are not interrupted. Repetition is a human tendency that allows us to master skills. When we observe babies repeating an action, instead of assuming they are struggling, need help, or might be bored, we can allow the opportunity and time for repetition.

Abstract Images and Imagination

Abstraction is the ability to see beyond the concrete, to interpret and generalize. It means envisioning ideas, concepts, or things that are not physically present. From a very early age, we are able to see things that are not right in front of us and imagine solutions to our needs. The baby learns they have a mother or father even when that parent is absent. They look for things that are not present.

This need and ability to imagine also helps us solve our problems and meet our own needs. To imagine and abstract requires a knowledge and understanding of reality. The baby is able to understand what a cup is and what it is used for because they have seen one, used one, or seen another person use one. A baby of 7 months who has used a cup before will try to drink from another object shaped like a cup. From very early on, we will observe babies using remote controls as phones.

While this tendency becomes stronger and more apparent as the baby becomes older, it is present from birth. So babies too need many hands-on experiences, because their ability to imagine and abstract is built on this.

3. Sensitive periods

A sensitive period is a moment of time when the baby develops an irresistible attraction or interest in something. It could be an action/skill or a particular aspect of the environment. We can usually tell when the baby is in a sensitive period because they show intense repeated interest in that area. Sensitive periods are like spotlights that focus the baby's absorbent mind on certain aspects of their surroundings.

There is a sensitive period for movement, from rolling over to crawling and walking. There are also sensitive periods for language, introduction of solids, and small objects. Each of these sensitive periods allows the baby to gain new skills and grow more independent.

Some of the sensitive periods in infancy are:

Order: Babies are in a sensitive period for order. They seem to crave order in tangible and intangible ways. A baby who is always placed on the left side of their bed might notice and react negatively when placed on the right side. We can help the baby by preparing an orderly environment where everything has a place. We can also be as consistent as possible in our processes and routines when caring for the baby. Just as with helping them get oriented (see page 16), we provide landmarks or points of reference to help the child absorb the order. These points of reference could be auditory (a sound or a song) or even olfactory (a scent that tells the child it is time for bed or another that signals time for food).

Movement: From birth, children are in a sensitive period for movement. In the first year of life, they pass through and master many stages of movement. They learn to reach, grasp, roll, crawl, sit, stand, and walk, along with many stages in between these ones. There is a lot of practice that is required to progress through each stage of movement. We can help the baby maximize this period by preparing a safe environment where they can move and also allow time and opportunity to move.

Language: This is another sensitive period present from birth. It is associated with the human tendency for communication. Because of our need to communicate, from birth the spotlight is on language so that the baby can acquire the skills needed for communication. If we observe a baby of even 3 months when an adult is talking to them, we will see how they focus on the sound and watch the movement of the adult's lips. They work hard to make their own sounds and create language. Most of this work is not seen in the beginning, but it is happening.

We can help by talking to the baby from the very beginning and using rich, beautiful language. We don't need to dumb down sentences or use imaginary words. Instead, we use the most beautiful words we can, name objects that the baby encounters, talk to them about what is happening around them, and also listen and acknowledge when they communicate using sound and babbles.

From the beginning of the baby's life, we can get into the habit of conversing with our baby. When we pick them up in the morning we can say, "Good morning, sunshine! Did you sleep well?" Wait for a response. It might be a smile or a slight movement, and you can respond accordingly: "Yes you did. Today we are going to take a walk to the park, but first, let's change your diaper. May I pick you up?"

Eating solids: This includes the introduction of solids and learning about their bodies. There is a time when the baby starts to show interest in food, reaching for our food and literally drooling. This is also usually around the time when the baby's teeth are coming in. This is the ideal time to gently begin the process of introducing solids.

Assimilation of images and small objects: During the period from birth to age 3, children seem to be very interested in details and small objects. They enjoy looking at images and will stare intently for extended periods. We can provide images for the babies at their level and give them time to enjoy them. When we notice our baby staring at something, if we are carrying them and moving, stop and give them time to take it in. We will notice when they lose interest. Take slow walks and just allow them to look. As they get older, they may also enjoy looking at book illustrations that have rich details.

4. Observation

Now that we know the nature of the baby's mind, their needs and tendencies, and how the sensitive periods work, we can only put this knowledge into use in our parenting by observing.

When we observe the baby, we will start to see these characteristics at work and catch glimpses of what might be going on inside the baby. Observation is really the key to implementing Montessori with our baby. It is what helps us get to know our individual baby and respond appropriately.

Observation allows us to:

- **Understand and follow the baby's development:** When we observe the baby, we can notice subtle changes in their abilities and provide an environment and activities that offer the right challenge. It is through observation that we can tell if the baby's human tendencies are being served. Are they able to explore freely? Are they getting opportunities for repetition?

- **Notice the baby's efforts and abilities:** See how the baby interacts with the environment: How are they using their senses to interact with the environment? Observing with their eyes? Tasting? Touching? Testing? Trying to modify? Are their actions intentional? What might be their intention?

- **Identify sensitive periods:** Where is the baby's interest and activity focused right now? What are they constantly returning to, repeating, or concentrating on?

- **Recognize and remove obstacles to the baby's development:** What are the obstacles to their movement, communication, and activity? What might be interfering with their independence?

- **Know when to help and what kind of help to offer:** For example, if the baby is trying to crawl, but their clothing is restricting their movement, we can choose alternate clothing or gently help them remove a foot from the hem of their clothing.

Junnifa discovered the power of observation with her first baby.

During her son's first 3 months, he would nap on her bed. He usually slept for about 2 to 2.5 hours. Around 3 months, she decided to move him to his floor bed in his room (we explain the floor bed in detail later on page 59). She would hold him in her arms until he fell asleep and then lay him down. She thought naps would be a good way to transition him to his room, and then they would gradually move to night sleeping in his bed. However, when she would put him down for his nap, he would wake up around 40 minutes later. This was much shorter than his usual 2 hours, so she immediately thought the floor bed was not working. She talked to one of her Montessori mentors, Pilar Bewley, who asked Junnifa what she had noticed when observing her son. Junnifa realized that she hadn't been observing him at all.

So when she put him down for a nap in her room the next day, she stayed and observed. She noticed he slept around 40 minutes and then he woke up, lifted his head, looked around, and then went right back to sleep and slept for a little more than 2 hours in total. The next day, she did the same but in his room. She put him down, and right around 40 minutes, he woke up just like the day before, lifted his head, and looked around, and she noticed a change on his face. He did not recognize where he was. He was disoriented! He started to cry, she picked him up. . . . She had figured out the problem.

Over the next couple of days, Junnifa and her son spent more time in his room when he was awake. She now knew that he woke up around the 40-minute mark during his nap, so she would stay close so that when he looked around, he would see her—his landmark—and he would go back to sleep. She also put a picture of their family on his headboard and gradually started watching from a distance. He would wake up, look around, stare at the picture for a little while, and go back to sleep. Junnifa stopped checking after a few days, and he would only make a sound when he woke up after about 2 hours. Observation helps us understand our baby's behaviors, needs, and tendencies, and how to respond to them.

(continued on page 24)

SOME THINGS WE CAN OBSERVE

MOVEMENT

- Physical response to visual or auditory stimuli
- Reflexive movements; intentional movements

FINE-MOTOR SKILLS

- How they grasp and hold objects
- Which fingers and which hand they use
- What grip they use on a rattle or spoon
- What fine-motor skills they are practicing, such as using their pincer grip or fingers against palm

GROSS-MOTOR SKILLS

- How they come to stand or sit
- How they walk—distance of legs or arm movements
- Balance
- Whether they choose gross-motor activities
- Whether the environment helps or hinders their movement

COMMUNICATION

- Sounds they make to communicate
- Smiling
- Crying—intensity, volume, duration
- Body language
- How they express themselves
- Eye contact during conversations
- Language used
- How we respond to their communication

COGNITIVE DEVELOPMENT

- What they are interested in
- What they are practicing and learning to master
- The activities they can complete
- How long they stay with an activity
- Times they repeat an activity or explore in another way

SOCIAL DEVELOPMENT

- Interactions with others—siblings, other babies/children, and adults
- Whether they observe others
- How they ask for help
- Whether they initiate interactions
- How others respond to their attempts
- How they respond to people they don't know

EMOTIONAL DEVELOPMENT

- When the baby cries, smiles, and laughs
- How they are best comforted or comfort themselves
- How they respond to strangers
- How they deal with moments of separation
- How they manage when things do not go their way

FEEDING

- Breast or bottle, including amount or length of time feeding
- What they eat and how much
- How is/was schedule established
- Who is feeding the baby
- How the baby detaches from feeding
- Whether they are passive or active eaters—being fed or feeding themselves
- Whether self-feeding is encouraged or taught
- If eating solids, what foods they are offered and how often
- Response of adults to feeding attempts, communication attempts, body positions

SLEEPING

- Sleep/wake rhythm
- Night schedule
- How they fall asleep
- Quality of sleep
- Position during sleep
- How they transition to waking—length of time, temperament upon waking

INDEPENDENCE

- Symbiotic relationship with mother and other family members
- Whether there are aids or hindrances to the growth of independence

CLOTHING

- Whether the clothing helps or hinders movement and independence
- Whether they try to put on or take off their own clothing
- Whether they express preferences for their clothing

SELF-OBSERVATION

- Record our communication—what we say and how we interact with our baby
- What comes up for us as we observe our baby
- How do we respond if our baby does not eat or sleep
- What we say when our baby does something we like or don't like

(continued from page 21)

We can observe on-the-go and informally. Whenever we spend time with our babies, we can watch them with a desire to truly see and understand. We can also set out time to routinely formally observe and write what we see, like a scientist studying their movements, their sounds; the things they focus on; how they eat, sleep, play; and any social interactions.

Observation leads to an even deeper understanding and love for the baby, and a respect for their abilities.

- When we are actively observing, we can try to be as invisible as possible so that we are seeing the baby's actions independent of our presence.

- When we notice that the baby is focused on something, even something as simple as looking at their own hands or playing with their feet, it is important to not interrupt. When we observe, we start to recognize the baby's amazing capabilities, and it can be tempting to praise or acknowledge in that moment, but as much as possible, we should remember to enjoy observing and not interfere with or break the baby's focus.

5. Prepared environment

Dr. Montessori called the spaces we create for learning "the prepared environment." When we look at our baby's needs, we can set out exactly what they need for their development, and we can adjust them as our baby grows. This can be indoor physical spaces, outdoors in nature, and even the people in our baby's life. A rich place for learning, where they feel safe and secure to explore.

> "The period of infancy is undoubtedly the richest. It should be utilized by education in every possible and conceivable way. The waste of this period of life can never be compensated. Instead of ignoring the early years, it is our duty to cultivate them with the utmost care."
>
> —Dr. Alexis Carrel (quoted by Dr. Montessori in *The Absorbent Mind*)

TO PRACTICE

- Are we being thoughtful about what our baby will absorb?
- Have we noticed any examples of our baby reflecting back what they see or experience?
- What familiar points of reference are we providing to help our baby orient?
- Are we slowing down and allowing our baby time and opportunity to take in the details of the environment?
- Are we making time to get to know our baby better by observing them?
- Can we begin to look at our spaces—our prepared environment—to see what we are offering our baby?

FROM CONCEPTION TO THE FIRST 6 WEEKS

3

We know that there will be a range of families who will be coming to this book. In the past, Montessori has held a fairly traditional view, centering the mother as the primary caregiver. Of course, this traditional arrangement does not reflect many of today's families. Raising our babies the Montessori way is possible no matter who takes on the role of primary caregiver and in families with equal co-parents. The same goes for mothers who choose not to or cannot breastfeed, adoptive parents who were not present for gestation or the early weeks or months of a baby's life, and for parents who return to work outside the home not long after the baby is born. The promise of this book is to give everyone the tools to adapt the Montessori principles and apply them in ways that work for their individual family constellations.

We encourage all new parents to read the following sections, whether they are carrying the baby or not, as there are helpful things to learn about the baby in utero and about the birth mother's experience.

CONCEPTION:
PREPARING THE BABY'S FIRST ENVIRONMENT

In utero is our baby's first *prepared environment*. Even before we conceive, we can give a lot of thought to the physical and emotional environment in which we welcome our baby.

Physically, we want our bodies to be strong. We can spend time learning about how to care for our body to get ready to carry a baby (for a birth mother), how to make healthy sperm (for a birth father), and how to get emotionally ready to welcome the baby (including for adoptive parents or parents who are not carrying their child).

We can also prepare our emotional environment, adding the ingredients of love and acceptance so our baby arrives knowing that they are welcomed and loved. When a baby is unplanned, the work of the adult is to come to a place of acceptance during the pregnancy so that the baby feels wanted and loved. We can say to the baby we are conceiving or that has been conceived, "You are so wanted. You are so loved."

Part of preparing our environment to welcome our baby is getting to know what is involved in caring for and raising a baby. Parenting is a challenging 24/7 job for 18-plus years of life. At the same time, it is also beautiful to bond with a child and help them grow into the best version of themselves. We can read books. Even better, we can spend time (preferably full days) in someone's home helping to look after their baby to see what it involves.

If we have a partner, we can begin conversations before conception and during pregnancy about our hopes and dreams for our family and, even more important, the values and vision for our family. Who will care for the baby, and how? Why are we bringing a baby into this world?

We can also examine our expectations and prepare ourselves (as much as possible) for change. We may be used to being in full control of our lives. We may need to consider that there are things we may need to forgo—at least for a little while. We may need to work on ourselves to build a space for inner peace, which we can tap into on those days when things get a little chaotic.

We can slow down and turn inwards. If we are trying to conceive, we may need to make space in our lives. We can consider making some changes (scheduling less, finding more space in the day, doing some breathing or meditation, finding time for quiet reflection) to allow our body, our minds, and our hearts to slow down to be ready for conception. Ready for our baby.

DURING PREGNANCY:
THE BABY'S FIRST ENVIRONMENT

How can a baby grow so perfectly? How can the cells divide, each knowing exactly what it needs to do? Pregnancy and birth are likely the most complex and naturally intelligent processes our body is capable of.

Along with wisdom gained in our Montessori training which covers conception and pregnancy, one of our favorite sources for this topic is Pamela Green—a Montessori educator, birth doula, and assistant midwife for over 30 years. (A doula provides guidance and support to mother and baby during birth.) Her expertise and knowledge informs much of what we share here.

Even in utero, our baby's life is already unfolding, and we can learn so much from them and about them. Here are ten things we can do during pregnancy to get to know our baby and prepare for the transition to parenthood.

1. Acknowledge that our baby is already taking in so much.

There is already so much our baby is absorbing in utero through their developing senses. They are not passive. They are taking in their first environment.

The table on the following page outlines some of this development, "What baby is already taking in while in utero."

2. Connect with and welcome our baby

We can talk with our baby, sing to them, massage them by rubbing our belly, and build a connection when they are in utero. Our voices, the music, our touch, our movement, and the rhythms of our bodies will all become important points of reference for our baby out of the womb. These connections create a safe, loving, and accepting emotional environment in utero, making our baby feel welcome. We can play an instrument, play some favorite music, dance, read to them, and notice any ways our baby responds.

If we have a partner, they can connect with the baby by touching and massaging the belly, talking, and singing to the baby. If there are other siblings or family members, they can regularly connect with the baby through touch, talking, and telling stories, jokes, or songs. We can notice if the baby responds differently to the resonances of our voices.

If we have other children, it can be easy to forget we are pregnant, because we are busy attending to everyone's needs. We can make time to check in during the day to listen to our baby, get the other children involved, and perhaps make a special time in the evenings for extra connection.

Prenatal yoga can be helpful to take time out of our week to turn inward, slow down, and connect.

And as the birth nears, we can dance to welcome the baby with the whole family or celebrate our baby's impending arrival with rituals or celebrations with dear friends.

For those interested, look for prenatal singing groups following the work of Marie-Louise Aucher. These can be for the mother and their partner, too. There are many physiological benefits in addition to connecting with the baby through our voice and resonance. The singing can also be helpful during labor (ancient wisdom connects the opening of the throat to the opening of the cervix), and singing can continue after birth too as a way to connect with our baby.

WHAT BABY IS ALREADY TAKING IN WHILE IN UTERO

TACTILE SENSE

- At 5.5 weeks, the embryo is sensitive around the mouth and nose.
- By 12 weeks, the entire body is able to feel (with the exception of the top and back of the head, which are not extremely sensitive until after birth).

VESTIBULAR SENSE (I.E., SENSE OF BALANCE AND MOTION)

- By 10 weeks in utero, the baby moves parts of the body in response to internal stimulation.

SENSE OF SMELL

- At 28 weeks, the fetus can smell, e.g., the food the mother has eaten.

SENSE OF TASTE

- Taste sensations are experienced in utero via the amniotic fluid. Some researchers say babies can taste what we eat from around 21 weeks.

VISION

- From 32 weeks, electrical impulses can pass along the baby's optic nerve allowing some vision in utero, e.g., light vs. dark.
- A baby's vision is very primitive at birth. They can focus to 12 inches (30 cm), which is the distance from the mother when they are held for feeding, and cannot yet track visually.

HEARING

- By 23 weeks, they can hear sounds (our voices, singing, music, etc.) outside their mother's body.
- From 30 weeks in utero to a few months after birth, hearing cells can be damaged by prolonged loud noise.

3. Learn to observe our baby in utero

We can observe how our baby responds to stimuli in their first environment. For example, when our hands are on our belly, we can pause and see what movement the baby makes. We may feel them responding to our touch, moving toward our hand, or increasing activity. Sometimes they move away from voices and touch that they do not recognize. We may notice patterns to their sleep-and-wake rhythms in utero.

This is going to be our work once they are born, to observe them and meet their needs accordingly, and we can begin this process now. We can be open and curious. We may choose to use a journal to note down our observations.

4. Provide a healthy in utero environment

Just as we are careful to prepare the home environment after birth, we can think about the environment we are creating in utero.

Are we getting enough good nutrition and rest so that the baby can grow and thrive? Are we looking after ourselves to maintain our own optimal health—our diet, exercise, rest?

When we are pregnant, our baby will also absorb our emotions—the highs and the lows. It's not always possible to prevent large emotional swings—life happens. Yet, as much as possible, a stable and predictable emotional environment in the adult(s) will help our baby thrive and grow.

It's so important to look after ourselves, let caregivers look after us, and be okay with sometimes having to cancel a social engagement when we need to rest. Are we able to receive care from others (a partner, friend, or professional like a chiropractor, osteopath, midwife, or doula)?

If there are lots of highs and lows, look for extra support from professionals. Some people find it useful to work with someone—for example, their doctor or a psychologist—before and after the birth to attend to their mental health as they go through this enormous transition.

5. Prepare for our baby's first environment outside the womb

Nesting starts, and we begin to set up the physical spaces in our home to welcome the baby—a time to create a warm, simple, loving space for them, without getting drawn into the commercialization of having a baby. Babies do not need a lot.

We can prepare as many things as possible before the baby is born, while we have more time. Junnifa had boxes sorted by month with clothing and some simple activities that she had made or purchased. Then, when she was tired after birth and busy with the new baby, it was easy to pull out the box as the baby grew and have some things at the ready. For example, items for the parent (such as nursing pads in the early months), activities for our baby at different ages, clothing in different sizes, and other supplies like bowls and cutlery for eating (around 6 months).

6. Choose our parenting community and support network

We can surround ourselves with people who support us and want to be part of our parenting community. Some Montessori playgroups and schools offer classes for expecting families, and they can be a great way to find like-minded families.

We will likely still receive unsolicited advice from strangers, friends, and family; however, we can prepare ourselves and respond with kindness when we are clear on our own choices.

During pregnancy is also the time to build our support network for the birth. Who do we want as part of our birth team? Who will make us feel safe and supported? We might consider having a doula to support us through the birth—some offer pro-bono work to lower-income families.

We may wish to attend breastfeeding groups to learn from other women who are breastfeeding their babies, and also to establish a network and find specialists if we need support after the birth.

And who can help us arrange meals and take care of laundry and cleaning after the baby is born? It's a good idea to organize this ahead of time in case we get overwhelmed or are too tired to arrange things after the birth.

7. Explore our birthing options

During pregnancy we have time to explore our birthing options. And though our options may vary depending on our location or circumstances, it is important to know that we have choices. Seek them out. Use them.

We can look at the kind of environment we choose to give birth in, both the physical and emotional.

The physical space might be at home, at a birthing center, or in a hospital. We look to see if the space will support the kind of birth we want. Some may want a birthing pool available. Others want room for a birthing ball. Can we make the space feel like home? Is there space to move? How much freedom of choice is there?

The emotional environment will be created by those around us during the birth process—including whichever support partners we choose.

How we give birth is a personal choice. We cannot manage all the outcomes, yet we can feel empowered to set up the birth environment—where and with whom—as we choose.

Once these choices are made, we don't hand over our birth. We remain active participants, looking at what we want, realizing the things that are important to us— for example, choosing our own positions—and understanding what our options are through the whole process. We need to be able to ask for what we want and to have someone know what these choices are, in case we need an advocate for us during the birth (if we are not able to ask for these choices ourselves).

8. Take the time to explore our stories around birth and parenting

In her Preparation for Birth classes, doula and Montessori educator Pamela Green discusses allowing space for families to explore their ideas about birth and parenting. Many of these will be generational stories inherited from our own family or society. Some of these stories will come with fear or anxiety, others with acceptance. It's important to investigate these stories.

We may wish to talk with our mother to learn more about her experience. For those with parents who are no longer living, this work can be done by exploring what we have been told about our birth.

BOOK RECOMMENDATION

Ina May Gaskin's books, *Ina May's Guide to Childbirth* and *Spiritual Midwifery*, give so many examples of positive birthing experiences and an understanding that pain in birth is the only time we experience "good pain," pain that will bring our babies into the world. Listening to and reading these birth stories show us that a positive birthing experience is possible.

We can explore our ideas through art like working with clay, drawing, belly casting, or painting. We can make mandalas, write letters, light candles.

There is also the choice to rewrite the negative stories we have heard and internalized and turn them into strong, positive ones. When we feel relaxed approaching the birth, our baby will experience this, too.

9. Transition to being a parent

Growing a baby takes energy and love. It is a special time when, if possible, we can try to slow down and enjoy. Pregnancy is a transition period. A time to transition to parenthood. Or, if you are already a parent, a time to transition into a larger family. We don't need to become "all about the baby," but we can take time to get to know our baby while they grow in utero and include them in our daily life.

We can educate ourselves on the physiological changes. Understanding the changes that are happening to ourselves and our baby during pregnancy and birth can fill out the picture as we transition into parenting and learn about our baby and our new relationship.

10. Make additional preparations

We can physically prepare for birth. There are options like hypnotherapy and active birthing. In our Montessori training, they advocate for RAT (respiratory autogenic training), a special breathing technique to manage the pain during birth. The mother learns to link the breath to relaxation and practices during pregnancy until it becomes automatic. Some describe the birth using RAT as pain-free.

If possible, take a first-aid training class for children and babies before the baby comes. It can give us valuable information and help us feel confident in the event of any emergency. When we feel prepared, we can give a feeling of safety and security to our baby. And there will be more time to do this during pregnancy than when the baby is born.

And the rest of the work is on ourselves—to heal from our past, to connect to our baby, and to prepare to welcome our baby with so much love, respect, and acceptance. That is our wish for every baby in the world.

THE BIRTH

Birth is often seen as a painful, scary medical procedure to be done in a hospital. But when we hear that it can be a beautiful and connecting process, one where we will meet our baby, we are able to look forward to the birth and let it unfold.

While the suggestions that follow are about making choices to have the birth experience we want, it can often be very difficult to make this a reality. Obstacles include health insurance restrictions, lack of coverage and high out-of-pocket expenses, and limited access to birthing centers or home birth expertise, just to name a few. When possible, we can look for a doctor or midwife who will support us in having the kind of birth we choose. And if it doesn't work out or isn't possible, we can remember that we are doing our best and that delivering a healthy baby is the ultimate goal.

The physical environment will play an important role in the birthing process. To feel safe, the mother generally wants privacy, familiarity, some warmth, and a place where she can introspect. We can look at creating a sacred place for birth—lights dim, a quiet space in which to focus inward, perhaps with soft music. If not birthing at home, we can bring some items to the birth center or hospital to create a familiar space. And there may be a birthing ball, a birth pool, and other materials to help during the birth. The birth environment will be unique for each person, a place where they have a feeling of trust and safety and where there is freedom (of choice and movement).

Mother and baby work together, the baby moving down, rotating, and descending as an active participant. When a mother is left to herself and given freedom, she may move, make sounds, sing, find her own rhythm, and breathe at her own pace. If a mother has practiced relaxation or hypnotherapy in the prenatal period, these tools can help her go deeper into herself. The mother turns inward with every contraction, in a process of surrendering and acceptance. Getting closer to welcoming the baby.

The birthing mother can be very aware of her surroundings. Even sitting with her eyes closed, she can notice anyone coming into the room, lights turning on, or people speaking. So we aim not to disturb her, moving and talking quietly, keeping the lighting and temperature consistent. And if there is an interruption, it can cause the labor to slow or stop completely.

Partners, family members, and birth attendants (midwives, obstetricians, doulas) make up part of the birth environment and can hold space for the mother and baby. This means they are available, present, observing, but in a non-intrusive way, not interrupting the process. If they need to step in to assist, they do so gently, quietly, swiftly, and then retreat.

Pamela Green, birth doula and Montessori educator, describes it like a dance. The attendant moves in a synchronized way with the laboring mother, gently does their work, then moves away. An experienced birth attendant will focus on the mother more than measurements. They look for cues like how high the baby is and how it lowers, and focus on how to get the baby into good alignment, not just focusing on dilation.

When the baby crowns, the mother and partner can bring their hands to feel the baby's head. A mother can be allowed to receive the baby and bring them up to her chest. Interestingly, most times the mother will bring the baby to the left side of her chest, bringing the baby closest to their mother's rhythmic heartbeat, which is so familiar to them from in utero. The baby is transitioning from their inner life within the womb to being out in the world.

Ideally, the baby is on their parent's chest, skin-to-skin, until the cord stops pulsating. If left alone, the umbilical cord eventually narrows to a point where it can then be cut.

There is wonder, bliss, joy, and relief in the mother's face. And the baby is a perfectly formed human being, with their own character and personality. If present, the partner joins them as a new family unit, and once all is stable they can be left to be alone together.

When this connection time has taken place, the birth attendants can be called back over to weigh the baby and take measurements. These attendants are the baby's first social contact outside of their family. They can do this in a positive, loving, and respectful way by getting the baby's permission before handling them. They can come close to the baby's face to make eye contact, tell them what is about to happen, and if the baby is not ready, they can wait.

Once weighed and returned to the parents, the baby left skin-to-skin can make their way to the breast for the first attachment. This can happen in the first hour or two. A midwife or nurse can support this first attachment if needed.

Perhaps we are wondering if this special experience can be created in a hospital environment. It's absolutely possible when we are able to choose our collaborative care team. Many hospitals now allow rooming in, partners staying in the room overnight, and other choices around the birth.

JUNNIFA SHARES LESSONS
FROM HER BIRTHS

My three births were very different but each beautiful in their own way.

My first son was born in a birthing tub at a wonderful birth center, after about 6 hours of labor and 2 minutes of pushing. He was born into water and *en caul*, which means his sac was intact.

SOME THINGS THAT STOOD OUT TO ME:

- I remember being very conscious of the work my baby was doing during the labor. It was our first collaboration. I was very in tune with his movements and moved in response. He worked hard to gain his independence from my womb, and I was his helper. This knowledge made a difference for my labor, as I was following his lead and conscious that he was working even harder than I was.
- I had a midwife that I trusted and who trusted me. I still hear her voice saying to me "just relax, your body knows what to do."
- My husband and mum—my two strongest pillars of support—were there with me through every step, and that made a big difference.

My second son was born in the hospital after a few hours of laboring in the birth center. I had always heard that the second labor would be shorter than the first one, and so when it became much longer, I worried that something was wrong.

My mum was also not around, and I had left my older son in the care of extended family members. So I was very conscious of wanting to get back to him. The labor process was beautiful again, but I could feel a stall and so we decided to transfer to the hospital. Something about the drive must have helped, because as soon as I got to the hospital, I felt he was finally ready to come out.

I remember the significant change from the birth center to the hospital. The lights were bright, the nurses and doctors were very loud, and when I told them the baby was ready to come, one nurse roughly checked me and told me I was hurting/tearing myself by attempting to push. It was such a different experience from the calm and trusting feel of the birth center with my midwives, but I remembered my midwife from my first birth, who told me my body knew what to do. I insisted that my baby was coming, and he was out about 2 minutes later. I refused the post-birth injections to the chagrin and criticism of the doctor. When they came to check on the baby and me a little while later, they expressed surprise at how alert and strong we both were.

My third child was born in a regular bathtub. It was my shortest labor and fastest birth. She literally popped out.

MY LESSONS FROM THIS BIRTH:

- Trust our body and our instincts.
- Make care arrangements for our other children that allow us to truly relax and labor for as long as needed.
- Find caregivers (midwives/doctors) who share our values and mutual trust.
- Make sure our pillars of support are present.
- Contrary to popular belief, sometimes the labor for a second or third child is much longer than the labor for the first or previous child. Knowing and accepting this can make a difference in our endurance.
- Sometimes, a drive or a walk around the block can change things up for our labor and trigger transition.

I had been worried after the experience of having to transfer to a hospital with my second child. I prayed and prayed and prayed for a quick labor because again I wanted to get home quickly to my two other children, who were both under 3 years old. I remember driving to a shop to make some purchases. I walked out of the shop and saw a big double rainbow. I don't know why it had such an effect on me, but I cried and told my boys that the baby would be coming today. I was not ready, but I just knew. I went home and put the baby's clothes in the washer, got everyone ready for bed, and we laid down as it rained heavily outside.

I remember thinking that this would be the last time that I would go to bed with two children.

A few hours later, I woke up and messaged my midwife that it was time. She seemed doubtful and told me some things to do, but I told her the baby was coming soon and that I was heading to her.

I got there and lay down for a little bit and then felt the need to throw up and use the bathroom. My daughter popped out 40 minutes after I arrived.

MY TAKEAWAYS WERE AS BEFORE:

- Our baby actually does most of the work, observes, pays attention, and listens.
- Trust our body and our instincts.

All of my births were vaginal, and I had no tears. I moved around while laboring and also labored partly in water. I was very active during all of my pregnancies and tried to eat healthy and stay happy.

I wish you births as beautiful as mine or better.

Some additional notes on birth

We may have preferences for the birth, and we can make them clear to others who may need to represent us during labor. At the same time, know that things can change, and the safe delivery of the baby is the most important thing in the end.

In a vaginal birth, know that:

- our bodies are made to birth children.
- we can work with the naturally occurring hormones, like oxytocin, which allow our bodies to transform during labor.
- we can move if we want to, eat if we can, relax in any way that works for us.
- no two births are the same—what helps for one person or even for our first birth may be different in following births.
- in the first stage, we can picture the cervix opening and thinning to make way for the baby to enter the world.
- in the second stage, we can visualize the baby moving down and out.
- we can be surrounded by people who will encourage us, massage us, feed us, and make us feel comfortable.

Sometimes babies are delivered by caesarean birth—this can be a choice or a necessity. When it's a necessity, there can be a grieving of sorts for some mothers who wished for a different delivery. It's important to let these feelings come up. And also be happy for the safe delivery of our baby into the world. With a caesarean birth, extra assistance may be required to help with lifting things during these first weeks, because there is likely to be additional pain related to the surgery.

Babies born by caesarean have not passed through the vaginal tract, which usually would help remove fluid from their lungs, as well as receive important natural bacteria for their immunity. Some midwives will help get some of these important bacteria from the mother through a process called "seeding" and apply the bacteria to the baby at the time of birth.

BOOK RECOMMENDATION

Mindful Birthing: Training the Mind, Body, and Heart for Childbirth and Beyond by Nancy Bardacke

SYMBIOSIS—THE FIRST 6 TO 8 WEEKS
WITH OUR BABY

"The newborn is most utterly sensitive, misunderstood and treated too hurriedly.

His most profound needs are not acknowledged.

The first days of his life are the most important."

—Adele Costa Gnocchi, *Quaderno Montessori*, volume 39, 1993

In Montessori, the first 6 to 8 weeks of the baby's life are called **symbiosis**, which means "a life together." This is such a beautiful way to see these early days, welcoming our new baby into our home, getting to know and adapt to them, and them to us.

In science, mutually beneficial symbiosis is when two organisms live in a way that benefits both parties. For example, coral and algae have a mutually beneficial symbiotic relationship—the coral provides algae with shelter, and the algae gives coral reefs their colors and supplies both organisms with nutrients.

Applying this to these first weeks of the baby's life, the parent–baby relationship is **mutually beneficial**—when the baby is nursing, the baby receives the perfect food, and the feeding helps contract the womb. Holding the baby can help replace the feeling of emptiness that can be experienced after the birth. A father, partner, or other caregiver can be involved by protecting and caring for this new family unit—they become like the gatekeeper, taking calls and messages, offering practical support like getting supplies, providing physical care such as bathing the baby or allowing the mother to sleep, as well as bonding with mother and baby. We are becoming a family.

We have time to **bond** with the newborn through feeding, singing, bathing, gentle touching, and caring for them.

The baby develops **trust** through close contact with us, being held, and having their needs met.

By simplifying the environment and activities for these first weeks, we are reminded to slow down. To connect. To establish a relationship with our new baby. To get to know what they are telling us. To be together and talk—about who we are, where they are, and what is happening. To be looked after. Many cultures have rituals for the first 40 days after birth, and we can create our own.

The strong attachment built during these first months gives a solid foundation for the months (and years ahead). After the first months, the baby is ready to start experiencing more from the world around them, including being introduced to extended family and friends.

"Developing the right type of attachment during the symbiotic period paves the way for natural detachment, and psychological birth happens."

Dr. Silvana Montanaro, *Understanding the Human Being*

It's important to find ways in which the mother (and co-parent) can be supported at this time. It is different for every family, but there can be an enormous emotional and physical impact after the birth. Sometimes the love we expect to feel is not immediately present—there can be baby blues or some post-partum depression. Even with a smooth birth and easy connection, there is less time to sleep, clean, or even shower with a newborn in the home. This blurriness is both the beauty and the struggle of this time. If one is able to do so, thinking ahead to have family, friends, or a paid helper to assist and support can be invaluable.

Tips for the Symbiotic Period

1. The home environment

- During the symbiotic period with our newborn, the baby is making an important transition from being in utero (where life was largely consistent in terms of warmth, food, and ambient lighting) to being outside the womb (where life is more unpredictable and noisier, and often colder and brighter).
- In the first days, if possible, it can help to keep the home a little warmer than usual and the lighting a little dimmer. We can also be aware of limiting the stimulation for the newborn, perhaps receiving fewer guests and allowing time to connect and learn about the new baby in our lives.
- A thin, quilted pillow, called a *topponcino*, is a favorite for many parents. The topponcino can be used starting at the birth and through the first few months at home during the symbiotic period to ease this transition period for the baby. It's a little longer than the baby and a little wider, made of natural fabric, in which baby

can be held or laid down upon. The topponcino can
become a point of reference for the baby and gives a
soft layer of protection. The baby finds security and a
familiar scent—their scent and the scent of their parents,
siblings, and family—in this thin cushion. It prevents
overstimulation when handled by family and friends,
and it allows the baby to be transferred from arms to
bed without triggering their startle reflex. Parents using
the topponcino say they take it everywhere. Instructions
for making your own topponcino are included online
at workman.com/montessori, or you can find them
available for sale online.

Topponcino

- If there are older siblings in the home, it may not
always be possible to create a calm, quiet environment during the symbiotic period.
However, the baby will be learning about their siblings, adjusting to the rhythms of
the house, and finding their place in this home.

2. The adult(s)

- We can begin to observe our baby and their early rhythms.
- We learn to feed our baby and to help them transition to sleep.
- We can sing and dance with baby—our voice and movement will be familiar to our
baby from in the womb.
- We can create a special bathing time.
- We should allow time for breastfeeding—this is a way of communicating with our
baby with our full body (not while scrolling on our phone) and a time to rest.
- We can allow time for skin-to-skin moments with both parents—it's calming
for baby and parent; promotes the parent–baby bond; regulates baby's heart rate,
breathing, and temperature; it can stimulate an interest in feeding; and can help build
immunity.
- We can share our wonder of the world around us.
- We can find ways for our partner (if we have one) to develop their own bond with
baby. Partners have their own unique way of being with the baby and are another
special and familiar person for the baby to connect with. The way they move and talk,
bathe, and sing may soothe our baby in a new way, and even may have a different way
of holding our baby over their shoulder, providing relief to baby's belly.
- We can receive care from others, such as cooking, cleaning, and washing, so we
can provide care for the baby and take time to rest. For some, it may be family and
friends. Without extended family around, we may have to be creative to make this
happen, and it's a good idea to arrange this ahead of time before the baby arrives and

we become overwhelmed or too tired to ask. We can get an organized friend to make up a roster for meals, request gift vouchers for food service as birth gifts, have meals in the freezer before the baby arrives, and we may be able to afford someone to come clean every couple of weeks, or think about arranging a babysitter or neighbor who may be able to look after an older child while we rest. Some countries have home visitors in the first week or two to support the family—and where this is not available, we are making it happen by building this support network ourselves.

- Keep things simple—keep visitors and appointments to a minimum.
- We can journal our experiences, for ourselves and our baby. Symbiosis also allows time to process any trauma from the birth experience or feelings of loss from not being pregnant anymore that may come up.
- For some, the natural feelings of love for their baby take longer to form. There are also the baby blues a few days after birth and the possibility of post-partum depression. Please seek help from a doctor if needed and accept support from others. It is not a weakness. It is the kindest thing we can do for our baby.
- For adoptive parents, the symbiotic period may come later, when the baby is welcomed into the home. It is possible to consciously create this special connection by blocking out 6 to 8 weeks. To become a family. To build trust and bond. To learn about the new baby, and again for them to get to know us.
- If the baby is adopted, it may be possible to ask the birth mother for any points of reference from in utero (i.e., music played during pregnancy, or to voice messages to the baby).

3. The newborn

A newborn has many memories—tactile, auditory, visual (though limited)—from prenatal life. We can offer experiences in the first weeks that are familiar to our newborn, to help them orient and to continue to stimulate their senses. Here are some ideas in the symbiotic period to help them adjust from in utero to the external environment.

Tactile experiences

- We can keep baby's hands free as much as possible, because their hands will come to their mouth area, just as they did in the womb.
- The baby is sensitive to every touch on their body—these are completely new sensations. So we handle them with the lightest touch, with the most efficient movements, and we slow everything down so the baby can learn these new processes, like having their diaper changed, having a bath, and getting dressed.
- Clothing should be very soft, made of natural fibers, without hard fastenings, and not needing to be pulled over the baby's head. If you can manage it, cloth diapers are soft

against the baby's skin, better for the environment, and will allow them to feel the natural wetness when they poop or pee (feeling these natural body sensations will be useful later when toileting). If we use disposable diapers, we can allow the baby plenty of time to go diaperless while lying on a soft blanket or towel.

- We can use a topponcino (see page 42) as a point of reference and to soften the stimulation to the baby.

- During our baby's short waking periods, we can give them time to be held and time to stretch on a movement mat. A movement mat is a thin mattress for the baby to lie on, around 1" high and large enough for the baby to stretch their limbs in all directions (see page 57 for more on setting up a movement area). When outdoors, we can take a padded blanket to provide a place for movement on the go.

- Gentle baby massage can be comforting and connecting.

Auditory experiences

- The baby has auditory points of reference from the womb—the main one is our voice(s), which they have heard throughout pregnancy. We can continue to talk to and sing to them.

- The maternal heartbeat and digestive sounds will be familiar—we can re-create them by allowing the baby to lie on our belly.

- Bird sounds can be appealing to a newborn.

- Playing music—either from a music box or soft, recorded music (especially music that was played in utero).

Visual experiences

- A newborn baby can see a distance of about 12 inches (30 cm). We can hold the baby close to allow them to focus on our face. Human faces fascinate babies—in research studies, babies begin to make sucking motions when presented with facial features.

- If the baby is facing a light source, a hand between the light source and the baby will look dark, and the fingers can move very slowly. A baby will observe this for a very long time, until they avert their gaze and show that they are done.

- Mobiles also provide visual experiences. The mobiles should be lightweight and move with the natural air currents in the room. There is a beautiful series of Montessori mobiles that we'll explore later in this book, going from a black and white mobile to simple colored mobiles to ones beginning to represent dancers or things that fly. (For more on mobiles, see page 134.) These are not placed over their sleeping area, but where they can explore them during awake times.

- The baby will begin to observe any siblings in their environment, not in focus at first, but soon tracking their movements. Their siblings become points of interest for them from the first days, and they will be fascinated by them, sometimes for long periods.

Many newborns do not want to be put down. They are very attached and love to be kept close. Symbiosis is the time for snuggling and comfort and being close. At the same time, we can also begin to offer our baby the chance to spend some time on their movement mat, especially when they become more wakeful after the first 2 weeks.

We can use the topponcino to transfer the baby from our arms to the movement area, keeping the topponcino underneath them. We can also start by lying down with the baby on our belly in the movement area. Then we can try the next time to move them from our belly to the movement mat next to us. They will still be able to see, smell, and hear us. If they are uncomfortable, we can lay a hand on them, look into their eyes, provide our sweet words or song. And over time, they will feel more comfortable lying down on their movement mat with us a little farther away. This same method applies to helping our baby get used to lying down in their sleeping area. (See page 59.)

TO PRACTICE

1. What steps will we take to prepare ourselves for birth?
   - physical preparation, e.g., nutrition, rest, etc.
   - arrange support from others
   - read about positive birth experiences
   - make a birth plan with alternatives for different outcomes

2. What can we prepare for the symbiotic period (the first 6 to 8 weeks)?
   - how can we transition baby from in utero to the external environment?
   - how can we adjust the home (e.g., temperature, lighting, etc.)?
   - how can we adjust ourselves (e.g., handling baby gently, slowly)?
   - how can we support their senses at birth (tactile, auditory, and visual)?
   - how can we allow time to learn about our new baby, and them about us?

THE VOICE OF THE NEWBORN:
AN INTERVIEW WITH KARIN SLABAUGH

In memory of Grazia Honegger Fresco (September 30, 2020)

Since 1992, Karin has been an early childhood educator. She now specializes in the care of newborns based on the work of the very first Montessorians trained in the 1950s. She has observed newborns for more than 500 hours, studying their behavioral language, their communications, and their incredible sensitivity, which is observable in how they respond to their caregiver and environment.

What does Dr. Montessori's principle "education from birth" mean?

It means removing obstacles from natural development and allowing children to self-regulate and self-develop from the moment of their birth.

Will you talk to us about your love of newborns?

The newborn is the purest form of human life that exists. A newborn begins learning at birth—even before, actually. At birth a baby is completely unconditioned, because learning is basically experiencing and creating habitual responses to what life's sensations are offering. So right after birth, as soon as the senses begin to take it all in, all of these new stimuli of the world outside the mother, newborns respond to all of this. Whether they feel trust or love, or whether they feel fear or terror, all of these experiences are recorded and "learned."

You talk of a newborn baby's ability to look into a person's eyes.

In the 1960s American developmental psychologist Robert Fantz demonstrated that newborn infants not only could see but also had clear-cut visual preferences. Visual ability is what makes it possible for the newborn to find the breast, which is his source for survival, by finding the dark circle of the areola. The black pupils and contrasting whites of the eyes on the mother's face are another visual target that give a newborn an important point of reference that his limited visual ability can capture. Babies at birth are programmed to look for their mother's eyes. This is how they make the first bond.

Can you describe for us the "first alert state" you have observed in newborns right after birth?

During my research, I have observed maybe 100 newborns in the hours after birth. When a baby has had an unmedicated birth, and if the environment is not too bright and the baby is allowed to spend his first hours in mother's arms, he often is very alert. To be in this position, on her body, skin-to-skin, warmed by her body heat, smelling her colostrum, listening to the sounds of her heartbeat and her voice, looking into her eyes, held and contained by her embrace, he can begin to take in the reality of being on the outside. In this position, though he is no longer on the inside, he is in similar conditions. After he gets his bearings, he may begin to open his mouth and thrust his tongue and turn his head, all reflexes that will help him find and attach to the breast for the first time.

Can you describe what you have felt when looking into the eyes of many newborns?

During the second hour after birth, many of these babies were very much alert and wide-eyed in the incubator, and I would place myself within 12 inches (30 cm) of their face to allow them to be able to see me. They were looking for their mother's face, of course. It was sad for me to be there in place of their mother. But I would describe it as a privilege to have "met" eyes with so many tiny people, and with whom I felt such a deep connection simply from the act of staring at each other.

Can you give new parents some ideas for how they can treat children with respect and dignity from birth?

The first thing that comes to mind about respecting a newborn is to respect the process that the newborn has to go through to find his or her individual rhythms. As he has never eaten before or slept before outside the womb, he needs a period of time to establish his own rhythms that are going to come out from the inside of his being. So we have to be very careful not to impose a rhythm for this person, or else we completely interrupt and prevent this person from finding a natural rhythm on his own.

So what we can do as parents, from birth, is to really focus on what it means to observe another person in order to understand what he or she is communicating. Newborns communicate with their body language and they communicate with their vocalizations, so they have a large repertoire of communications that we can learn to read, learn to understand. But it's a very different language, and like learning any new language, it takes effort and time. It is not just the language of crying—even more so, it is the language of behavior. It's a bit like a cat or a dog who has a bark or a meow. That is their vocal language, but they have a lot of behaviors—they go sit by the door, they get really happy in their whole body. They look sad and depressed when they want to go outside for a walk and they know we are not taking them out. So there is a lot of communication that we can read in a newborn's expressions and movements that doesn't come from crying, but comes from how his autonomic nervous system is responding to the various stimuli. Their body language tells us how they feel, what they need, even what their preferences are, and this is the language that we have to learn in order to respect a newborn.

Treating a newborn with dignity, now that's a very interesting question. Would you like to be handled by others, say, during a hospital stay, as if you weren't there, moved about and touched without being addressed, without being told what was happening? Dignity is offered simply by taking into consideration what the other person is needing or feeling, and acting accordingly. How often do we really take into consideration the real and urgent needs of the newborn to be able to process all of the new stimuli and feel safe throughout this transitional period of adaptation, being newly outside the womb, a reality that is 100 percent different from the world in which he lived during his entire life?

Could you describe how we can do our best to change a newborn's diaper without him crying?

Crying is simply an expression of fear, discomfort, or physiological dysregulation. A newborn has a high level of sensitivity to sensorial input such as the temperature of the air, movement that happens too quickly, or the sensations from the clothing that is touching him. The newborn skin is very sensitive. What we have to do is to take into consideration this person's high sensitivity to stimuli. Now, of course, over time there is an adaptation, so throughout the course of the days and weeks and months all of these actions and feelings become normal. So if you pay careful attention from the beginning—from the very beginning—to do all of these things in a way that, in your best attempts, does not provoke crying, does not cause an expression of dislike for the experience, then you are conditioning him (creating a learned response) of understanding that these things happen regularly and they are not uncomfortable.

Many parents make the mistake of working really rapidly through a diaper change so it is over very quickly, and also so the crying is over quickly, and then they can soothe the baby. But that is a very different thing from attempting to act in a way so that you don't even provoke the upset feelings.

As for some practical advice, just slow down, more than you can even imagine is necessary. This is the key: to move through everything you do with a newborn at 5 percent of your normal speed. Don't allow yourself to get stressed and feed off of the crying baby's anxiety, rather, offer a calm energy that he can feed off of. This is what is called co-regulation. Talk to him about what will happen before it happens. Before picking him up, talk to him about how you are going to pick him up. Before each action, pause and look into his eyes, at a distance of 12 inches (30 cm), to see how he is doing, what he is thinking. If you want to see what this looks like, at the very beginning of Bernard Martino's documentary, *Loczy: A Place to Grow* (available on the internet), there is a scene where the caregiver prepares a newborn for a bath. This gives you an idea of what this level of sensitivity to the newborn person looks like.

Birth is the first experience that is very much a shock to the newborn's senses, coming out of the mother's body and coming into the world. It can provoke a response of crying and does most of the time, but it doesn't have to. This is what Frédérick Leboyer was able to show the world in his books and the film *Birth Without Violence*. His films show births where babies come into the world with wide-open eyes, curious about where they are, looking around in the dim light, and they often do not cry.

So if a baby at birth can come into the world without sensations that are disturbing to him and that make him cry, then every event, every diaper change, everything you do with the newborn, if you consider his basic needs, the urgent needs of this person, those things that should not be ignored, then you can have a very different outcome. What does a newborn need for the level of light in the room in the moments after his birth? What does a one-day-old-baby need for the amount of noise around him? What does a newborn need on his third day, concerning the level of stimulation from a diaper change, with his clothing being taken off for the fifteenth time? What does the newborn need? That is the question at the root of this.

SETTING UP
THE HOME

4

SETTING UP MONTESSORI-STYLE SPACES

Never underestimate how much we can use our homes to create an inviting, cozy, attractive, and engaging space for our baby.

Montessori educators use the classroom as a "second teacher." We get the classroom to do a lot of the work. We take the time to prepare activities in a way where the children can see what is available; the whole space is prepared with such love and care, and the children respond by treating it with respect; and there is beauty in the space, with living plants and artwork placed at the child's height. Dr. Montessori called her first classroom *Casa de Bambini*—"children's house." The classroom can make the child feel like they belong and are important.

We don't have to completely transform our homes to look like Montessori classrooms, but we can create intentional spaces in each area of the home to make our baby feel special, to welcome them, and to give them a sense of security as each space becomes a point of reference for them.

This can be achieved in even the smallest of homes. Small or difficult spaces are opportunities for creativity.

BABIES DO NOT NEED THAT MUCH

There is a general idea that we need a lot of of furniture, clothing, toys, and supplies for a new baby. We can buy fancy feeding cushions, cribs with matching chests of drawers, a changing table, a baby bath, and more. Then we need a stroller that collapses, one we can push while jogging, and maybe one for traveling too.

One of our favorite things about the Montessori approach is that it aligns with the idea of *less is more*. Buy only what we need, keep things simple and beautiful, and perhaps put the extra money toward a higher quality, or more natural, version. These special things can be used by any future children in the family or donated or passed on to another family. And they are much more sustainable for the environment.

Tips for setting up your home

1. **Baby-sized.** Look for small furniture that the baby will learn to use by themselves—like a low bed to crawl in and out of (see pages 59 and 64). By the time our baby learns to sit, we can have a low table and chair where they can eat, play with their activities, and pull up on. We want the baby's legs to reach the ground with their feet flat on the floor, so we can trim the legs of the table and chairs if they are too high.

2. **Beauty in the space.** Display art, photos of the family, and plants at a low height for the baby to enjoy. (Make sure the plants are safe for curious babies who want to put them in their mouths or move them to where the baby can see them but not reach them.)

3. **Independence.** To help our baby move from dependency to increasing independence in the first year, we can set up simple activities on a low shelf or in a low basket so the baby can learn to choose for themselves. Older babies will be able to roll, wriggle, or crawl to fetch things they want to use, and we can look for ways to make it easy for them to help themselves.

4. **Attractive activities.** We can create inviting, age-appropriate activities for each stage of our baby's development, beautifully arranged on shelves, rather than in toy boxes.

5. **Less is more.** Displaying only a few activities helps develop the baby's concentration. Display only the ones the baby is working to master, so they don't feel overwhelmed.

6. **A place for everything and everything in its place.** When we have a place for everything and everything is in its place, the baby learns where things belong (and eventually, as toddlers, where to put them away).

7. **See the space through their eyes.** Get down to the baby's height in each space to see what it looks like from their perspective. Remove messy wires and clutter.

8. **Store and rotate.** Create storage that ideally is out of sight or easy on the eye—think floor-to-ceiling cupboards that blend in with the wall or containers that can be stacked in a storage area or behind a couch. Keep out a few activities, store the rest, and rotate them when the baby is looking for new challenges.

CREATE "YES" SPACES

In Montessori classrooms, we like to remove obstacles to the child's development. When we set up our home, we can do the same. What we create are "yes" spaces where our baby is free to explore safely, we are okay with everything they can touch and reach, and the chance of us having to say "no" is limited. (The term "yes" spaces originates from Janet Lansbury, a RIE—Resources for Infant Educarer—educator and author.)

People love to come to Simone's classroom with their babies because they know that the space has been carefully prepared so the babies can explore freely with little danger to them. Everything is set up with the babies in mind—low furniture they can pull up on; open spaces for them to practice rolling, scooting, and crawling; no wires to reach; no loose cords to look out for; and only objects that are safe for them to put in their mouth.

In our homes, we can:

- remove anything we do not want our baby to reach—this may mean storing it for some time or moving it to a space the baby cannot access
- lie on the floor to see what the baby can see and reach
- make the space inviting to explore with a few simple activities on a low shelf, including baskets of objects that are fun to investigate
- if we cannot make every space a "yes" space, we can make one large area of the home a "yes" space for the baby, where they can move freely. We may need to be creative, for example, using our furniture to create a safe boundary for this area or having a gated-off area
- if we need to gate off an area, avoid brightly colored plastic room separators and look for subtle options which will feel light in the space

We want to allow the baby (from birth) free movement and unobstructed vision. So we prefer not to use baby boxes, playpens, or cribs in our homes—these contain the baby's movement, and the bars do not give a clear view of the whole space from the baby's perspective. We even prefer not to use a high chair. Controversial, we know. These containers have been developed for our convenience, not the child's.

Simone's Montessori trainer, Judi Orion, said that the only time we might want to use a playpen is for the adult to stand in if we are ironing (meant quite literally!). If we need to use the bathroom, place the baby in their "yes" space, where we know they will be safe and have space to explore.

AT-HOME STARTER SET FOR MONTESSORI BABIES

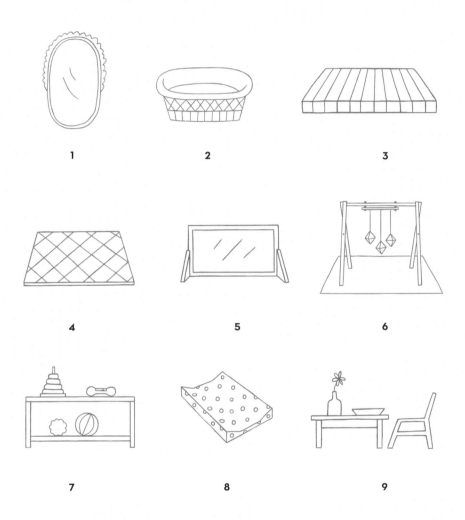

1. A topponcino (a thin, quilted cushion) 2. A *cestina* (also known as a "Moses basket") for sleeping (newborn to 3 months) 3. A low mattress for sleeping 4. Floor mat for movement 5. A long horizontal mirror in the movement area 6. A place to hang a mobile 7. A low shelf to display simple activities 8. A changing mat—have just the changing pad and store when not in use 9. A low table for eating food (once baby can sit)

Because we value giving freedom to our baby, we need to ensure that the home is safe for our baby. Household chemicals are securely locked and out of our baby's reach; cords from curtains are tied and out of reach; electrical wires are hidden by plastic tubing that can be adhered to the wall; furniture such as shelving is secured to the walls; and window locks are installed. If there are stairs, we may wish to have baby gates across the opening so that the baby only practices on the stairs with supervision.

> "Remember that a supportive environment is sometimes distinguished more by what objects are left out, than by what are included."
>
> —Susan Stephenson, *The Joyful Child*

OBSERVE, STORE, AND ROTATE

One of the secrets to the success of our intentionally created spaces is to limit the number of activities available for our baby to the ones they are working to master. We can display a limited number—about six of their favorites—on a low shelf in their movement area. It's easier for our baby to choose from a smaller selection, the activities will be just the right challenge for them, and there will be less for us to tidy up.

Then we observe. When we notice that they are no longer interested in an activity or it appears to be too easy or difficult for them, we can store it for another time and bring out a different activity.

Storing mobiles can be a little more difficult because they get easily tangled. One idea is to display them on the wall on small hooks when they are not being used. They make an attractive wall display too. We can then hang the mobile the baby is interested in on a mobile hanger above their movement area.

We'll look more at which activities to choose in chapter 6. For now, remember to observe, store, and rotate.

ROOM BY ROOM

Entrance

- Low hooks in the entrance where we can hang the baby's coat, hat, bag, etc. As our baby grows, they will have naturally absorbed that this is where these things belong.
- A basket for the baby's shoes once they are walking.

Living room

Movement area

- A movement mat, where the baby can stretch and move their limbs, reach for their toes, observe a mobile, and look at themselves in a low mirror (see page 45). This is a great alternative to a bouncer chair, which limits the baby's free movement and exploration. Avoid propping them up with pillows, which which may limit them from moving freely.
- Once the baby is crawling, the movement mat can be removed to allow free movement and the movement area becomes the whole room (always check for safety).
- A low mirror hung horizontally to support development of the full visual body schema (i.e., learning what parts make up their body and how they look as a whole).
- A place to hang a mobile—this could be from the wall, attached to furniture, or hanging off a wooden frame suspended over the baby.
- A basket containing up to five or six board books.
- When baby is getting ready to pull up, we can provide sturdy furniture to pull up on and cruise along, for example, a heavy ottoman or coffee table, or even a horizontal bar on the wall with a mirror behind where they will be delighted to practice pulling up and cruising while seeing themselves in the mirror.
- We can hang art low on the wall. They enjoy gazing at familiar scenes and objects, so attractive pictures of plants, animals, or photos of the family are always favorites. Vintage pictures from old books placed in a frame can also be a beautiful choice.

- As our baby gets older, the low table and chair (see Kitchen section below) may be placed in the movement area for pulling up on, for activities, and for eating. As our baby gets close to walking, don't be surprised if the chair becomes a support that they stand behind and push along.

- There is a trend to buy colorful foam squares to cover harder surfaces, and we question whether this is necessary. These foam squares can become tripping hazards as our baby begins to pull up onto their feet, and the colors can add a lot of visual noise to the space. Instead, the movement mat provides a soft surface for our baby to explore when they are not yet crawling. Once our baby is on the move and trying to put themselves into a sitting position unassisted, they may get fewer bumps than we would expect. And remember that when there are bumps, they are learning about the limits of their bodies. Babies relearn how to navigate physical space with every new stage of development—it is the natural process.

Kitchen

- We can set up a low cupboard or drawer to store the baby's plates, bowls, cutlery, and glasses. They will learn where their things can be found before they begin to walk.

- Before the baby is walking, we can keep a basket of items such as a whisk, a wooden spoon, a metal spoon, or a small pot and lid, where the baby can sit and explore while we are working in the kitchen.

Eating area

- Once the baby is sitting, a low table can be used for eating food. Cut down the legs of a low table and chair so that the baby has their feet flat on the floor. We can add a vase with a flower to make eating time a special occasion.

- The low table and chair could be used for snacks and also for mealtimes if that works for the family.

- Simone likes to include the baby at the family table at mealtimes to introduce them to the social aspects of eating. A tray-less high chair with baby attachment (or similar) allows the baby to share mealtimes with the family and is a good alternative to a traditional high chair because the baby will soon be able to climb up into it independently and there is no tray distancing them from the table.

Bedroom   *Sleeping area*

- A floor bed—a mattress about 6 inches (15 cm) thick that is placed on the ground. Low frames are also possible to find, like ones for futon mattresses, or ones with raised edges that prevent the baby from rolling out but is low enough for a crawling baby to climb out of by themselves. See more about floor beds on page 64.

- For a newborn, the cestina (Moses basket) can be placed on the low mattress from birth—the baby learns this is the place for sleeping, a point of reference. The cestina may be used for the first few months or until the baby grows out of it.

- In order to keep the space calm for sleeping, it's not recommended to hang a mobile over the sleeping area.

- If the baby sometimes rolls off the mattress, have a soft surface on the ground next to the mattress. (Check that the space complies with SIDS guidelines outlined on page 63.) *Note:* We have observed babies move to the edge of the floor mattress in their sleep, feel the edge of the mattress, and move away from the edge, just as adults unconsciously do during sleep.

- SIDS guidelines currently recommend that the baby sleep in the parent's bedroom. Some people have an area in the baby's bedroom for daytime naps, which can assist with the eventual transition into this space for night sleeping.

- Some families may choose to co-sleep—either in the parents' bed or in a co-sleeping attachment. If possible, a family bed that is close to the ground will allow the baby to learn to crawl out safely as they grow. (Look into additional SIDS risks when co-sleeping.)

Note: Not all families feel comfortable using a floor bed. If this is the case, then we recommend moving the baby into a toddler bed as soon as they are able to climb in and out of it independently (at about 12 to 15 months old). We can begin with daytime naps to orient the baby to their new sleeping place. And we can sit next to them until they fall asleep for the first few days to help with orientation and then begin to move out of their room.

Quiet play area/movement area

- A low shelf with a few quiet activities or a basket of board books—once our baby is wriggling and crawling they can explore these upon waking.

- If space allows, a movement area could also be set up in the bedroom. (See page 57 for more on setting up a movement area.)

Changing area

- A place for changing diapers—a changing pad/cushion can be placed on the ground (if the adult has no back problems) then stored when not in use; or it can be placed at the height of the adult's hips on a table or set of drawers. (Always have one hand on a baby when they are at a raised height.)

- Have all the things for diapering at the ready, for example, a basket with clean diapers, wipes/cloth wipes, any creams, a place for dirty diapers.

- A low dressing stool can be useful once the baby is sitting steadily (from about 9 months). The height of the stool is very low so the baby can have their feet flat on the floor. This allows the baby to have a clear place for dressing; enables collaboration during dressing; and, as they become more independent, it will allow them to have more success when putting on pants and underwear and when dressing themselves. A wooden stool will be sturdier and easier to use than plastic.

- By the time a baby is standing, they may resist lying down on a mat to be changed—then we can change them in the bathroom while they stand up and we sit on a low stool (space allowing).

Feeding area

- A place for feeding—if space allows, a comfortable adult chair is ideal for feeding in the night. This allows the baby to remain largely undisturbed. Have a glass of water, tissues, etc., on hand for the nursing mother.

- We can also choose to lie on the floor bed to feed.

A note on decoration

- Decorations can be simple and attractive.

- We can hang a couple of realistic pictures at the child's height, for example, of animals, nature, and familiar people. A Montessori principle is to have artwork that depicts real things our baby sees and experiences in their daily life. It will be some time before they will be able to imagine things that are not in front of them.

- Homemade elements like bunting or something meaningful to the family can also be hung to add some cozy, personal touches.
- It's possible to have something bolder like patterned wallpaper and still create a cozy space—we then may wish to have a more neutral shelf or furniture to create calm and make it easy for the activities to stand out and be attractive for the baby to explore.

Bathroom

- While it will be some months before the baby is using this space independently, we can already set things up for how they will be used as they grow, for example, their toothbrush in a special place and a mirror where they can see their face as it is cleaned.
- Around 12 months, some babies show an interest in using the potty, and we can offer this when we change their diaper or training pants (cotton underpants with extra padding to catch a little pee). Other children will be much older. Always follow the child. The toileting area will be added to as they become a toddler (see page 69).
- Some people do elimination communication with their baby from the first few days (using a baby's cues to know when to offer them a potty) and would want to include a potty earlier in the bathroom for the baby to use.

Outside

- A soft blanket or picnic blanket for the baby to lie on when we are at the park, the beach, the forest, or anywhere outdoors. Babies love to lie under the trees and watch the shadows change and the movement of the leaves and branches.
- Many babies enjoy going for walks outside in a baby carrier or stroller. We can talk to them about what we see and enjoy quiet moments listening to the world around us. In the early months (up to around 3 months old), we will have our baby facing us as we walk so they can see where we are and we can talk with them. Soon, we can face them away from us so they can experience more of the world around them. With a stroller, we can stop and come stand next to them when they are looking for us.
- A sitting baby can enjoy the swings at the playground (or at home if space allows).
- Once a baby can pull up to standing, it won't be long before they can push a wagon (which can be used inside or outside). Avoid jumpers or baby walkers where the baby is placed in an upright position, putting pressure on their hips. Wait until they can pull up and push the wagon by themselves.

At first, these changes to our home might seem quite unattainable. We might ask, "Won't my baby pull everything out now that they have everything accessible to them?" Yes, they probably will at first. And then they will lose interest, or we can show them what they can play with instead. We make sure to babyproof cupboards that have dangerous chemicals or objects. For the rest, it is a matter of trust. They will find some things that are not meant for them, but that is their job—to explore the world around them.

So as much as possible we create "yes" spaces and babyproof unsafe things, and then the baby will learn by experimenting that it hurts when fingers get closed in drawers, and we will be there with loving arms to soothe them if needed.

TO OBSERVE

- Does our baby look relaxed in the space? Bored? Overstimulated?

- Lie down next to our baby to look from their perspective. What do we see? How can we make the space interesting to them without it being too "busy"?

- Can our baby see us? Being able to have us in their eye line can make a baby more secure to explore on their own.

- Do we need to adjust the space as our baby grows? Are they moving off the movement mat? Maybe it is time to remove it? Can they pull themselves to standing? Does the mirror need to be changed from horizontal to vertical?

- Are there any obstacles to their development that we can remove (e.g., that limit their freedom of movement)? A playpen? A crib?

- Does any activity need to be changed? We can store those that are not being used and rotate them again when we see our baby looking for something new.

From these observations, is there something new we learned about our baby? Is there anything we would like to change as a result? Something in the environment? Another way we can support them? Obstacles we can be removing? Including our own intervention? Observe joy!

SIDS GUIDELINES FOR SLEEP

These are the current SIDS guidelines from the American Academy of Pediatrics (AAP).

1. Baby should sleep on their back for every sleep.

2. Baby should sleep on a firm surface.

3. It is recommended that babies sleep in the parents' room, close to the parents' bed, but on a separate surface designed for infants, ideally for the first year of life, but at least for the first 6 months.

4. Keep soft objects and loose bedding away from the infant's sleep area.

5. Consider offering a pacifier at nap time and bedtime—studies have reported it reduces the risk of SIDS.

6. Avoid overheating and head coverings for infants.

7. Avoid the use of commercial devices that are inconsistent with safe sleep recommendations. Examples include, but are not limited to, wedges and positioners and other devices placed in the adult bed for the purpose of positioning or separating the infant from others in the bed.

8. Do not use home cardiorespiratory monitors as a strategy to reduce the risk of SIDS.

9. There is no evidence that swaddling reduces the risk of SIDS.

FLOOR BED QUESTIONS

Won't my baby roll out of the floor bed?

- If the floor bed is new for our baby, they may indeed roll off the floor bed. Luckily, the bed is close to the ground, so there is little chance that our baby will be hurt. If the floor bed is used from birth when our newborn isn't moving that much, they will learn the limits of the mattress as they grow.

- After a couple of times, our baby will learn to unconsciously feel for the edge of the bed—they are learning about their body, their environment (the edge of their bed), and their strength (how gentle they need to be to stay on the bed versus falling off).

- We can also lay a soft blanket on the floor if we have hard floors— make sure it is not loose or easily tangled as it could be a SIDS hazard.

- If our baby has just learned to roll, we may want to roll up a towel and place it lengthwise underneath the mattress along the edge that is not against the wall.

- Some people use a mattress frame that is high enough to stop our baby from rolling out but low enough that they will be able to climb or slither out on waking.

Won't they get out of bed to play in the night?

- They may crawl out of bed during the night when they are wakeful. That is one advantage of the floor bed. They can play with some activities, then crawl back to bed when they are done (or sometimes they happen to fall back to sleep on the floor of their room). Keep the room babyproof and offer quiet activities for them to explore.

How will I get my baby, who crawls/walks, to stay in a floor bed?

- A baby who has always had the floor bed as their point of reference will be clear that this is the place where they rest and often even crawl to their bed when they are ready to sleep.

- If the floor bed is new to them and they are already crawling or walking, we can help by introducing the floor bed for them to explore. Then at sleep time, when we see their tired signs, we can lay them in their bed. We can sit next to them, perhaps with a gentle hand on them, and enjoy relaxing with them as they learn their new place to sleep. After a few days, we will be able to move farther from their mattress, and eventually we won't need to sit with them for them to stay in bed.

- Over time, they will enjoy being able to choose to get up to play and not need to call out to us, and we will trust them. It's hard to believe that they will choose to sleep. But remember all the Montessori families who have experienced just that.

We live in a warm climate—what about bugs in their bed?	• Light-colored flooring in the sleeping area (or a light-colored rug) will make it easy to see any bugs. Also, keep the room clean and close the door when the sleep area is not in use. • The floor bed has the advantage in warmer climates of being cooler for our baby because it is close to the ground.
We live in a cool climate—won't they get cold on the floor?	• Block any drafts coming under the door with a draft snake or a rolled-up towel. • Have a woolen underlay under the sheet. • Dress the baby in warmer pajamas with socks (this allows them to have freedom of movement in their feet). • Use a warm sleep sack until it becomes a tripping hazard once the baby is crawling or walking.
Do you need a frame around the mattress?	• It's a personal preference. • A frame can look nice and a low lip around the mattress can help to keep the baby from rolling out. A frame can also keep the mattress off the floor to provide air circulation. • Putting a mattress directly on the floor is also okay.
What size should the floor bed be?	• It can be a crib-sized mattress or larger. • If there is space, many families enjoy a larger floor bed so they can lie down with the baby to nurse or soothe.

TIPS FOR TRICKY SITUATIONS

When there are older siblings

One of the most common questions about setting up a Montessori-style home is how to use the space with children of different ages. In this case, we are working to meet the needs of all the children in the home in these (sometimes small) areas.

1. **Use higher shelves for older siblings.** We can look for shelving that is three shelves high—the lower shelves can be for the baby to use or can hold activities with large parts that are safe for all ages; and the higher shelves can be used for activities with smaller parts for the older children.

2. **Look for containers for small parts that the baby cannot open.** We can use things like a screw-top jar or a container with a tightly closed lid to hold small nails for hammering; small blocks like LEGOs for building; and other small parts, like little pegs, that are used by the older siblings.

3. **Make a space where each child can go to be by themselves if they wish.** An older child may get very frustrated with a crawling baby who seems intent on destroying the building structure they have created. Even the baby may wish to be left in peace instead of being dragged around by an older sibling or dealing with a sibling who keeps interfering and taking over what they are playing with.

    It might be that building materials are brought to the dining or kitchen table, out of the baby's reach; a blanket can be placed over the back of some chairs with a sign that says "Private," and we can show the baby the sign and tell them, "It says *Private*." Or we can create an area for the baby using some low shelves or a floor rug to mark their area and have a separate area for older children.

It's not going to be argument-free. Think of it as giving the children many opportunities to practice problem-solving and finding ways to meet everyone's needs. And we can continue to adjust our spaces as our children grow and find ways to make it work even better for everyone.

Small spaces

It's almost more important in smaller spaces to have a place for everything and everything in its place. Otherwise the space quickly becomes cluttered and uninviting to our baby.

If space is tight, we have the opportunity to be creative.

- We could roll up the sleeping mattress each morning to create more space.
- There could be space high on the walls that we could use to mount some storage (paint it the same color as the walls and it's barely visible).
- Some of the furniture might be unnecessary and could be taken out of the space, at least for now—for example, a desk or couch that is used infrequently.
- Look for light-framed and light-colored furniture that can give the appearance of more space.
- We can arrange a toy swap with friends. In some places, it may be possible to rent toys for a monthly fee rather than buying things that need to be stored.
- And clever storage will also play a big role in a small space, keeping out only the things the baby is using right now.

Getting rid of the clutter

When we start with setting up our homes Montessori-style from birth, we have the advantage of not having a lot of extra toys and baby stuff before we get started.

We may still have quite a lot of our own things that we could streamline to make space for a calmer, less cluttered home to welcome the baby.

It can be a good idea to see what we no longer need and remove it to create more space for curious babies, who are natural explorers. And to be conscious of what we bring into our homes for the baby.

BOOK RECOMMENDATION

There is good reason Marie Kondo's decluttering method has become so popular: It works. She encourages us to only keep those things that spark joy or are useful. And for those things we are going to let go of, we can say "thank you" for the joy we felt when we received them. To read more, we recommend her book *The Life-Changing Magic of Tidying Up.*

WHAT'S NEXT:
PREPARING THE HOME FOR A YOUNG TODDLER

It won't be long before our baby becomes a young toddler on the move. Here are some ideas for setting up the home for young toddlers so we can be ready for what is coming next.

Kitchen

The young toddler loves to be involved in what is going on in the kitchen. They will want to be able to see what is being prepared and to help in simple ways, so a stepladder or learning tower can be useful once they can stand steadily.

They will start to be able to carry a plate, glass, and cutlery to their snack table, so have these in a low drawer or cupboard. We can also set up an area where they can help themselves to a glass of water (a water dispenser or jug with a small amount of water, a cloth at the ready, and a small glass) and a simple snack (look for containers that they can open themselves).

Bedroom

The young toddler may want more space to explore and move in the bedroom when awake. If an adult chair was being used for feeding, this may need to be removed to create more space. We can make sure the activities on the low shelf are becoming more difficult, to challenge them. Again, choose quieter activities for the bedroom area.

As the young toddler is likely to be pulling up, standing, and even climbing, make the space as safe as possible. Think about having window locks installed if necessary, ensure bookshelves are attached to the walls, and remove any items we don't want them to reach (toddlers can be remarkably resourceful).

Living room

The horizontal mirror will likely no longer be used in the movement area and could be reused in the entrance area and hung in a vertical orientation (perfect for checking themselves before leaving the house). Similarly, if the movement mat has not already been removed, it can be cleared away to make space for more exploration and movement.

Young toddlers love to climb—if space allows, a climbing frame like a Pikler triangle with slide will get a lot of use. For smaller spaces, it's possible to find versions which fold up for storage, or can be hung high on a wall out of the way when not in use. Alternatives like wooden stepping stones, a balance beam, or rocker are also wonderful opportunities for toddlers to practice their movements. A wagon for pushing is popular for young toddlers learning to walk.

Keep updating the activities provided for them to master and rotate ones from the storage area when new challenges are needed.

Reading books becomes a favorite activity for many young toddlers. Think about creating a cozy book corner with front-facing bookshelves displaying a small selection of books and have cushions, a bean bag, or comfortable low chair to read in. We can rotate books when needed with others from a bookshelf or storage area to keep it interesting without being overwhelming to a young child.

Bathroom

Young toddlers want to be able to wash their own hands, reach their own toothbrush, and possibly climb into the bath by themselves. Having a low step stool at the ready will be very useful.

Some young toddlers may show interest in toileting—then it's time for a potty (or a step to reach the toilet), a place for wet clothing, dry underwear, and cloths for cleaning up at the ready.

Entrance

Now is the time—if not already—to get the entrance ready with some low hooks for a bag, coat, hat, etc. A basket down low for shoes and another for items like scarves and gloves will be helpful for toddlers who like to know where things belong so they can be found easily.

The mirror from the movement area can be relocated to the entrance area, hung vertically. A small table with tissues and sunscreen can be handy for last-minute leaving-the-house checks.

Outside

The young toddler is becoming more and more active. Once they are standing and walking, a whole world opens up for them to explore. We can begin to provide opportunities for running, cycling (e.g., a small tricycle they can push with their legs by themselves), jumping, hanging from their arms, sliding, and swinging.

Simply exploring a garden or going for a walk in the forest will be rich experiences for young toddlers. Look out for rocks, shells, feathers, and other things to find in nature to start a nature collection. And they may start to show an interest in working in the garden and helping to pick homegrown vegetables, giving water to the plants, and raking up leaves.

BENEFITS OF SETTING UP
A MONTESSORI-STYLE HOME

We're always surprised at how setting up our homes in this way creates a lighter, calmer space for the family. In addition, setting up our home in this way:

1. Provides a sense of security for the baby by offering consistent points of reference in the home
2. Allows the baby to absorb beauty and feel that we care for our home
3. Gives a clear place for everything and everything in its place—beautifully arranged with everything needed at the ready (also in the adult spaces)
4. Enables the baby to absorb aspects of their culture through artwork, ceramics, and other cultural elements found in the home
5. Allows the home to become an aid to move from dependence, to collaboration, to independence
6. Helps the baby learn their effect on the world by using spaces set up where they can move their body, explore spaces, and try out different activities
7. Gives a sense of belonging to the baby, being included in all areas of the home and family life

By being intentional in creating these spaces for our baby, we have laid the foundation for the coming months and years. There is one last thing about setting up our homes—the work is never finished. Our babies become toddlers, and our toddlers become children and then teenagers. Yet there is now a strong base in place from birth that can be adjusted easily as our child grows.

TO PRACTICE

- Can our baby use their spaces in an independent way as much as possible (e.g., a movement mat instead of a bouncer chair)?
- Are our spaces beautiful and clutter-free for our baby to experience?
- Can we place attractive activities in a way that our baby can see what is available and begin to learn to choose for themselves?
- Do we have a consistent place for feeding, changing, bathing, and sleeping?
- Have we created sufficient storage so we can rotate activities and store items that are not being used?
- Have we laid down on the floor next to our baby to see what the space feels and looks like from their perspective?

**ENVIRONMENT
0 TO 5 MONTHS**

1. Floor bed
2. Center for changing and clothes storage
3. Receptacle for rubbish or dirty clothes
4. Shelves
5. Adult chair
6. Movement mat with mirror
7. Mobile

**ENVIRONMENT
5 TO 9 MONTHS**

1. Floor bed
2. Center for changing and clothes storage
3. Receptacle for rubbish or dirty clothes
4. Shelves
5. Adult chair
6. Movement mat with mirror
7. Ottoman
8. Weaning table and chair
9. Bar on wall

ENVIRONMENT
9 TO 12 MONTHS

1. Floor bed
2. Center for changing and clothes storage
3. Receptacle for rubbish or dirty clothes
4. Shelves

5. Adult chair
6. Ottoman
7. Weaning table and chair
8. Bar on wall
9. Basket of balls

These rooms are based on illustrations by Gianna Gobbi in the AMI Assistants to Infancy training.

A MONTESSORI HOME FROM THE
BABY'S PERSPECTIVE, BY ZACH, 16 MONTHS OLD

*We see here how the home setup has aided his development and joy in exploration
from birth. Enjoy this "interview." (imagined and transcribed by his mother, Pilar Bewley,
Mainly Montessori)*

Welcome! Come on in. . . . I'm Zach, and this is my home. I was born in my parents' bedroom
upstairs and have spent my entire life—a whopping 16 months—living here. I love what my
parents have done with the place, and I want to share my favorite spots with you.

Let's begin in the kitchen. When I started being strong enough to open the drawers on my
own, my mom had to do some rearranging. She moved all the chemicals to the bathroom
(the only cabinet in the house with a childproof lock). She put her glass containers in a higher
drawer so I wouldn't accidentally break one while playing with other containers, and she
moved the silverware (except the sharp knives) down to a low drawer so I could have access
to it. Other than that, she left everything else as it was. A few times I tried investigating the
delicate items she had in some of the drawers, but she would come over and tell me, "No,
those are not for you." She would then show me which drawers I could play with. Now I know!
I got my fingers caught in the heavy drawers a couple of times, but now I'm really skilled at
closing them.

Next to the kitchen is the little wooden cupboard where I keep my toys. My mom found it at
a swap meet, and I love it because it's the perfect size for me! We keep my cars in one basket
on the floor and my balls in another. Mommy says baskets are great, and I agree! I especially
like to dump everything out of them and then put things back (or walk away and leave a giant
mess behind, depending on my mood).

Next to my toys is my weaning table. This is where I had my first meal with a bowl and a spoon!
When I first used the table, at 4 months of age, I needed help sitting up. Now all mom has
to say is "It's time to eat!" and I run to my table, pull out my chair, and sit down on my own!
Sometimes I share my weaning table with my friend James. We have so much fun eating lunch
together! My dad and my aunt Debbie made the weaning table from plywood he had lying
around in the basement. They also built my Learning Tower [a Montessori stepstool], which
we move into the kitchen when I need to wash my hands or help with the cooking. I hope one
day I can be as crafty as they are.

I have breakfast and dinner with Mom and Dad at the dining room table. I have a Tripp-Trapp
chair that was a present from my grandparents, aunt, uncle, and cousins. I love knowing that
my entire family has contributed to my independence. I am learning to climb in and out of the
chair on my own, and it's so nice to share meals with Mom and Dad. We always light a candle
and use real china, silverware, and glasses. I love feeding myself, which can get a little messy,
but it's also a lot of fun. I've broken a couple of glasses and plates, but now I have a lot of
respect for them and am so careful that I am now in charge of taking the plates and silverware
to the table when it's time for dinner!

Careful with those steps. You might want to hold on to the low railing my dad installed so I could go up and down them on my own. This way, I can get to the bathroom when I have to use the potty. Here's my little toilet. I have another one upstairs. Here are my underwear and my books. Mom and I spend a lot of time here, reading books, singing songs, and waiting for me to do my business. When I pee or poop, I proudly empty my potty into the toilet on my own, while my mom flinches and tries to pretend like she's not dying to help me.

Oh, look, right outside the bathroom is the dogs' water bowl. I used to make a giant mess every time I walked by—I couldn't resist turning over the bowl and spilling the water everywhere! I'm much more mature now; I notice when it's empty and take it to my mom so she can fill it up. She didn't understand me the first time I took it to her and said "agua." She told me, "No, there's no water in the bowl right now." Moms can be so dense! I persisted, and eventually she understood and got really excited at my new "level of awareness," which is what she called it when she told Daddy. Call it whatever you want, Mom, but someone had to give the dogs water!

Let's go upstairs. Mind the gate at the bottom of the stairs, which nowadays is only used for keeping the dogs downstairs. We still use the one at the top of the stairs when Mom has to take a shower and I am hanging out upstairs.

Here's my bedroom. I slept on a floor bed for many months. It was a crib mattress placed on the floor, and I really enjoyed the freedom it gave me to explore my room after my nap or if I wasn't feeling sleepy. Unfortunately, I am a big-time roller, and in the winter I would roll out of bed and get very cold sleeping on the wood floor. My parents found the perfect solution: this neat bed from IKEA! Instead of using slats to raise the mattress off the floor (like the original design intended), my dad came up with the idea of putting the mattress on the floor so that there would be a low wall surrounding it. There's a little entry/exit built into one end of the bed's frame, but I'm also really good at climbing in and out of the side of the bed (I landed on my face the first few times I tried this, but now I'm a real pro). Next to the bed is my stool and my laundry hamper. Mom says I'm a wiggle worm; she tries to get me to sit down to get dressed, but I often end up running around the room half-naked. However, I do love to put my dirty clothes into the hamper!

In the upstairs bathroom, I have a stool to reach the counter so I can brush my teeth, and I also have another potty like the one downstairs. In my parents' room, I have a few toys on a shelf, which I mostly use only when Mommy is getting dressed. This was my movement area when I was younger; I had my mobiles, mirror, and a bar for pulling up and cruising. We'll soon turn it into a climbing wall so I can give Mom more heart attacks and start bouldering!

Well, that's it, folks! I hope you've enjoyed the tour of our Montessori home. Thanks for visiting, come back soon!

HOME TOUR

Let's take a look around the home of Nicole, founder of the site The Kavanaugh Report. There are four children in the family, and we can see how the space is set up to meet the needs of, and include, the youngest member of the family.

Pictured here with a DIY black and white mobile, inspired by the Munari mobile, and the topponcino.

BEDROOM

The bedroom area is calm and relaxed. A mattress on the floor serves as the floor bed, a sheepskin with a wooden mobile hanger as a movement area, and low shelves can display simple activities. Botanical artwork is down low for the baby to enjoy when awake, and an adult feeding chair is in the corner so the baby can be fed in their room during the night. The space is baby-proofed so it is safe for baby to explore upon waking.

MOVEMENT AREA

A soft carpet is used as a movement mat where the baby can have free movement, stretch, and explore their body and the things around them. A mirror allows them to see themselves, take in their body schema (how their body is made up) and also allows the baby to see their siblings busy alongside them. There is a bar on the wall when the baby is ready to pull up to stand and cruise.

A low shelf with some objects to explore is at the ready— an object impermanence box with a ball, grasping beads, a palmar grasp cylinder, a basket of objects, and some simple board books.

A plant and wall hanging soften the space to make it feel cozy and inviting.

FEEDING AREA

A low table and chair provide a baby-sized space for their first meals and snacks. A tray with a small glass and pitcher of water is at the ready, along with some flowers and a cloth placemat showing how we prepare even the baby's feeding area with love and care.

The table height is about 12 inches (30cm) and the chair seat height is about 5 inches (13cm), so their feet can reach the ground.

FAMILY ROOM

This photo shows the baby being included in the family's life. The baby has the space to do their explorations—lying on a sheepskin with a grasping object to investigate—while also tracking their siblings and parents going about their play. In the background, we see a bookshelf with books from the older children and a large puzzle on a mat next to the baby, nearby enough to see but out of reach for safety.

CHANGING AREA

The baby's clothes are easy to see and, once wriggling, the baby can make their way over to indicate which one they would like. This also establishes a sense of order once they are dressing more independently, as they learn where their clothes are stored. We do not need so many clothes and can rotate these seasonally and as the child grows.

On the top of the low shelf is a changing pad for diaper changes, which can also be placed on the floor as the baby gets bigger. Once they are standing, we can change their diaper as they stand (for example, with us sitting on a low stool). It takes some practice, but babies might feel more vulnerable lying on their back. Standing confers a sense of agency, and lying down makes the baby more passive, being acted upon. It involves them, and often leads to less resistance to diaper changing.

PARENTING THE
MONTESSORI BABY

5

TRUST

Like many parents, Junnifa spent a lot of time thinking of and researching the best gifts for her son's first birthday. Her wish list included wooden stacking blocks, a tricycle, and musical instruments. Then one day, while observing her almost-1-year-old, she realized that the best gifts for the first year cannot be bought; they are not material, but psychological. They are the basic trusts. These gifts are made even more special because they can only be given in the first year and only under the right conditions.

The two basic trusts are the *trust in the environment* and the *trust in self.*

Basic Trust in the Environment: This first basic trust is usually acquired by the end of the second month of life, which also marks the end of a very important time in the baby's growth, the period of adaptation to their new world. During this time, the mother and the baby depend on each other to meet both physical and psychological needs—this is the period of symbiosis we discussed in chapter 3. This stage lays the foundation for the child's personality and their view of the world and life. A child who has basic trust in the environment will approach life with optimism, security, and trust in the world as a good place where they can thrive.

Basic Trust in Self: This second basic trust is usually acquired by the ninth month, which marks the end of exterogestation, or the external pregnancy. The child will have spent as much time outside the womb as they spent inside. The basic trust in self lays the foundation for confidence and strong self-esteem. The child who has basic trust in self will approach challenges with confidence in their abilities. They will not be discouraged by failures. They will be curious and approach the world with an exploratory attitude.

We can give our baby this gift by helping the child develop independence and providing opportunities for movement, exploration, and communication.

Each time the baby succeeds, a deposit is made in their basic trust in self. It is important that we do not interrupt our baby or try to "help" our baby too much, for example, by putting the bell or ribbon of their tactile mobile in their hands. In addition to creating themselves and building their basic trust in themselves, the baby is also building their ability to concentrate. This process should be respected.

We can prepare an environment that will enable the baby to acquire basic trust in self. We can also continue to observe the baby to notice changes and then adjust the environment to balance challenge with their ability to succeed. We also continue to model the behaviors and social expectations for them and provide the baby with feedback for their actions. We talk to the baby, sing to the baby, and, even more important, listen to and converse with the baby. The parent observes the child for verbal and nonverbal cues of hunger, care, sleep, etc., while responding and providing language. Gradually, the baby improves their ability to communicate. It may be a word, or a sign, or a gesture, like bringing over their bib when they are hungry. They know they can communicate and make their needs known—another deposit in their basic trust in self.

And then one day, before they turn a year old, we will be together and our baby will smile at us and walk or crawl away. They look back at us now and then but continue to move away with purpose. They go out of sight and we wait for them to come back, but they don't. We go to check and we find them. They are sitting down and exploring their shelf or sitting at their table and having a snack. Maybe they are drinking from their glass or in their reading corner, flipping through a book that they have chosen by themselves.

And then we realize that they have received the best gifts for the first year. They trust the environment and themselves. They are optimistic and know that the world is a good place, and they trust in their abilities—so they are not afraid to explore independently. The foundations for a good life of happiness, lifelong learning, and exploration have been laid.

And while the role of the parents remains paramount, any informed caregiver of our baby can support us in giving of the two gifts of basic trust.

ACCEPTANCE

Imagine the feeling of visiting a place and before you get there, a message comes from your hosts telling you how much they are looking forward to having you. And when you arrive, you find them waiting excitedly and you see that they have beautifully prepared the home for you. Wouldn't it make such a difference for your stay?

We can welcome our babies in this way, and in so doing, we send them a message of acceptance that will stay with them for the rest of their lives and lay a foundation for all future relationships and transitions. We can send this message of acceptance through our interactions with our babies, and this can start from the moment of conception. When we rub our bellies while pregnant, spend time talking to the baby in utero, call the baby by name, read books, and sing to the baby, we send the message that we accept them and are looking forward to welcoming them. Being happy and as relaxed as possible during pregnancy helps keep our hormones balanced and also sends the message of acceptance versus stress and unhappiness.

This message of acceptance can continue to be sent after birth by the way we prepare ourselves and our environment for the baby. The time spent holding the baby, the way we look at them, touch them, love on them, and give our undivided attention during caregiving are all ways that we continue to send the message. They can sense that we waited for them and are happy to receive them.

This message sent and reinforced during pregnancy and after birth tells the baby that they are wanted and that they have come to a safe place. Dr. Silvana Montanaro, one of Dr. Montessori's infancy collaborators, believed that this message stayed with the child through life and gave them an optimistic view of the world that allowed them to adapt positively.

RESPECT

Respect is not a word that many people associate with babies or children in general, but Dr. Montessori believed that "Children are human beings to whom respect is due, superior to us by reason of their innocence and of the greater possibilities of their future." (*Dr. Montessori's Own Handbook*)

Montessori parenting is based on respect. Respect for the child as they are, and for the innumerable possibilities of their future.

There are many ways to show our babies respect starting from birth.

Respect our baby's body: The first interaction the baby has with the world is often through touch, and this continues to be the predominant interaction during the first year. Babies are touched a lot by their caregivers. We touch them when we feed them, change them, and hold them. This provides many opportunities to show the baby respect.

We can start by asking permission before handling our baby, picking them up, or handing them to someone else, especially a stranger. We might say, "Hello, baby, may

I pick you up?" When we ask a baby if we can touch or carry them, we can usually tell if they accept or reject. We can stretch our hands toward them, make our request, and wait. There is usually a change in their gesture or body. If they smile or move in our direction, we take it as a "yes" and pick them up. Then we can say, "Thank you," or otherwise acknowledge their acceptance verbally. If they frown, look away, or just shrink back, we can say, "No worries, maybe next time." In this way, we tell the baby from the beginning that they own their body and have a choice in how it is handled.

When carrying the baby, we do not yank or forcefully carry them. Instead, we carry them as gently and gracefully as we can. Our hands can teach the baby peace or violence. Gentle, slow, deliberate hands communicate respect and teach peace.

Physical care, including diaper changes and baths, provides lots of opportunities for respect.

Thank our baby: We thank adults for many things but often don't have the same courtesy when dealing with children. When we get into the habit with our babies, it will stay. And guess what? They are absorbing it and will adopt it too.

"Thank you for letting me hold you."

"Thank you for being here and spending time with me."

"Thank you for napping and giving me a break."

Trust our baby and their abilities: We can trust them to control their bodies, and we do not put them in positions that we feel they are not ready for. We can trust them to make choices about how to move and interact with the environment we create for them. We can trust them to problem-solve and we do not always rush in to help or provide a solution to their struggles.

When we respect the baby's abilities, we invite collaboration at every stage. It can be waiting for our newborn to find the nipple; saying something to our 3-month-old and waiting for their acknowledgment; putting the fork in the avocado for our 7-month-old and waiting for them to pick it up and bring it to their mouth; or holding out the arm of their shirt and waiting for our 9-month-old to put in their hand. All these small gestures tell the baby that we trust their ability. The gestures also support the baby's development of functional independence. We offer as little help as possible and as much as necessary, observing before intervening and allowing the baby to solve problems.

Observation is a form of respect: When we observe our children before responding or to understand them, we are effectively saying to them, "You know something I don't. Show me. Help me understand more about you."

Respect their individuality: Each child is unique, different in their timelines, personality, and expressions. Simone has two children and Junnifa has three—and we marvel at how different they each are from their siblings. Even if you provide the exact same environment and treat them the same, each child will be their own unique self. When we accept this from the beginning, we are able to accept and respect each child for the unique individual they are. It can be so hard not to compare or have expectations of one child based on another. Instead, we can observe our babies to understand and support their uniqueness. One unexpected way in which our children's personalities can differ is with sleep. We might have a baby who winds down easily and just goes to sleep or one who just doesn't want to miss a thing and so fights sleep with all their might. Even this aspect of individuality can be respected. We respect it by first accepting that this is how our baby is, and then finding ways to help them thrive in their individuality.

Consider the baby's needs: We want to always have the baby's tendencies and sensitive periods in mind and try to understand which of these might be motivating the baby's actions. (For more on sensitive periods, see page 18.)

Follow our baby's rhythms: Each baby is different and will have to find their own rhythm. We can respect this by providing situations that make it possible for them to do so and to allow time in our busy days to prioritize this. This includes rhythms around food, sleep, diapering, and the day in general. From birth, we can notice the baby's cues, build routines around them, and stay consistent.

Encourage our baby's activity: In her book *Child in the Family,* Dr. Montessori invites us to "respect all reasonable forms of activity in which the child engages and try to understand it." But how does one determine what is reasonable, and how do we try to understand it?

If an activity is safe, we can consider it reasonable and then we can stop to observe. This is how we can try to understand it. If we observe our baby touching something, watching something, moving in a certain way, and generally exploring, we respect their activity by not interfering or intervening.

Often babies can struggle but not necessarily need help. When we observe, we will learn to tell when they are asking for help, and then we can offer just the right amount of assistance. With babies, when we watch them play or try to reach for something, they might make little sounds indicating their effort and maybe a little bit of a struggle. As parents, our first instinct is usually to step in and help. Instead, we can first take a moment to observe, and often, when we hold ourselves back, we are rewarded by the evident joy when they succeed without our interference. And they are, too.

Knowing that all of the baby's activities are the work that they do to develop themselves, we respect their effort and protect their concentration by not interrupting. Sometimes even our words of acknowledgment can be an interruption. We respect our baby's exploration by sitting back when they are active, observing to understand and support them better.

"Never help a child with a task at which he feels he can succeed."

"Every unnecessary help is an obstacle to the child's development."

—Dr. Maria Montessori

ALTERNATIVES TO PRAISE

Praising our babies can be a hard habit to break or avoid. Often when our children do something, we feel the need to acknowledge it in some way. Many times our instinct is to acknowledge by praising, but when we do this, we teach the baby to look to us for how to feel about their efforts.

In Montessori we are wanting to build a child's intrinsic sense of self rather than having them look for or get used to external praise and validation. Instead of praise, saying "Good job," or clapping, we could try the following alternatives with our babies:

1. Don't do anything. This allows the baby to enjoy the moment in their own way.

2. Sportscast—say what we saw the baby doing: "You put the ball in the hole."

3. Describe what you observe about the baby's feelings: "You look content/excited!"

4. Acknowledge our baby's effort: "You worked on that for a long time" or "You did it."

5. Give a gentle smile.

6. Offer encouragement: "I knew you could do it."

7. You could talk about what comes next: "I see you are done. Shall we go get ready to nap?"

8. Or talk about how it feels: "I'm so excited for you. You did it."

Respect the baby's pace (slow down): Respecting the baby's abilities also means understanding that it takes children a little longer to process and figure out things, so we give them "tarry time" to process and try. When we say something to our baby, it can take 8 to 10 seconds for them to process it, so we can build this time into our interactions and wait for their response.

It also takes longer to involve a baby in dressing, feeding, and other moments of daily life. Yet, we often save time when we involve them, because they may not become upset so easily, and we are laying the foundation for them to develop concentration, focus, skills of independence, and to explore the world around them.

Respect the baby's choices: When we respect the baby, we give true choices as often as possible and respect what the baby chooses. We do not impose our thoughts or emotions and instead listen to hear and understand them. This can start from as early as 3 months with our babies. We can offer two shirts and see which one they gesture or smile toward. We can offer two books and see which one they choose. We put two rattles within reach and let them choose which one and how to use it. For an older baby, they will select an object from a selection of 3–5 items in a basket. Offering a choice is a form of respect, and then we respect the baby's choices.

This helps us already practice for the choices our baby will make as they become a toddler, preschooler, school-aged child, and beyond. We won't give them the choice of which country we might live in or which school they attend, but we will give them age-appropriate choices.

> "Now we must learn how to care for the newborn child. We must welcome him with love and respect."
>
> —Dr. Maria Montessori

HAVING KIND AND CLEAR BOUNDARIES

"Freedom within limits" is how we help our Montessori children develop self-discipline, and, like other ideas, we start with this at birth. We try as much as possible to give the baby freedom within the limits of safety and their abilities.

Offering our baby choices, giving time and opportunity for movement and activity, and letting them feed themselves are some of the ways that we give our baby freedom. "Freedom" can be a difficult word to understand, as we are often used to it meaning "freedom from" something, like rules or having to work. In a Montessori context, we give the baby/child "freedom to" do something—like freedom to choose, to move, and to express themselves. It's not a license to do whatever they like—it's freedom within the rules of our family and society.

So with all of these, we also set limits or boundaries. Here are some of the ways that we set boundaries with babies:

Limit the options or choices: When preparing the baby's environment, we consciously only include the items that are safe for them to use. When we offer choices, we limit them to options that we have approved and that are acceptable to us.

Keep them safe or give safe alternatives: Babies are still getting to understand the world. They do this by exploring, and sometimes they will explore beyond the safe areas of the home or space or do things that are unsafe. In these situations, we can stop unsafe behavior and redirect unacceptable actions. For example, if a baby crawls to an electrical outlet, we tell them it is unsafe and carry them to a safe part of the room. A baby who is throwing inappropriate objects can be redirected to a basket of balls or objects more appropriate for throwing.

Respond to the need or message being communicated: The baby's behavior is usually their way of communicating something. It might be a need or a message. A baby who is throwing objects might be communicating a need for more gross-motor movement, and a baby who is throwing food might simply be communicating that they are full or not interested in the meal. Our response would be based on our observation and interpretation.

Modify the environment or a process: If our baby often pours the water out of their cup while they're not drinking, we can modify our process by keeping the cup by our side until it is time for the baby to drink, or pouring just enough for one drink and taking the cup back once the baby is done. If our baby keeps going back to an electrical outlet, we can make sure it is protected or maybe move a piece of furniture in front of it. In this way, we set limits using the environment.

Be prepared to repeat ourselves: We have only a few limits because we will need to repeat ourselves many times until our baby's will is developed enough to stop themselves, for example, from touching something they want to explore. Their prefrontal cortex, which is responsible for inhibiting themselves, is in the earliest stages of development and will be developing into their early twenties. So we need to be their prefrontal cortex.

Teach them what to do, rather than tell them what we don't want them to do:
Remembering that babies are new here and just figuring out how things work, we can
see ourselves as their guides, here to help them and show them how things work. With
this in mind, when the baby goes beyond our boundaries or limits we can see this as an
opportunity to teach them appropriate and acceptable behavior. This understanding can
make a difference to how we respond. If we are teaching the baby what is acceptable, we
might say. "The water stays in the cup. Put the cup down here," instead of "Don't pour
the water," or "Why do you keep pouring the water?"

We might model like this: "I see you are done. Let me show you where the cup goes."
Modeling is so important in helping the baby figure out the boundaries.

A NOTE ON POSITIVE LANGUAGE

This is a great time for us to practice saying things in a more positive way. Children
tune out when they constantly hear "don't" and "no" all the time. So we tell them what
we want them to do: "Let's keep your feet on the ground" rather than "Don't climb
on the table." In addition, it's simpler for them to process our request. When we
hear someone say, "Don't put your hands on your head," first we think of our head
and then need to work out where to put our hands instead.

Start now, and by the time they are toddlers and we are seeking their cooperation
more and more, it will be automatic.

ENCOURAGING CONCENTRATION

Babies can concentrate. Given free time and a prepared, orderly space, they can concentrate from birth. So we create the following conditions that support concentration starting from birth.

1. Ensure our baby is sleeping enough

Babies from 1 to 12 months old need 14 to 15 hours of sleep. We can guard our baby's sleep. Watch for signs that they are tired, and help them wind down and sleep. Once asleep, avoid waking them up. Without enough sleep, it is hard for babies to focus, even if the environment is well prepared.

2. Keep our baby hydrated and well nourished

Once babies are eating solid food, they need balanced meals that include carbohydrates, protein, fat, fruits, and vegetables. They do not need processed foods and sugars. Even as adults, we find it hard to concentrate when we are hungry or have had too much sugar. We can also teach our baby, as soon as possible, how to get water when they are thirsty. A baby as young as 7 or 8 months old can crawl to a small cup of water or a bottle with a straw.

3. Prepare an orderly environment

Order on the outside leads to order on the inside. Babies need order. This means an uncluttered environment, a place for everything and everything in its place. Order makes it possible for the baby to make a choice. It also makes it possible to focus. If we have hoarding tendencies, we can try to limit our clutter to one room or storage area that the baby doesn't spend time in.

4. Allow the baby to experience peace and quiet

What is the noise level of our home? Are there times of the day when the baby can experience silence and peace? A time when no one is talking on the phone, the radio is not on, and neither is the TV. When pots are not clanging, and everything is quiet and still. Can you imagine it? These can be the best times for concentration. Junnifa tries to make sure her family has many times like this daily, when the only sounds they can hear are the whir of the unavoidable fan for the Nigerian heat and the baby's voice as they hum while they explore. Even an hour of this daily is good for the soul (of both adult and baby).

5. Limit passive entertainment

We don't need to constantly entertain the baby. It becomes exhausting for the adult and can be detrimental for the baby. Babies learn through active experience and by doing instead of being entertained. So we provide an environment that encourages our baby to engage themselves. This can start at birth. Toys that entertain also affect concentration. These are the toys that sing, flash, beep, talk, and do all sorts of things at the press of a button. This kind of entertainment leads to passivity and takes away that sense of wonder and accomplishment that comes from direct discovery. Magda Gerber, founder of the RIE approach, described it well when she said that we want passive toys and active children, not active toys, which lead to passive children.

6. Avoid screens before age 2 and have little or no screens after age 2

You can try this experiment. Put on a cartoon or a typical children's television program. Take out a stopwatch and count how many scene and color changes happen in 3 minutes. The real world moves much more slowly. Children can get used to this stimulating pace and will struggle to slow down and focus. This passive entertainment is often very noisy.

Our babies are sensorial learners best suited to learning through their mouths and hands, so we can turn off screens and let them discover this beautiful world we live in.

7. Choose simple and developmentally appropriate toys and materials

For babies, many of the skills they concentrate on building are ones that require no materials at all. Some examples include when a baby first discovers their hands and stares at them for extended periods of time, or when they are learning to turn over and can sometimes try more than 30 times in a row. The majority of a baby's explorations fall in this category and require nothing but space and uninterrupted time. Mobiles and very simple toys that the baby can explore in different ways also support the development of concentration.

8. Observe

In all things Montessori, observation is important. We observe to make sure the baby gets enough rest, to make sure they are not hungry or dehydrated, to see when they are overstimulated, to identify their interest, to identify their developmental stage and support it, and, most importantly, to recognize moments of concentration and respect them.

9. Avoid interrupting

Once we have recognized concentration, *we do not interrupt.* Not to help, not to congratulate, not to correct. We can simply smile to ourselves, enjoy their achievements and process, and watch from a distance. During their development, concentration is fragile. It is easily broken, and when the baby experiences this a few times, they can stop trying to concentrate. It is so beautiful to watch a baby completely absorbed and engaged in something.

FREEDOM OF MOVEMENT

One significant way to give freedom to a baby from birth is by giving freedom of movement. We have already talked about it a lot in this book, but it cannot be overemphasized. There are many benefits, including the development of strong gross- and fine-motor skills, increased body awareness, confidence, determination, and an early start to learning problem-solving, among other things.

The following are some of the ways we allow freedom of movement for our baby:

Offer food and wait for baby to accept and take it. If breastfeeding, from birth, the baby can be placed on the tummy and chest and, if we wait, they will find and move toward the breast by themselves.

Avoid swaddling. Babies move their limbs freely in the womb, so we allow them to have freedom to do so from birth. We all have a startle reflex in the beginning because we are no longer constricted by the womb, but we will gradually work it out. If necessary, we can swaddle loosely so that the baby feels covered or cocooned but still has some freedom of movement.

Avoid containers or restrictive devices like bouncers, exersaucers, or similar items. There are times like when we are cooking or busy and need to have the baby close by. In these moments we can wear our babies, use a blanket on the floor, or even use a small bath in the kitchen. If we do find it necessary to use a container, minimize the time the baby spends in it.

Allow free time for movement. Put the baby down on the floor on a blanket or mat or on the bed. They can be put on their back and on their belly. Observation will tell us if the baby is okay. Prepare a movement area where they can freely and safely explore. We can also set up temporary movement areas as needed so that the baby can always be around us in different parts of the house.

Try not to prop our baby into sitting, standing, or other positions that they cannot get into by themselves. When not being held, they can either lie on their backs or on their stomachs. They will come to sit up, pull themselves to standing, and walk when their own bodies can manage this.

Avoid putting toys into their hands. Instead, we can hold or put the toy close enough that they can reach it with some effort, but not too far away that they get frustrated.

Choose movement-friendly clothes. These are comfortable and not too big or too tight. They have minimal fastenings and decorations, which can make the baby uncomfortable if lying down, slithering, or crawling. Leave the feet and knees exposed as much as possible.

Remember that each baby will develop at their own pace. The goal is not to make a baby move faster. Whenever they do move, they will do so with control and confidence.

A SECURE ATTACHMENT

Dr. Montessori saw life as a series of attachments and separations, like pregnancy (attachment) and birth (separation), or breastfeeding (attachment) and weaning (separation), right through to a teenager needing their family as a base (attachment) but gradually spending more time with friends (separation).

Attachment

A secure attachment is the optimum kind of attachment that the baby can develop with their caregiver. It is an innate human need, which babies seek to achieve from birth.

SOME TIPS FOR FORMING SECURE ATTACHMENTS

CONNECTED PREGNANCY LAYS THE FOUNDATION

Even in the womb, the baby receives messages of acceptance. When the mother is happy, relaxed, and makes efforts to connect with the baby (rubbing her stomach, talking to baby, responding to baby's kicks, etc.), messages of acceptance are transmitted, and this lays the foundation for a secure attachment.

RESPONSIVE PARENTING BUILDS TRUST

Contrary to some beliefs, we will not spoil our baby by responding to their needs. Instead, we will be helping them form a secure attachment. From birth, our baby will communicate their needs to us using their vocalizations, facial expressions, and other body language. It is important to spend time with the baby and observe to understand what they are trying to communicate, and then respond appropriately and as quickly as possible. This helps the baby acquire a basic trust in their environment. This is the feeling of security and the knowledge that their needs will be met in this place. It allows the baby to go from self-preservation to attachment.

RESPECTFUL AND CONSISTENT CAREGIVING FOSTERS SECURITY

A large portion of the baby's first year is spent receiving care in the form of feeding or diapering. These times provide a great opportunity to connect with our baby and in doing so, support their formation of a secure attachment. Feeding the baby on demand, notifying them before we pick them up or handle them, and handling them respectfully when we dress and undress them are some ways that we can help form a secure attachment. We can also be consistent with other caregivers such as babysitters or day care workers, having limited, consistent, and well-selected people to care for them.

SPENDING TIME TOGETHER CREATES A BOND

Spending time with the baby and being truly present creates a special bond. Nursing provides a special opportunity for bonding, and while breastfeeding is ideal, bonding doesn't necessarily require that the baby feed at the breast. Skin-to-skin touch, eye contact, holding the baby, observing, and responding to the baby all foster a bond.

There is a great deal of research that supports the notion that a secure attachment sets the foundation for the baby's overall well-being and emotional, intellectual, and social development. A securely attached baby is joyful, curious, and interested in exploring their environment. They will deal with separations more positively and will grow up to be happy, empathetic, creative, resilient, and better able to self-regulate and learn. They will also have a positive sense of themselves and be able to form and maintain more positive relationships throughout their lives.

Separation

It is up to us as parents to observe signs that we can allow our baby more distance to explore safely from this secure base. We can allow them to stretch and move on a mat as we observe; to attempt to reach for things to explore; to slither and crawl away, and come back; and to make little expeditions, then longer ones as they become confident babies and toddlers.

WHEN OUR BABY CRIES

Our baby's cry can trigger strong reactions in us. This is natural and one of nature's ways of protecting our babies. Other things, like our emotional state and our childhood experiences, can affect the way we react to our baby's cry. It is important to move beyond an instinctive reaction to a calm, respectful response. How can we do this?

Take a moment to calm down. Our baby's cry can trigger our freeze, fight, or flight mode. This is not a rational mode, so it is important to take a moment to take our brains out of that mode before responding. It can be a deep breath and a reminder to ourselves to calm down. If the baby is not in danger, we might even step into another room, a bathroom, or a closet and shut the door for a minute or until we feel calm enough.

Next, we can acknowledge our baby. Even before we get to them, we can calmly say, "I hear you, Solu. I am on my way." When we get to them, we can assess and respond. Sometimes our presence is enough to calm the baby down. Sometimes we have to pick the baby up and hold them. Tell them we are going to pick them up and then pick them up and hold them close. Our words are important, and we can choose them carefully. If we know why our baby is crying, we might say, for example, "You bumped your head and it hurt." When we say things like "You're okay" or "Stop crying," we can inadvertently negate, brush away, or ignore the baby's feelings. Instead, allow the feelings and let the baby know that we hear them, we recognize their feelings, and we are there. In this way, we accept and respect their emotions.

It is important to try to understand our baby's cry. Our baby's cries are their way of communicating with us. In the beginning, our baby's cry is uniform, but by the second or third month, it becomes differentiated.

These cries are usually trying to communicate a need, whether it is hunger, tiredness, or discomfort.

We can try to understand and respond appropriately. There are often other signals that our baby gives us before they even start to cry. We might miss them in the beginning, but as we start to observe, we start to see these cues and can anticipate our baby's needs and, in doing so, help them to communicate without needing to cry.

CHECKLIST FOR WHEN OUR BABY CRIES

- Calm ourselves down.
- Acknowledge baby's cry.
- Observe if they need help.
- If needed, comfort with our presence and by holding them.
- Allow our baby's feelings and name them.
- Respond to their need.

BEING THEIR GUIDE

Modeling: Montessori parents, like Montessori teachers, can be our child's guide. This means that we are neither their boss nor their servant. As guides, when we prepare the physical environment for them, we can guide them and model to them how to engage with it, but then we step back and allow them figure it out in their own way. It is a fine balance, and it requires some practice to find the line of allowing exploration and knowing when to intervene. We are not the boss, so we do not dictate how our babies will engage, but we are also not their servants, so we do not rush in to solve every problem. We give them the reassurance of our presence and availability but step back to allow them to figure things out. We offer just enough help when necessary but not too much.

We are always modeling how to engage with the environment and show up in the world. We drink and eat in the baby's presence to model how to use a cup and cutlery. They watch our movements, our conversations, and interactions, and they absorb them.

Knowing this reminds us to be mindful of our actions. To prepare ourselves to be the best version of ourselves. And to apologize and acknowledge when we aren't. "What I should have done is . . ." or "What I should have said is . . ."

When we acknowledge how we are feeling, we are modeling to our baby how to be authentic with feelings and emotions. Some days are hard, and it is okay to be sad or frustrated or tired. We can say that to our babies and then model to them how to find calm by finding it for ourselves (see chapter 8).

Removing obstacles: One of our roles as guide is that of an obstacle remover. We are responsible for identifying and removing obstacles to our children's optimal development. This requires observation and in many cases selflessness. Some of the obstacles actually make our adult lives easier but might be an obstacle for the baby's development. A pacifier might be helpful sometimes, but it can soon become an obstacle that can interfere with the baby's need to communicate and the process of acquiring the skills for communicating. Putting the baby in front of a television might give us a break for a while, but again, it interferes with the baby's optimum development and becomes an obstacle.

We have to be willing to remove the obstacles we identify. Disorder, noise, disproportionate furniture, and things that constrict the baby's movement are some obstacles.

We can also be an obstacle when we put pressure on them to do something like performing on cue. Simone remembers saying to her son, "Show Nanny and Poppy how you can clap/wave/point to the dog." She loved that her son rarely did what she was commanding him to do. So she stopped these "tests" and saw his refusal to perform as a reminder that babies will show their skills in their own time. They are their own person.

We can also be obstacles when we interfere and don't allow opportunities for independence, or when we react instead of observing and then responding.

Being their guide means:

- Giving space for our baby to work it out for themselves
- Being available when needed
- Being respectful, kind, and clear
- Trying not to change who they are
- Supporting them and helping them learn skills where needed
- Using gentle, slow hands and waiting for their response
- Setting limits by modifying the environment instead of having to limit the baby
- Giving as little help as possible and as much as necessary
- Listening and responding (pausing first before we act) rather than reacting (acting straight away without pausing to check ourselves or the situation)

FRAMING THEIR VIEW
OF THE WORLD

In many ways, our babies see the world through our eyes in their early years. They come to define safe and unsafe, good and bad, and other qualities by watching us and listening to us. They reflect what they see and hear from us.

We can be intentional in the messages we pass on about different subjects. For example, when it comes to gender, we can be careful not to unconsciously assign qualities like strength, beauty, or specific interests to one gender over the other. Girls can be strong and boys can be caring. Boys may enjoy playing with dolls and girls may enjoy playing with vehicles. By the way we talk to our babies, the way we dress them, and the opportunities we offer them, we can frame the way they perceive gender and the roles they assign to each gender. Research has shown that there are actually very few differences in the first year between girls' brains and boys' brains. The differentiation begins around a child's first birthday. Some of the ways that we can give them a balanced view are by using gender-neutral pronouns when reading books, avoiding labels like "pretty" versus "handsome" and by seeing each child as capable regardless of gender.

This framing also applies to how we view or label our baby's abilities and character. When we say things like "You naughty baby," we might be joking or not mean it seriously, but it still sends a message. We can instead frame it differently: "I see you are struggling with . . ." In this way, we don't define our baby by a temporary situation. When we trust our babies and say things like "You can do it" or show them that we trust them by allowing them freedom and to struggle to work something out, we frame their view of themselves as capable.

A HANDY CHECKLIST
FOR FOSTERING CONNECTION
WITH OUR BABY

NURSING

- Skin-to-skin contact
- Eye contact
- Observing and responding to our baby's cues

TWO-WAY COMMUNICATION

- Let them know what we are doing
- Wait for their response
- Incorporate their response into our actions

GENTLE HANDS

- Be slow and deliberate when handling our baby
- Collaborate with our baby to dress, bathe, etc.

QUALITY TIME

- Take advantage of caregiving activities like feeding and changing to connect with our baby
- Make time to observe and understand them better
- Spend time just holding and enjoying our baby with no agenda

GOING SLOW

Babies, by nature of their abilities and speed, invite us to adopt a slower pace of life. To support them optimally, we in a sense have to move at their pace. Once our babies are slithering or crawling, instead of picking them up to go to a different room, we can tell them where we are going and invite them to come with us.

It takes longer to involve our baby in their care, to talk them through our actions, to wait for their response, and to do many of the other things we have talked about in this book so far.

We can view this time of slowing down with our baby as an inconvenience, or we can take advantage of it and slow down and enjoy this time. We might enjoy it so much that even when this stage passes, we find opportunities and ways to slow down in the midst of our regular lives.

Some of the ways we can slow down with our babies are:

- Using slow, gentle, and deliberate hands when handling them
- Speaking slowly and clearly so that they can hear each syllable
- Waiting for their response after we speak to them
- Letting them move by themselves and do things by themselves, regardless of how long it takes. We can take these moments to observe them and marvel.
- Stopping to observe before reacting when they struggle or fall, or when we are tempted to intervene
- Stopping for them to stare at things that catch their attention, regardless of how long it takes
- Taking slow walks that allow both baby and us to enjoy the sights, scents, and sounds of nature
- Doing nothing while baby naps. Not trying to catch up on laundry, not catching up on our emails, just sitting in the silence and enjoying it.
- Making some of the baby's materials by hand. There are so many options for materials available commercially, but there can be something soothing and special about making something for our baby by hand. We could sit next to our baby's movement mat while we are working, so they can see us while they do their own explorations.

- Putting on some music and dancing slowly with the baby in our arms or just dancing while baby watches
- Making time to read something daily. It could be something about our baby or just anything that interests us.
- Taking a nap or going to bed early

When Junnifa thinks back on the first years of her three children, one word comes to mind: *joy*. The pace of their family life was slow. Each baby had time and freedom to explore and develop, which led to joy, and a baby's joy is contagious. We hope you too get to experience this joy.

Our baby's first year can feel long and demand so much of us, because we are learning so much and doing so much to support another life. But in our experience and that of everyone we've asked, in retrospect, the time always seems to have flown by. We can find moments of connection and joy, and enjoy the journey.

TO PRACTICE

- How would we like to give our baby the gift of basic trust?
- Can we see our baby for who they are and accept them in their individuality?
- Can we see and treat our babies with respect?
- Can we be intentional in the words that we say to them?
- Can we find opportunities to connect with them?
- Can we enjoy them and enjoy the journey during this special and transient time?

MONTESSORI ACTIVITIES FOR BABIES

6

PART ONE

INTRODUCTION TO ACTIVITIES

HOW WE CAN SUPPORT OUR BABY'S DEVELOPMENT

For more than a century of observing babies, Montessori parents and educators have documented the ages and stages of development in children. We can use these stages as a guide as we observe our own baby's development—and prepare the environment with activities that support these developments.

WHY WE CHOOSE ACTIVITIES FOR OUR BABY

These Montessori activities will help our baby's brain development (by three years old, a child's brain will have reached 80 percent of it's adult volume—an enormous amount of change over a small amount of time). However, the purpose of these activities is not to make our babies "smarter" or to help them reach milestones before their peers. It is to treat them as the unique human they are, to support their developmental needs, to establish a secure attachment, and to help them transition from dependence, to collaboration, and then to independence.

The main areas of development that we can support during infancy are movement and language. Activities can support their intellectual and psychological development—our baby learns to make connections (e.g., "When I hit this with my foot, it moves"), their understanding of our language grows, their bodies are challenged, and they build confidence and trust in the world around them.

The activities presented in this chapter are organized by age, but these are just guidelines. Every baby will develop at their own pace, on their unique timeline, and that is okay. We want to support our baby on their own path—not try to speed up or slow down their individual process. If we are concerned about our baby's development, we can seek support. This is not a bad or shameful thing; this is giving them and us the tools that they need to thrive.

HOW TO CHOOSE ACTIVITIES FOR OUR BABY

1. Read about their current stage of development.

2. Observe our baby.

3. What are they developing/practicing/showing interest in right now?

4. What can we offer to support this?

When choosing activities for our babies, there are several things to consider:

Choose natural materials. Babies explore with their mouths, so the things they use will inevitably end up in our baby's mouth. Therefore it is important to choose materials that are safe to be tasted and chewed. Natural materials like wood, fabric, rubber, and stainless steel are usually safe. The texture and temperature of these materials also provide different sensory feedback. Metal is cold and smooth; wood is warmer and can feel different depending on the grain and finish. If the object is painted, check to make sure the paint is safe. We can also look for materials that are stained with natural/food-based dyes. Natural materials also last longer and can be enjoyed by multiple children.

Consider the size of the entire object as well as any components. The object should be a size that the baby will be able to manipulate. Check that all the components are securely attached and will not be choking hazards. A choke tester can be used to check the size of objects offered for children under 3 years. This is a cylinder that is 2.25 inches long by 1.25 inches wide (5.7 cm long by 3.2 cm wide), about the width of two fingers. A toilet paper tube can also be used to check for safety. If it can fit in the toilet paper roll, it is probably a choking hazard.

Choice of beautiful materials. In chapter 2 we talked about the baby's absorbent mind and how it takes in everything. With this in mind, we can offer beautiful materials or find ways to beautify less-than-lovely materials. Many things can be repurposed to make materials for the baby, e.g., empty water bottles, food boxes, and cans. We can improve the aesthetic value by using colorful tape on the edges, tying a ribbon around it, or covering it with nice paper.

Variation in qualities and functions. We can offer an array of activities that are different from one another. This can be variations in color, size, weight, texture, or shape. They can also vary in function, for example, some objects that make sounds and others that don't, some that bounce and others that don't, some that are elastic and change shape when manipulated and others that don't. Through our baby's explorations, they start to understand the properties of things and how they work.

Most of the materials we choose for babies are intuitive to use. We don't need to show them what to do. Our role is to set up their play environment, prepare the toys and materials, and make them available and accessible at the ideal time. When our baby is working on the skill that the material supports, they will naturally do what it calls for. This time of exploration is the time during our baby's day when they can be in complete control. They can choose if, how, when, and what to engage with. They can experience being in control and the effects of their actions and choices. It is important for our baby to experience this control as part of their daily life. This is how they build trust in themselves and their abilities—trust that they will carry with them into adulthood and rely on when they encounter challenges.

If we notice our baby struggling with how to use a material or not showing interest, it could be that they are not ready, so we might put the material away and try again a little while later. For babies, there is not really a right or wrong way to use an object. As long as it is safe, we allow their exploration and discovery.

One way that we can guide our baby's exploration without showing them directly is by ensuring the baby finds materials in their correct and complete state whenever they spend time in their movement area. So if we have a puzzle, for example, it would be in its regular place when the baby finds it. They might not put it back properly and that's okay, because that is not the goal at this stage. The goal is in the process of the baby touching and using their hands in different ways. This changes as they become toddlers, and at that time, we change the way we prepare the activity. Even though the baby might not complete the activity, they are absorbing how it should look when they first see it put together, and as they explore, they will find that they know exactly what to do.

One of the human tendencies is self-perfection. We want to push ourselves to do better and feel successful. This tendency is present even in babies. We all enjoy activities that are at the edge of our abilities. If it is too easy, we become bored, and if it is too hard, we become frustrated. The right material for our baby is just a little beyond their current ability so that it requires effort but is not hard enough to be discouraging. We can observe our babies as they use activities and see how they react. As much as possible, do not interfere or offer help even if it looks like the baby is struggling. As long as they are not frustrated, we should sit on our hands and observe. If we notice frustration, we observe to see what might be causing it. For an older baby, we might model and then observe again, or we might remove the material and try again later.

"The struggle is essential."

—Nichole Holtvluwer, Radicle Beginnings

Limiting the number of activities. Limiting the number of activities allows our baby to concentrate and not get overwhelmed. In the beginning, our baby's age can be a guide for the number of activities we can make available. We could have one activity out for a 1-month-old, two for a 2-month-old, etc. Ideally, we do not want more than five or six things available at a time in one place even for an older baby. As the baby reaches about 7 months old, the activities might not all be in one place. We might have four on one shelf in their play area, a basket in the kitchen, and maybe two activities in their room. We can store most of the activities and rotate a few out at a time. Every time an activity comes out of rotation, it feels new or like a long-lost friend.

Maintaining and restoring the environment. When our baby plays, they will usually move from one thing to the next, leaving behind a trail. We talk about order a lot, and with older children we usually show them how to put one thing back before getting another. We don't do this with our babies because they are not yet able to put things away, and we don't want to interrupt their concentration as they move from one thing to another. We can wait until the baby is done completely and then tell them we are going to restore the activities. They watch us as we do this and are absorbing this. When they start walking and are able to collaborate, we can invite them to put the things back together and show them how to do it. One day we will observe them starting to do it independently.

With older children, we also create order by putting the materials on trays that the child can carry to a table. For babies, this can be an obstacle because they are not able to carry the tray yet or might be more interested in the container than the activity.

Quality over quantity. There are so many possibilities for materials and toys that we can offer our babies. However, many of them are only enjoyed for a short period of time, and others are easily damaged. Instead, we can choose a few quality options over many not-so-great ones. We can invest in materials that can stand the test of time by considering:

- The materials they were made with. Natural materials often last longer.
- The construction. Babies bang, throw, and drop materials, so we want well-constructed objects that can withstand rough treatment.
- The flexibility of use. We want materials that our baby can continue to use in different ways even as they get older.

Quality doesn't have to mean expensive. We can find really lovely options in markets selling handmade items and also in secondhand shops, or we can make some of them ourselves.

"Each rattle, grasping toy, toy, puzzle, and other piece of material has been chosen for a specific purpose. It is up to the adult to watch carefully to see that the challenge is not too easy as to be boring, and not too difficult to cause frustration and giving up."

—Susan Stephenson, *The Joyful Child*

Our role is to prepare the environment, not to entertain

The foundation for independent play is laid during our baby's first year. The Montessori phrase "Help me to do it myself" applies to everything the baby does including entertaining themselves. "Help me to entertain myself." A parent of an older child of between 2 and 6 years old might ask, "How can I get my child to play alone?" While it's never too late to teach our child to be independent, starting when the child is a baby is the surest route.

It is important to understand our role in the baby's play. We are to gain knowledge about our baby's development, prepare the environment, link the baby to the environment, and allow freedom and time for the baby to explore. We avoid entertaining or initiating the baby's activity. What does it mean to link the baby to the environment? It means that we simply put them in the movement area or in the space where they have freedom to explore. We first study to know more about the baby's natural development so that we can prepare an environment that is suited to their needs. We then observe to find their rhythm and see when they are awake, alert, satisfied, and happy. This is when we put them in the movement area, which is already prepared for them. Once we have put them there, we gently withdraw ourselves and observe.

In Montessori, when we make an activity available to a baby, we say we "present it." The term highlights that we are giving or making available something special to our baby.

WHEN TO OFFER ACTIVITIES TO OUR BABY

1. They are alert.
2. They are full.
3. They are happy and comfortable.

What if the baby does nothing and is not interacting with the materials? This is perfectly okay. We often expect the baby's play to be noisy and busy. This is not always the case. Many times the baby's activity may be calm and not very obvious to the undiscerning eyes. If the baby is calm and happy, we don't need to interfere. Sometimes the baby's interest is on a different aspect of the environment than what we expected, for example, a container or an object close by or a sibling. We trust that they know what they need and we still do not interfere.

Junnifa remembers once observing an infant watching a mobile at a parent–baby class. The Montessori mobiles are designed to be moved by air currents, so they move very slowly. The baby was so calm and relaxed while watching the mobile's floating butterflies. The baby's parent was sitting alongside of them, watching. After some time, the parent must have felt that the baby was bored or not getting enough stimulation, so he started to blow the mobile to make it move faster. It was a well-intended gesture, but the mobile began to move too fast for the baby's eyes and neck. The baby soon looked away and started to cry. In a world that is so fast-paced, loud, and full of stimulation, many of us don't remember how to sit with stillness or enjoy moments of slowness, and we can unconsciously impose this on our children when we try to entertain them. Remember to observe them to see when they are ready for a change, rather than use our own feelings as an indication that it's time to move on.

As much as possible, we avoid placing toys in the baby's hands or rattling them above their faces to get their attention or entertain them. We place an item within view and within reach, leaving it up to them to choose to reach for it. This is practice for them in making choices and requires persistence and patience. When we allow these choices, we are allowing the baby to follow their own initiative and laying the foundation of intentional and purposeful actions.

When we focus on entertaining the baby, we make their concentration impossible. Often we entertain by talking or moving, and we can soon get tired and stop before the baby is done. When babies entertain themselves, they are in control of this aspect of their day and can choose what, how, and for how long they engage with each activity. We try not to interrupt or interfere, even to compliment or praise. Babies are amazing, and when we prepare the environment and observe, they will do amazing things. We have to learn to celebrate internally or maybe wait until we can tell a partner or friend or relative to recount and celebrate, or we can surreptitiously take a picture. But as much as possible, do not distract the baby. When we observe them, we will start to notice that they know when they have made an achievement, and they can acknowledge it in their own way. When we have a strong reaction, whether positive or negative, we inadvertently teach them to look to us instead of themselves for how they feel.

Babies enjoy stillness and quiet. We can protect this and help them continue to enjoy it by allowing them to sit with stillness and seek activity when they choose to.

The baby is the main actor in their play. They are their own entertainer. This means we avoid toys that talk or light up and make all kinds of sounds when buttons are pressed. We choose materials that come to life because of the baby's action. We also don't use the television as an entertainer.

If we keep these ideas in mind and help our baby learn to entertain themselves, we will lay the foundation for them to be able to do so as they get older. And there are many other moments when we can interact with, hug, and connect with our baby—what we like to call moments of connection—when we are changing the baby, feeding the baby, bathing them, and watching the world go by. These are not moments to rush through, but rather where we establish the foundation of our relationship (see page 102).

OUR ROLE IN OUR BABY'S PLAY

We study to understand the natural course of development.

We prepare an environment where our baby can be free to move and explore.

We identify ideal times to bring our baby to their movement area.

We observe our baby's play to understand them better.

We watch to see when they are tired, hungry, overstimulated, or soiled.

We foster concentration by not interrupting or interfering with their activity.

How to help if our baby is stuck or struggling

Let's say a baby is trying to turn over and we notice they are struggling to get their hand unstuck. If they are making an effort and struggling, observe but don't interfere. If they start to get frustrated, we might get closer, tell them what we see, and offer to help. We can then give just enough help, like helping to take out the hand but still leaving them to turn over themselves. We offer just enough help and never take away the baby's opportunity to succeed at something they set their mind to.

FURTHER NOTES ON ACTIVITIES FOR BABIES

1. Spontaneous exploration with objects

The materials we offer here are specific in supporting the development of gross- and fine-motor movement. In addition to these materials, we can allow opportunities for the baby's free exploration and open play. We call this heuristic-style play.

Usually, as the baby's mobility increases, they can move to examine things in the environment. We can allow this exploration and notice what holds our baby's attention the longest. Often the materials being explored are not necessarily toys. Junnifa remembers her son running his hand through a shaggy rug and trying to grasp the strands, and crawling after light reflections from the window. She also had a few blocks in a basket that her son enjoyed for a long time and four small plastic bottles that she filled with rice, colored water, and glitter or colored water, oil, and beans. He enjoyed shaking them and crawling after them. She also remembers him rotating one of the wheels of his toddler brother's tricycle, which was parked in a corner; touching the ruffles on a pillow; and exploring a spinning top and a music box controlled by a string that can be pulled. Her babies often enjoyed exploring the tray, basket, or container that held the materials more than the material itself. She would provide two or three animal replicas in a basket, choosing animals that they have in their environment, e.g., cow, chicken, dog, and peacock (a common sight in Nigeria!). Junnifa's babies enjoyed looking at these, moving them around, and exploring them with their mouths.

We can observe our child in silence in their exploration and—sometimes—use it as an opportunity to offer them language around the names of the objects, how they sound or feel, or the child's experience. And then leave them to explore again uninterrupted.

2. Dressing for movement

Removing obstacles is one of our roles as adults. One obstacle that is sometimes overlooked is clothing. The wrong kind of clothing can interfere with the baby's experience and thus development of movement.

In the first three months, when the baby spends time on the floor on either their back or tummy, consider the placement of buttons, zippers, and other accessories. Make sure they are not situated in such a way that they dig into the baby's body or they feel it in a *Princess and the Pea* way.

Choose clothes that are not too tight and allow for free movement of all limbs. The baby will involuntarily flail arms and kick legs, and we can select clothing that allows for these movements.

Swaddling can impede the baby's movements and interferes with the use of the Moro (startle) and fencing (neck) reflexes. If we do choose to swaddle, we can leave room for some movement of hands and legs.

When our baby starts to slither or crawl, they use their knees and toes for traction. At this stage, the baby has usually adapted to the temperature, and if it stays moderated, choosing clothing that allows movement becomes a priority. Shorts, onesies, or other clothes that keep the knees exposed are most suitable. Dresses and long shirts can trip the baby, especially when they are beginning to crawl.

Feet are better left exposed. They are used for a lot of transition positions, and shoes can interfere with both the baby's perception of the feet and their development. Remove their socks and allow the baby to dig in their toes as they scoot and crawl and get a better grip as they climb on the stairs, a Pikler triangle, and other obstacles. If necessary use nonskid socks or thin, flexible-soled shoes that allow feet to move. As cute as mini sneakers look, they are not helpful for a baby to move, crawl, or walk.

Hands are best left exposed, too. As tempting as it is to cover a newborn's hands to stop them from scratching their face, having their hands near their face is a tactile experience they had in utero. Keep them uncovered as much as possible.

PART TWO

LANGUAGE ACTIVITIES

Language refers to both verbal and nonverbal communication. We act on our human tendency to communicate by expressing ourselves and understanding others. Language is also connected to other human tendencies.

- It helps orient ourselves in both new and familiar environments.
- It helps us explore.
- It helps us adapt to our environment.

Let's think about these tendencies from our baby's perspective. From the time our baby is born, the sound of our voice lets them know someone familiar is close—it orients them, consoles them, and makes them feel safe. It invites them to look around and explore to find the source of the voice, and soon they start to replicate the sounds we make and become like us, adapting to their new environment.

At birth, we are wired to learn the languages we are exposed to.

Junnifa remembers being amazed by the process of developing language with each of her children. Her third child was immersed in two languages, and by age 2, she understood everything said to her in both languages and could speak in sentences.

To develop spoken language, the baby needs the ability to speak (functioning vocal chords), to hear the sounds we make (check their hearing often, especially if they have ear infections in the first year), a desire to speak (so we should respond to their efforts to communicate), and rich language (the input we provide). We need little or no materials to do this in the first year. One of the most important things we can do is to provide rich language for our baby and show our babies that we listen to them.

Our work to support our baby's development of language actually starts before they are born. The development of language starts in the womb. At about 23 weeks in utero, the fetus starts to hear sounds. It can hear the mother's breathing and voice, as well as other voices and sounds in the external environment. If we speak to the baby, sing, and even play music while they are in the womb, the baby recognizes these sounds at birth.

ACTIVITIES TO SUPPORT LANGUAGE
IN THE FIRST YEAR

- Speak to the baby from the womb using rich language instead of nonsense words like "goo goo ga ga."

- Speak clearly and correctly so that our baby hears the distinct sounds that form the words.

- Check their hearing and create an environment conducive to hearing.

- Remove obstacles to communication, e.g., pacifier, television, and background noise.

- Acknowledge and encourage every effort at communication, e.g., crying, cooing, blowing raspberries, babbling.

- Sing, tell rhymes, read poetry, play music.

- Read books with real themes and characters.

- Model conversation with eye contact, expression, and body language.

- Involve our baby in daily life and allow them to listen to conversations.

- Make it a habit to come down to our baby's level or lift them up to our level when talking to them.

- Speak gently and respectfully.

0 TO 3 MONTHS

Speak to our baby

Our babies seem to be born with a special sensitivity to the human voice. Even from their first days, they will turn toward the sound of a familiar voice and are interested in other voices in their environment.

A significant portion of a baby's day is spent being held or handled. (By handling, we mean the interactions we have with the baby when feeding, bathing, and changing, or otherwise being with them.) These are wonderful opportunities to talk to the baby.

We can refer to them by name and talk them through our actions: "Metu, I'm going to pick you up. It's time for your bath. I'm washing your left leg and now your right one." We can also talk about their actions or reactions. "You smiled! You enjoyed that," or "You're pulling your ears, looks like you're sleepy." In this way, our baby starts to make connections between actions and words.

When we talk to our baby, we can make it a conversation. When we say something to them, we make sure we are making eye contact and then we wait for their response. It takes babies a little more time to process than adults. In the RIE philosophy, there is a concept called *tarry time*. It is a wait time that we give ourselves to allow the baby to process and respond. After we speak, we wait a little and observe for their response. They might make a sound or gesture and we can repeat it back to them or verbalize what we think they might be saying. We can poke out our tongue, and wait for them to make a movement with their mouth back. They are learning the art of conversation and that what they "say" matters to us.

> "When you speak to a baby . . . he will look directly at your mouth. When you speak to him, in the charming and affectionate way we all speak to babies, he will not understand what you are saying, but will feel emotion and be so thrilled that he will start to move his own mouth."
>
> —Dr. Maria Montessori

We can also point to items in the environment and name them for our baby. When Junnifa first came home with her babies, she gave them a tour of their home, showed them the rooms, and told them what happens in each one. She repeated this process often during their first year. We can give babies cues about their routines, share jokes, and just enjoy a conversation with them. It may seem like they don't understand, but the brain is making a lot of connections by figuring out how language works, how to form words, and how to repeat sounds. They are building their language bank and will eventually be able to express all they have accumulated. In Montessori, we use rich language and correct vocabulary even with babies, from their body parts to the breeds of dogs to the types of flowers we might see around us. We are limited only by our own knowledge.

If we want to raise a multilingual child, it can be preferable to have one person speak one language to the baby (instead of multiple languages). For example, one parent can be dedicated to speaking one language and the other person speaking another; or perhaps a grandparent or other caregiver might speak one language, while the parents speak another. Like with everything to do with babies, consistency is important. For more about bilingualism, see page 127.

We can start reading to our babies before they are born and continue after birth. The great thing about reading to the baby in the first few months is that it is not necessarily about the content but about hearing the phonemes (sounds) and the cadence of language. So we could choose a book that we want to read for ourselves and just read it aloud in the presence of the baby.

We can also choose simple books that have only pictures or minimal words and read by describing the pictures or illustrations. One fun idea is to make homemade books using familiar people or things. We can use a small album and put in photos of our family members or blank board books that we can fill with our own photos. We can look at the pictures together and tell the baby about each person. Many older children continue to enjoy looking through these books that they loved so much as babies.

It is important to check the baby's hearing soon after birth and continue to check it frequently, because colds and other infections can cause problems that affect hearing if not detected early. Many hospitals and birth centers offer hearing checks soon after birth. We can continue to check from time to time by calling out to the baby, clapping or ringing a bell from a distance, and checking for a response or reaction from the baby.

We can play beautiful music that our baby (and we) can enjoy. Dance with them, hold them, and sway them to the rhythm of a song. This supports our baby's development of language because identifying rhythms is part of learning language. Junnifa had some beautiful music boxes that she would play at different points during the day. One of them was transparent and you could see the mechanism moving inside, and her babies watched intently as they enjoyed the music. Another music box was controlled by pulling a string, and as it played, the string retracted and got shorter. Her babies also loved this and learned very early (around 6 to 7 months) how to pull the string and listen. Provide music in different forms. If we live in a place that has birds, we can open our windows in the morning or take the baby out to the garden and enjoy the music of the birds and the other sounds from nature. This is also an aid to the development of language and rhythm.

Babies need to experience and absorb conversation happening between others. So we can keep them with us or close by when we converse with our partner, friends, or their older siblings. Wearing them in a baby carrier or sling when we are out and about also allows them to observe and listen to these conversations.

Remove obstacles

Loud environments or a space with constant noise, like a room where the television is always turned on, can be hindrances to language. It makes it hard for the baby to clearly hear words spoken in the environment and can also overstimulate the brain. Even background music needs to be filtered out by the baby. So instead of having music on constantly in the background, it can be better to make a moment to listen to music with our baby.

Pacifiers can also be obstacles to the proper development of language. It is hard to coo, babble, or speak when you constantly have something in your mouth, especially at an age when you can't remove it yourself. In the beginning, the baby's main means of communication is crying, and it can be tempting to offer a pacifier, but apart from potentially impeding the baby's communication, it can also send a message that we don't want to hear what they have to say.

If we choose to use a pacifier, we can try to limit its use by placing it in a box in the sleeping area. And we can gradually remove the pacifier by the end of the first year. A pacifier is often offered for a baby that likes to suck—then we observe to see the moment that they are done, so that we can remove it and they can communicate with us with their sounds and cries.

Tips for choosing books in the first year

- Sturdy board books are best for hands that are still refining their grasp and their ability to turn the page. These books can also withstand being chewed on.

- Start with black-and-white images, then, around 4 to 6 weeks, move to colorful images on a white background, and then to images with more details.

- We can start with books with no words, then move to single words, then short sentences.

- Choose beautiful pictures—a baby absorbs the beauty we present to them, including in books.

- Choose books about things in daily life: animals, sounds, smells, the seasons, the senses, vehicles. In the first years until around 6 years old, children understand the world around them from what they see and experience—and a good deal of research suggests young children prefer realistic books. So we like to choose books based on things that a baby would understand from the world around them, i.e., reality rather than fantasy.

- In a similar vein, we can (mostly) avoid books where animals or toys are doing things a human would do, e.g., a teddy bear is driving a car or an elephant is on roller skates. We want to give our baby as accurate information as possible.

- When the baby is around 1 year old, they may enjoy lift-the-flap books (but may still tear the flaps by accident). Interestingly, research shows the flaps distract children so they learn a little less from such books—but they are fun.

- If the baby is interested in turning the pages or reading the book backward, follow their lead. This will not last forever. We are getting them interested in reading even if we never finish the book.

3 TO 6 MONTHS

As the baby matures (around 3 to 4 months), we will notice that they pay more attention to and even stare at our face and mouth when we are speaking. It's like they realize the sound they hear is made by the movement of our lips and they are trying to figure out how it works. Give them opportunities to do this by talking to them slowly and at a level where they can see our face.

Soon after, we will notice that they are not only interested in watching our mouths when we speak, but they also start to move their mouth and try to imitate our mouth movements. If we stick out our tongue or make fish lips or any exaggerated gestures to the baby, we will notice that they try to imitate it. Engage them by making these gestures and acknowledging their efforts with a smile or another gesture for them to imitate.

We continue to talk to our baby, but when we talk to them, we remember it is a conversation and not a monologue, so we pause and give them the opportunity to respond. Babies are very capable of responding vocally or with their gestures. Their responses become more noticeable around 3 to 4 months. When we observe a response, we can acknowledge it and incorporate it in our response back to the baby. We can repeat the sounds they make, or smile back at them, or say what we think they are trying to communicate. This tells them we are listening and also models conversations. It lets the baby know that we care about what they say and that they can always talk to us.

Repeating the sounds they make back to them is different from "baby talk" (like "goo goo ga ga"). When we talk to the baby in baby talk, we talk to them as if they don't understand anything else. Although we'll naturally use a singsong voice with babies—sometimes called "parentese"—we don't need to over-exaggerate this. Babies like the sing song tone and yet we still want to treat them with the same respect as a friend, a partner, or any other person.

Around this time, the baby also starts to produce vowel sounds—their first sound that is not crying. These sweet sounds called *cooing* (for their similarity to bird sounds) are delightful and can be acknowledged by the adult. Maintaining eye contact, we listen, and when the baby stops, we acknowledge by repeating the sound and talking back (e.g., "Ahhhh . . . I hear you. Ooo really? Tell me more") and then giving them a chance to talk. This encourages the baby's efforts at communicating and models the back-and-forth of conversation. Again, this is a conversation, not "baby talk." The baby's hearing should also continue to be checked periodically.

Around 4 to 5 months, a baby who is given freedom to produce sounds, acknowledged, and encouraged to communicate will also start what we think of as vocal gymnastics. They scream and test the limits of their voice. These sounds may become irritating to us, but they will pass. As much as possible, allow them to make these explorations rather than telling them to stop screaming.

They also "blow raspberries" (make sounds by fluttering the lips), blow spit bubbles, and make funny sounds. All of these are steps in their development of language and can be encouraged. This is how they work on regulating their voices and figure out tone, pitch, and volume. They are also practicing coordinating their diaphragm, mouth, tongue, and lips. We can encourage such attempts by blowing raspberries in response. This is fun and will usually elicit a lot of laughter and giggles, and it provides a wonderful opportunity for bonding. As before, it is important to continue to talk to the baby, sing, and read books to them.

Around 3 to 6 months, the baby may begin responding to specific pages in books. They may smile at a favorite page or try to imitate the faces on the page.

Around 5 to 6 months, the baby adds consonants to the vowel sounds and produces their first syllable. The first consonants are usually *m*, *n*, *d*, and *p*, so the baby might produce "mama," "nana," "dada," or "papa," much to the excitement of the parents. This reaction causes the baby to continue to repeat these sounds.

This can be a good time to introduce some sign language. Often babies understand so much more than they are able to express verbally, but they can use their developing motor skills to give simple signs to communicate. Babies are able to sign before they can speak, thanks to the early development of motor neurons that send signals to their hands. We can teach basics like "milk," "more," "eat," "done," and "sleep." We can say the words while also signing. Once they start signing these back after a couple of months, we can add a few more signs, and keep adding as our baby masters them.

BOOK RECOMMENDATION

If you are interested to learn more about baby signs, we recommend *Baby Sign Language Made Easy* by Lane Rebelo.

6 TO 9 MONTHS

From around the end of 6 months, the baby starts to understand words and can respond to requests like "Clap your hands," "Open your mouth," and "Say 'bye-bye.'" They know the names of family members and can react appropriately to statements like "Daddy is at the door" by looking or crawling toward the door. They also understand the different tones of voice and the word "no."

We can support them by continuing to talk to them and providing them with the correct names for things. We name things and sounds that they come across. For example, if they turn toward a ringing phone, say, "My phone is ringing"; if they look around at the sound of a dog barking, say, "Do you hear the dog barking?"; or when they are looking at a spoon we are holding, "That is a spoon . . . spoon. Spoon. Would you like to hold it?"

Singing provides opportunities to play with pitch, tone, speed, and volume. We can sing the same song with different voices, speeds, volumes, etc. And if we can play a musical instrument and sing, we can watch our baby open their mouth and sometimes match the sounds we make.

Babies up to around 7 months can reproduce sounds of any language although they favor the sounds of their parent language right from birth. These cooing and babbling sounds change around 7 to 8 months, when babies start to "purposefully babble" and try to practice the sound of their language (or languages). If we listen, we can hear some of the sounds. A lot of times they attempt to repeat sounds they hear. Again, all of this requires the baby's mouth to be free and the environment to be rich in language.

9 TO 12 MONTHS

By 9 months, babies understand many words even though they can't say them. They babble a lot and try to communicate more using signs and gestures. They appear to have a better understanding of object permanence. Research has shown that a 4-month-old can remembers that an object is there; what changes around 9 months is they become more capable of retrieving these "hidden objects." They will enjoy playing peekaboo games with us. Around this time, they also start to point with their index finger. We can name the objects as the baby points to them.

We continue to talk, sing, and read, and use clear and specific vocabulary. We can also play games with the baby by making sounds like shaking a rattle or clapping from different locations around the room and watching for them to turn or crawl in that direction.

Around this stage, the baby might start to get into things and explore cause and effect. Instead of saying "no" or "don't do that," we can practice positive language. For example, when our baby throws food while eating, we might say, "Food stays on our plate or goes in our mouth." If they seem to be done, we could say, "You seem to be done, I'll take the plate away." In Montessori we have a phrase to describe this: "teach by teaching instead of correcting." So instead of simply saying "no," we observe them trying out something in the moment, then wait to show them what to do instead at another time. We also try to tell them what to do instead of what not to do. This does not mean that we never say "no" to them. We just use it sparingly so that they know its importance.

12 MONTHS+

Around their first birthday, they may produce their first word, and shortly after they might know a few words, usually names of family members or requests, e.g. "water," "milk," "up!" etc. This is the product of a whole year of work! Remember that every child will learn to talk on their own schedule. The range for speaking their first word is wide (from 5 to 36 months) with the average first word spoken at 11.5 months.

Around this time, the young baby also starts to walk, which leaves their hands free to work. They can be included in practical aspects of the household, like cooking, cleaning, setting the table, and putting away groceries. Each of these activities provides opportunities for rich vocabulary, as the baby can learn the names of foods, fruits, vegetables, tools, utensils, processes, furniture, and also the particular vocabulary of their culture.

Materials like replicas (for example, model animals and tools) and eventually pictures can also be provided to introduce the baby to new words. Babies have an amazing ability to absorb language around this time, so we can introduce as many words as possible at this time. Talk, talk, talk. Sing, sing, sing. Read, read, read. Come down to the baby's level and listen when they speak.

LANGUAGE IN THE FIRST YEAR

- Speak to the baby from the womb.
- Speak clearly and correctly so that our baby hears the distinct sounds that form the words.
- Remove obstacles to communication (i.e., pacifier) and hearing (i.e., television); and check their hearing.
- Acknowledge and encourage their efforts at communication.
- Sing, tell rhymes, read poetry, play music.
- Read books with real themes and characters.
- Model conversation with eye contact, expression, and body language.
- Involve our baby in daily life and allow them to listen to conversations.
- Come down to our baby's level or lift them up to our level when talking to them.
- Speak gently and respectfully.

NEWBORN

- Will respond to soft or familiar sounds by listening; they will become still
- Will startle or blink in response to loud or unexpected sounds
- Expresses needs by crying
- Attempts to imitate facial gestures

MONTH 2

- Turns head toward sources of sound
- Focuses on caregiver while being fed
- Coos
- Frowns and smiles

MONTH 3

- Starts to make vowel sounds, e.g., aaaa
- Starts to show excitement
- Enjoys physical care routines like bathing
- Intently studies faces

MONTHS 4 TO 6

- Vocal gymnastics—spit bubbles, loud sounds
- Consonant sounds introduced in cooing to form simple syllables like "na," "ma," "ba"
- Coos have rhythm

MONTHS 7 TO 9

- Searches for and localizes faint sounds
- Understands "no"
- Can wave "bye-bye"
- Babbles tunefully in syllables and canonical babbling (where they duplicate the sounds, "ma ma," "ba ba")
- Turns to their name
- Can begin learning baby signs

MONTHS 9 TO 12

- Can play peekaboo
- Can respond to simple directions
- Can recognize several words
- Can recognize and point to body parts
- Can say some single-syllable words
- Can express wants and preferences without crying
- Can repeat baby signs
- Can point to alert us to interesting sights

OBSERVING THE DEVELOPMENT OF LANGUAGE

- How do they respond when they hear a familiar voice?

- How do they respond to an unfamiliar voice?

- Their cries: Do they sound different at different times? Can we differentiate them by cause?

- How do they respond to different sounds?

- What are they doing with their eyes and mouth when we speak to them?

- Observe the sounds they make. Are they vowel or consonant sounds?

- How are they making the sounds?

- How do they react to hearing their name?

- Are they making single sounds?

- Same sounds but strung together?

- Different sounds strung together?

- If we are also using baby signs, notice when they start responding and when they use the signs too.

- Notice how they respond when we read a book to them. Are there particular pages that hold their attention? What are they doing with their face or mouth while they look at the pages?

- Notice how they communicate pleasure or discomfort, with or without crying.

- Notice when they start to use words with intention.

From these observations, is there something new we learned about our baby? Is there anything we would like to change as a result? Something in the environment? Another way we can support them? Obstacles we can remove? Including our own intervention? Observe joy!

BILINGUALISM

Because babies have an absorbent mind and are in a sensitive period for language acquisition, infancy is a wonderful time to expose our baby to more than one language. They will take in additional languages with seemingly little extra effort.

If there is more than one language in the home, we can use the One Person, One Language (OPOL) approach. Each parent chooses their mother tongue when speaking with the baby, while the family uses one agreed-upon "family language."

We can also use an approach called Domains of Use. This is where we have agreed-upon times or places (temporal domains) when we use certain languages. For example, on the weekends the family chooses to speak English; out of the home they choose to speak the local language; and at home they speak the parents' mother tongues.

We need to spend around 30 percent of the week speaking any language that we hope our child will use as a literacy language. To increase our baby's exposure to any language, we might have a teenager read and play with them in that language, a caregiver who speaks that language, or play groups in that language. We can be creative.

Some parents worry that their child will have a language delay if they are being raised to be bilingual. When children have more than one language, the research shows that they should not have any learning delay. For comparison, a 1½-year-old who is monolingual may have ten words. The bilingual child may have five words in one language and five words in another. So it can appear that their language level is lower, even though they can say ten words in total too.

BOOK RECOMMENDATION

A Parents' and Teachers' Guide to Bilingualism, by Colin Baker is a book for anyone with questions about bilingualism or learning more than one language.

PART THREE

MOVEMENT ACTIVITIES

Movement is how humans explore and come into contact with their surroundings. Movement is also a means of self-expression, and it allows us to nourish ourselves, stay safe, and work to improve our environment. Movement in many ways is linked to our survival and progress, so we want to help our babies develop this skill to its full potential.

At birth, our babies already move. They move their heads, hands, and legs and stretch, but these movements are involuntary. They are not controlled or conscious choices. Many of the baby's movements at birth are linked to primitive reflexes. These are muscle reactions that automatically happen in response to stimulation. These reflexes are important because they signal that the baby's brain and nervous system are working. They also help the baby with different things needed for survival (e.g., feeding) until they can move voluntarily.

Babies need to train their muscles to move voluntarily. As the baby begins to move voluntarily, many of the reflexive movements that they are born with get integrated and disappear. (If movement does not develop naturally and optimally, some of these reflexes remain and can interfere with other areas of development later. It is helpful to know what some of these reflexes are so that we can check for their presence in the beginning and observe them as they get integrated and disappear, or notice if they remain. See page 271 for a list of infant primitive reflexes.)

The optimal movement for our baby to develop is voluntary and coordinated movement. This is movement that is initiated and directed by the baby. This is what we support with the activities we provide. We provide opportunities for the baby to train their muscles and control their bodies through repetitive movements.

The baby's role is to explore, initiate movement, enjoy challenging their body, and refine their coordination.

The adult's role is not to interfere with this exploration but to support it. We can set up a rich environment to support the baby at their current developmental level and provide some new challenges for them to reach for.

There are many different movement skills that our babies develop in the first year, each falling under the categories of gross-motor skills and fine-motor skills.

Gross-motor skills are the movement of our baby's body (including their arms and legs) in space: crawling, walking, waving arms, etc. These movements usually require large muscles. Gross-motor skills are necessary for their balance and coordination.

Fine-motor skills are the skills required for the movement of the hands, wrists, and lower arms. These are the unique rotations in these body parts that allow humans to grasp tools and work in a way that is different from (most) other animals. We can have a huge impact on the level of our baby's coordination and the development of the ability of their hands. Dr. Montessori referred to the hands as the instruments of human intelligence. She also said that whatever we want to give to the mind, we must give to the hands first. In essence, the hands and the baby's intellect are directly connected. When we help our baby develop their fine-motor skills, we are also supporting the development of their intelligence.

It is important to note that while we can support the development and quality of our baby's motor skills, there is a natural process to this development that every neurotypical baby follows. The process cannot be sped up, but it can be slowed down. Our goal is not speed, but rather to allow our babies to develop increasing control and coordination.

To understand this, let's have a quick science lesson. At birth, our baby has very limited gross- and fine-motor skills. Before the baby can control the muscles of a certain area, the axons in the nerves in those areas have to be covered with myelin, a fatty substance that insulates the axons, allowing messages to be able to be transmitted along the nerves. So as an area gets myelinated, the baby can gain control of that muscle. Myelination progresses from head to toe and from the chest out to the arms, hands, and then out to the fingers. The development of the baby's gross- and fine-motor skills follows the same progression.

So the baby gains control of their head before control of their torso, and has control of their torso before their feet, and they can move their arms before they can grasp with their fingers.

Kinesthetics is the ability to feel movements of the limbs and body. It is muscle sense. With repetition, the baby continues to feel the results and sensory experience over and over again. In the process, they incarnate these movements and also build dendrites and build dendrites for neuron to neuron connections, which helps their brain development.

The progression of myelin can be seen if we observe our baby closely—when we see them gaining increasing control of movement in their arms, hands, fingers, and legs. And we can prepare or modify the environment and provide activities to support the progression at each developmental stage as it arrives. By 12 to 14 months, all the axons are myelinized for movement, but the exact progress of their actual movements in each baby will depend on what their environment has to offer. A well-prepared environment where the baby has freedom to move and finds materials that encourage development and exploration will allow movement to progress optimally. We want to do more than allow movement—we want to encourage it.

Before we look at the activities, here is a guide to the ages and stages of the development of movement.

Remember: These are just general guidelines, and each baby will follow their own timeline, which might be plus or minus a few weeks or months.

Fine-motor skills can be seen developing in our baby as follows:

- **Reaching:** At around 3 to 4 months, our baby will have voluntary control of their arms.

- **Grasping:** At birth, our baby will have an involuntary reflex to grasp; at about 4 months they will be able to do it intentionally.

- **Raking:** At around 4 months, babies will scoop an object into their palm and then their fingers will wrap around it.

- **Thumb Opposition Grasping:** At 8 to 9 months, our baby will use four fingers with their thumbs. At 10 to 12 months, they will progress to the pincer grasp, first using two fingers and their thumb, then one finger and their thumb.

- **Releasing:** At 8 months, our baby will be able to voluntarily release an object into a small chosen space.

By preparing the environment and providing activities that support the baby's movement development, we also support the development of the following:

- **A "Can-Do" Attitude:** The baby will experience the feeling of being a conscious participant in their development of movement. Each successful acquisition builds the baby's confidence.

- **Self-Esteem:** In order to let children do these movements, the adult has to trust the baby. This trust becomes absorbed by the baby and helps them develop positive self-esteem. A safe, prepared environment makes it easier for the parent to trust the baby.

- **Body Schema Awareness:** Our baby will become aware of and get to know their body, its orientation, and the location of its parts.

- **Self-Awareness:** They will learn how their bodies work in relation to the environment. They will come to understand how to respond to their environment and become self-reliant.

ACTIVITIES TO SUPPORT THE DEVELOPMENT OF MOVEMENT

We do not need many things to support the baby's development of movement. The most important thing to have is knowledge of the natural process of development. This helps us to observe intelligently, prepare the environment, allow freedom, remove obstacles to movement, and notice early if there are delays or other concerns.

Remove obstacles

Removing obstacles is just as important as providing ways to support movement. We can:

- avoid dressing our baby in restrictive clothing (see page 113)
- avoid placing our baby in a playpen; instead, we can set up a "yes" space for them to explore
- avoid placing our baby in carriers such as strollers, car seats, bike seats, even baby carriers or slings for long periods of time
- avoid placing our baby in a "jumper," walker, or exersaucer; these devices put a lot of pressure on the baby's hips and limit the baby's control over their own movements
- avoid placing our baby in a position they cannot get into by themselves—e.g., sitting before they are able to on their own
- avoid holding our baby's hands above their head before they are ready to walk

0 TO 3 MONTHS

In the first month, our baby is adapting to this new world and orienting themselves. The best activity is just being held and snuggled by us, ideally at home or in an environment with very subdued stimuli, i.e., lights are not too bright; the space is quiet, with soft voices and maybe low music; temperature is regulated. This allows us to welcome and bond with the baby while allowing them to orient, feel safe, and build trust in their environment. This is important because if they feel safe, they are able to explore and engage with activities that we provide. We will notice when they start to feel oriented.

GRASPING AND DEVELOPMENT OF MOVEMENT

0 TO 3 MONTHS

Reflex grasp

Observe own hands

Grasp

3 TO 6 MONTHS

Intentional grasp

Manipulation

Clap hands

6 TO 9 MONTHS

Hand to hand

Release

Finger grasp

9 TO 12 MONTHS

Refined movement

Pincer grasp

They will be more relaxed, cry less, and start to look beyond us. Then we know that they are ready to spend more time on their movement mat.

Tip: We can use a topponcino when transitioning baby from arms to a mat or bed. This allows the temperature, feel, and smell to remain relatively consistent, so the baby is not disoriented or startled. Always lower the baby slowly and tell them what is happening.

Movement mat

By the second month, the baby could be spending a significant portion of their awake time on their movement mat. They can be placed on their back on a blanket and given the freedom to move.

If we haven't already done so, read about the movement area and how to set it up (see page 57). Many of the activities in this chapter can be presented or made available in the movement area.

Floor bed

A floor bed can support the baby's development of gross-motor skills because it allows and even encourages the baby to move. The floor bed is a Montessori alternative to a crib. It is very close to the ground and allows the baby to have a clear view of their surroundings. It can be used from birth, or the baby can be transitioned to the floor bed at around 3 months. Even families who co-sleep can use floor beds for naps and for part of the sleep cycle. Junnifa co-slept with her three babies but would put them on their floor beds at 7 p.m. and then bring them into bed with her when they woke up to feed at night. If we observe our newborn on their floor bed, we will notice that they move unconsciously. Often, we might find them in a different position from where we left them, but strangely enough, they typically don't fall off the floor bed. They move very slowly and seem to be aware of reaching the edge, and they will change direction or just stop themselves.

Grasping rattles

In the first 2 months, the baby has the grasping reflex that makes them wrap their fingers around anything that touches their palm. While breastfeeding or at other times, we can put our finger gently on their palm and they will wrap their fingers around it. We can offer them a small, light rattle or a narrow silk tube with batting inside. Remember that primitive reflexes become integrated with use, so this activity encourages use of this reflex while also bringing the baby's attention to their hand.

The visual mobiles

Visual mobiles are the main Montessori material used in the movement area for the first 3 months because they support so many of the baby's developmental needs during that time.

Montessori visual mobiles are a series of handmade mobiles that follow a specific sequence. They can be homemade or purchased and are made available to babies from the early weeks and rotated as the baby progresses in their development. The mobiles support a baby's development in several ways including:

Visual Sense: From birth, babies can begin to take in and explore their world with their eyes. While their vision is not yet acute at birth, it gradually improves, especially in a well-prepared environment. Visual mobiles provide an opportunity for the baby to both track (follow with their eyes) and focus on an object. They can also provide beauty and a point of reference for the baby. The development of vision also supports the development of both gross- and fine-motor skills.

Gross- and Fine-Motor Skills: In these early months, our baby is working on gaining control of their neck and arm muscles. As they watch the mobile, they will follow its movement initially with just their eyes and then with their head, turning from side to side, and then with their torso and entire bodies. Our baby will also eventually start reaching for the mobile. The movement is usually involuntary in the beginning, but they repeat it many times, building muscle strength and control.

Orientation and Adaptation: The mobiles are usually hung one at a time over the baby's movement mat, so they can provide a point of reference for the baby, as it is something familiar that they can recognize in the environment. The mobile is changed when they lose interest or when we notice progress that indicates the baby is ready for the next mobile. Ideally, the mobile could be changed within the baby's view. We can tell them we are going to change the mobile and then change it. Imagine coming to a room that you always visit and realizing that, without your knowledge, it has been changed. Imagine how disorienting that would feel. It is the same with babies—actually, even more than adults—so we try to make changes as respectfully as possible and in a way that does not disorient them.

Beauty: We have talked about the baby's absorbent mind and how the baby absorbs the things they see in the environment. The mobiles are beautiful, so they allow the baby to absorb beauty.

Below we describe four specific visual mobiles, but these can also serve as a guide for choosing or making other mobiles. Templates for the Munari, Gobbi, and dancer mobiles can be found at workman.com/montessori.

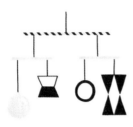

The black-and-white (Munari) mobile is usually the first mobile we present to the baby.

Research has shown that newborns prefer looking at high-contrast (black-and-white) geometric shapes. This is because the nerve cells in their brain that enable vision and their retina are not yet fully developed—studying the contrast helps them develop.

The Munari consists of black-and-white geometric shapes and a glass sphere that catches and reflects light and the other shapes. This mobile can hold the attention of a baby as young as a few days old for a long time. This mobile can be hung in the baby's movement area from birth, and they can start to enjoy it as soon as we feel they are ready. Junnifa felt her babies were ready around their second week.

The next visual mobile is called the **octahedron**. It is made of three octahedrons, usually in the three primary colors. The octahedrons are made using origami techniques or by cutting and folding paper into shapes. The shapes can be cut from red, blue, and yellow shiny paper (recycled gift bags work well). The reflective paper allows the mobile to catch and reflect light.

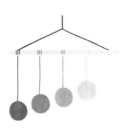

The third mobile is the **color gradation (Gobbi) mobile**, which is made of five same-sized spheres in progressively lighter shades of one color. The spheres are arranged in gradation. This helps the baby see the small color differences and can be fun to watch when put near a sunny window. Each ball casts a shadow on the next ball. Children love this mobile. It can be made by wrapping embroidery floss around spheres. We have also seen knitted, painted, and stained versions. By the time our baby is using the mobile (around the end of their second month), we may observe them starting to bat at the mobile with their hands or arms.

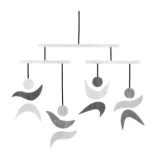

The **stylized dancers mobile** is the final mobile in the Montessori visual mobile series. Like the other mobiles, it holds the baby's attention for a long time. It is made of stylized paper in gold or silver and a contrasting primary color cut in the shape of a person. The way they move makes them seem like dancers (hence the name).

The mobiles described here are specific to Montessori. But we can make or buy any mobiles for our baby, keeping these qualities in mind:

- Select simple, beautiful, and interesting mobiles.
- Choose light mobiles that move with the air current and do not require batteries or electricity.
- Visual mobiles are for visual stimulation and do not need to have music. It is easier to hone one sense when the focus is on that particular sense alone. In this case, the sight is the sense being stimulated.
- Look at the mobile from underneath. Remember, this is the baby's view. What are they seeing?
- Select mobiles that have either geometric shapes or real animals/items that they will encounter in real life. Avoid cartoon characters.
- Things that fly or float in the sky can also be lovely, for example, birds, butterflies, clouds, and aircraft.
- Choose bright, interesting colors.
- Mobiles should provide different views from different angles.
- Ensure the mobile does not have too many elements and is not overstimulating. Less is more. Ideally, mobiles for the first three months should have no more than five or six items.
- Ensure the mobile is not boring or understimulating.

Ideally, the mobile can be hung over our baby's movement mat, because this is where they will spend a lot of their waking time. The mobile gives them something to concentrate on. The baby can be laid on their back under the mobile. We hang it at least 8 to 12 inches (20–30 cm) above them when they are a newborn. This distance (which is also about the distance between our face and our baby's face when they are breastfeeding) is the distance that the baby can see at birth. Their range of vision gradually increases, and the distance can be increased as they grow and their vision develops.

We can avoid placing a mobile over the baby's bed, because this is their resting place. A mobile is for "work," that is, working on their visual development.

When we put our baby on the mat under the mobile, we can observe their interest and interaction with the mobile. If they are enjoying it, we remember not to interfere. We can read a book or get some rest nearby. If they are crying or upset, we might need to adjust the mobile to see what works. One of Junnifa's children did not like to have the mobile hanging directly above him and would cry whenever he was placed under it. After observing him, she moved the mobile just off to the side, and that made all the difference. He started to enjoy it. If our baby is visibly upset by the mobile, move the mobile away, reposition the mobile, or try another day.

Mobiles and other activities are best offered when the baby is full (not hungry) and alert (not sleepy). In the beginning, they might observe the mobile for a few minutes and then lose interest. This is normal. The time will gradually increase. We've observed babies watching their mobiles intently for more than 15 minutes. Remember the baby is building concentration, so we try not to interrupt or distract. We don't need to constantly talk either. We know they are done when they begin to look away from the mobile, no longer appear relaxed, or cry.

We can rotate three to five visual mobiles over the course of the baby's first few months, perhaps after 2 or 3 weeks or as we observe that the baby starts to get bored or loses interest in a material.

We may notice they no longer interact with the mobile or that the time of concentration consistently reduces, or they might show signs of being upset when put under the mobile. These signs suggest it is time to rotate it out. We can bring back a mobile after a couple weeks and find that the baby is delighted with it again and interacting with it in a different way.

We can also hang up beautiful art or other images on the wall, low enough that the baby can see them. We can stand a book with black-and-white and other high-contrast images within the baby's view during the early weeks.

A tree makes a very special mobile. The moving leaves and branches make the light and shadows dance, and the baby watches, mesmerized. Similarly, holding up our hand with light behind it or making shadows for our baby to focus on can be enriching, too.

"The training and sharpening of the senses has the obvious advantage of enlarging the field of perception and of offering an even more solid foundation for intellectual growth."

—Dr. Maria Montessori, *The Discovery of the Child*

OBSERVE 0 TO 3 MONTHS

- What do their eyes do while taking in the environment, like when they see a familiar face or hear a familiar voice?

- What is their reaction when their body first comes in contact with the bed or mat?

- Notice when they start to turn their head from side to side. Do they prefer looking in one direction? What happens to their hands and legs when they turn?

- Can they lift up their head? Are they on their backs or tummies when they do?

- How do they watch the mobile? Do their eyes track it continuously or do they only watch when it comes back into view? Does this change with time?

- Do they have a preferred component of the mobile? Is it the same every time?

- Apart from the mobile, what else in the environment do they look at?

- How is their hand? Is the palm open or closed most of the time?

- How do their arms and legs move? Often the movement will be of the whole limb, not yet bending at the wrist, elbow, ankle, or knee.

- What do they do when we call their name?

- When they are on their back, what are their hands and legs doing when they turn their head?

From these observations, is there something new we learned about our baby? Is there anything we would like to change as a result? Something in the environment? Another way we can support them? Obstacles we can be removing? Including our own intervention? Observe joy!

3 TO 6 MONTHS

From 0 to 3 months, we provided activities to stimulate our baby's visual and auditory senses. Starting around 3 months, we can offer more activities to develop their grasp and tactile sense.

In the pages that follow, we will begin to distinguish between activities for fine-motor skills and gross-motor skills, even though many materials support the development of both. Myelination (myelin is the substance that coats the axons in the nerves allowing increased motor control) follows two paths. One path starts at the head at birth and moves slowly down to the feet, making gross-motor movements possible. The other path starts at the chest and slowly moves outward toward the fingers. These two processes mean that our baby is usually developing aspects of gross-motor skills and fine-motor skills simultaneously. By the third month, myelination of axons is occurring in the shoulders, upper trunk, arms, and hands. The baby's vision is also better, so we start to see the beginning of voluntary fine-motor skills.

Fine-motor skills

Around the beginning of the third month, we will start observing our baby making a larger range of hand movements. If the baby has mobiles, we will notice their efforts to reach for them. This is a good time to introduce reaching and grasping materials, starting with tactile mobiles.

Grasping materials support the development of the baby's fine-motor skills, specifically reaching and grasping. We know that from birth children grasp involuntarily as a result of the grasping reflex. If we put our finger in a baby's palm, they will close their fingers around it. This is an unconscious action. They become very interested in their hands around the time when their vision becomes clear. If we observe the baby, we will notice when they become almost fascinated with their hands. They will look at them for extended periods of time. Around this time, they also gain control of their upper body and are working on getting better at directing their arms. We will observe that they start to reach for and bat at their visual mobiles. We don't interfere with this exploration of their hands but can then make grasping materials available by exchanging the visual mobile for a tactile one and providing a selection of rattles.

The best tactile materials are simple and beautiful. In choosing, we can:

- Consider the size. The materials should not be too big. Our fingers can be used as a reference for width and length. Some objects might be bigger, but they should have graspable parts that the baby can hold and manipulate. They should also not be small enough to be a choking hazard. A toilet paper roll can be used to check. If an object can go through it, it is probably a choking hazard.
- Consider the material. Our baby will almost definitely bring the grasping materials to their mouth. This is how babies initially explore. Therefore we can make sure we choose materials that are safe for putting in the mouth, e.g., wood, cloth, rubber, and metals such as silver or stainless steel. Offer a variety that gives the baby different feedback. For example, stainless steel feels cool in their hands and mouth, different from how wood or cloth would feel.
- Grasping mobiles or rattles that make a gentle sound like a wood clack or a gentle chime are nice because they provide the baby with feedback for their effort.

Tactile mobiles

Tactile mobiles are designed to be manipulated by babies. Unlike the visual mobiles, which are fragile and made just to be looked at, tactile mobiles can be touched, grasped, and even brought to the baby's mouth. The baby can use a tactile mobile independently. It is hung within our baby's sight and reach, and they can decide to interact with it. It is also good for repetition because our baby can continue batting and reaching and then stop when they want.

Like the visual mobiles, there are specific Montessori tactile mobiles and a suggested sequence. We can also consider the qualities of these mobiles and apply them when choosing or using non-Montessori mobiles. Even a rattle can be hung as a mobile. With the grasping mobiles, the baby will be reaching, grabbing, and pulling, so it is helpful to attach some elastic to one end so that the mobile can stretch when pulled. It should also be hung sturdily so that it does not pull off and fall on the baby.

Bell on a ribbon: Attach a bell about the size of the baby's grasp to a ribbon and add a little bit (about 4 inches) of elastic to the end of the ribbon. We can hang this above the baby. Initially, their flailing arms will bat it unintentionally and it will jingle. This auditory feedback is satisfying and will encourage our baby to repeat the motion with some intent. With practice, they will get more accurate with their reach. The sound from the bell might be one of the first impressions that gives the baby the message that they can affect their environment. We can imagine it—the baby lies there watching the mobile, hands moving, and they hear a ding. They might not initially register that they caused the sound, but then it happens again and again and they realize, "Every time my hand hits the mobile, it makes that sound. I am causing that sound!" It then becomes a conscious effort: "I want to make that sound again. I will move my hand in the same way and the sound continues." We can observe the quiet determination with which our baby works, never giving up. They will continue to try and will one day grasp the bell and bring it to their mouth. This is why the elastic is important. It stretches as the baby pulls. If the mobile is hung near the baby's feet, they can also kick at it.

Ring on a ribbon: This is a wooden or metal ring attached to an attractive ribbon that the baby can grasp and pull toward them. Unlike the bell, which provides the satisfaction of a sound if the baby hits it both voluntarily and involuntarily, the satisfaction of the ring is experienced when the baby pulls it and brings it to their mouth. This is more advanced because it requires the baby to reach and grasp using their palm and fingers and then bring the ring to their mouth.

Remember that our baby has a tendency for self-perfection and wants increasing challenges in line with their development. We can offer materials requiring increasing levels of effort to serve this tendency.

Other grasping materials

Rattles can only be independently enjoyed when the baby's grasp is somewhat developed and they can slither or turn. Before that stage, babies are prone to dropping rattles and cannot pick them back up by themselves.

As the baby's reach and grasp develop, we can provide different rattles and safe objects of different colors, shapes, textures, and weights that call for the hands to be used in different ways.

Rattles can be made of different materials that provide different tactile impressions. For example, metal will feel cooler and smoother than wood. Keep in mind that the baby is going to bring these rings to their mouth, so choose safe materials.

Junnifa offered her children wooden balls, a wooden egg with wool knitted over it, interlocking silver rings, and cylinders made with dowels that can be grasped. Interlocking circles are easy for babies to grasp. Silver interlocking rings fit nicely in their hands, and they enjoy teething on them. A nipple teething ball made of safe plastic is easy to hold and perfect for a baby to use to massage their sore gums, and a variety of rattles provide different ways for them to practice their grasp.

Gross-motor skills

Movement Area: Floor time continues to be the simplest and most important activity to support the development of gross-motor movement at this stage (3 to 6 months). Floor time can take place on the movement mat in the baby's movement area, with a mirror that allows the baby to observe their voluntary and involuntary movements. This time spent in a safe space without any obstacles to movement helps our baby strengthen their muscles and perfect the control needed for movement. It gives them complete freedom and control of their body and allows for involuntary movements. The mirror allows the baby to observe their actions and the resulting movements. Their hands and legs can move as much as they want because they are not restricted. If we are carrying our baby all the time or if they are always restricted in well-intended containers (bouncers, exersaucers, walkers, etc.), they do not get the opportunity to master control of different movements.

There is often a debate within Montessori, RIE, and other gentle-parenting circles about placing the baby on their tummy, i.e., tummy time. There are some people who prefer not to lay the baby on their tummy because the baby can't get into this position on their own. The two of us think that it is important for the baby to spend time on both their backs and tummies, as long as we start from birth and give the baby opportunities to spend time on both sides. We can make tummy time more enjoyable for our baby by using a mirror so the baby can see their reflection, or by laying the baby on our body or lying on the floor next to them. We can also add interest by doing tummy time in front of a mobile. This allows our baby to look at the mobile from a different perspective. Tummy time allows our baby to build the core strength needed for most gross-motor movements and is also recommended by the American Academy of Pediatrics. We can notice when our baby is uncomfortable and make changes or pick them up as necessary.

Kicking activities: We can provide activities that encourage the baby to observe their feet and work toward control of their leg movements. A simple way to do this is to hang a tactile mobile or a kicking ball above our baby's feet. A patchwork ball also works well and can be used later for them to crawl after. Interesting objects like a bell, button, or ribbon can also be sewn to the baby's socks. These will catch the baby's attention, and they will work to bring them to their mouth, thus building their coordination.

Note: Always be careful of choking hazards and use small bells with supervision.

Provide interesting things in the environment for the baby to move toward. We can set up a shelf for the baby with materials that are attractive and developmentally appropriate. It should be within view but at a distance from the movement mat so that the baby has to move to get to the materials. If we put toys in the baby's hand, there is little motivation for them to move. We encourage movement by putting a toy or something that attracts the baby a little distance away from them. We do this even before the baby can move. They will keep observing it and, one day, they will attempt to move toward it and slowly but surely will succeed. Different babies find different techniques for moving. Some will slither, others will roll. Each of these techniques requires effort and perseverance from our baby, and they are the beginning of building characteristics that will serve them through life.

Slow-Rolling Object: When our baby starts slithering, we can provide interesting balls or rattles that roll, but not too fast nor too far. These rolling objects encourage our baby to move and provide them with the satisfaction of achieving a goal, subconsciously teaching them that they are capable of doing things for themselves. They reach and reach and reach and then they grasp! These little successes are deposits in our baby's confidence bank. They are building a basic trust in themselves and their abilities. Junnifa's babies enjoyed a rain stick, which made beautiful sounds as it rolled.

OBSERVE 3 TO 6 MONTHS

- Continue to observe the suggestions from 0 to 3 months.

- Notice their shoulders. Can they lift them? When they do, what is their hand doing?

- How do their arms move? One at a time or both together?

- Watch for when they start turning from tummy to back and back to tummy. Which came first? Which do they do more often?

- Do they turn with intention, or is it spontaneous?

- Pay attention to where we leave them and where we find them. Have they moved? How did they move? In what direction?

- Do we notice any development in their movement? Are they moving faster? Do they use hands when they move? Are knees involved?

- When they move, do they have a destination or goal? Do they reach it? What do they do when they stop?

- Notice their hands when they grasp. What parts of the hands are being used? Fingers? Palm? Thumb?

- What do they do with the object once grasped?

- How is it released?

From these observations, is there something new we learned about our baby? Is there anything we would like to change as a result? Something in the environment? Another way we can support them? Obstacles we can be removing? Including our own intervention? Observe joy!

6 TO 9 MONTHS

At this stage, myelination is occuring in the lower trunk, thighs, and down to the leg. It has also moved to the fingers. Like with other stages, the best way to support this development is by giving our baby time to spend on the floor with freedom to move.

Gross-motor skills

During this stage, our baby will start to slither and will then gradually transition to crawling. They will enjoy a wider space to explore and get more efficient with their movement and cover longer distances. We might leave our baby in one end of the room and find them on the other end. If our baby has been using a floor bed, they might learn how to get off it and find us when they wake up. One of the great joys of parenting is the first time our child wakes up from a nap and doesn't think to cry, and instead climbs off from their floor bed, listens to hear where sounds are coming from, and sets off to find us. Just think of the trust our baby must have in themselves and in their ability!

TIPS

This is a good time to childproof our home by:

- Lifting up curtains so our baby can't pull themselves up on them
- Making sure wires are not exposed
- Securing furniture to the wall so it won't fall on the baby if they try to pull up or lean on it
- Covering electric sockets
- Securing cupboards that we don't want our baby to open

Baby-sized furniture and pull-up bar

We have observed that crawling, pulling up, and sitting often happen in quick succession. Once our baby starts crawling, a few changes can be made to the movement area in preparation for these other movements. If we have placed a mat or rug in their movement area, we might remove it now because it can become an obstacle.

A **child-sized shelf** can be added to the movement area. The baby can pull up on the shelf, lean against it to work, cruise along it, and hold on to it to practice lowering into a sit or kneel. The materials on the shelf also provide motivation for movement.

Solids are usually introduced around this time, and a **child-sized table and chair** can be placed in the space for that purpose. The table can also be an aid for movement. Soon after Junnifa started her baby on solids, she would announce when dinner was ready and her baby would crawl to the table, pull up, and climb into their chair. We could also provide a sturdy stool or small **ottoman** that our baby can pull up on and push around, using it as a support as they get to their chosen destinations. A heavy coffee table is also a good support. We could install a **bar along the mirror**, which they can pull up on and cruise on. We can attach the bar at chest height for our baby and 2 or 3 inches from the wall to allow their hand to wrap around it.

We can give our baby a **basket containing balls** of different shapes, sizes, weights, and textures. They can explore in different ways, and often the balls roll, inviting our baby to turn, crawl, and move in different ways that support the development of coordination. Manipulating the balls also supports fine-motor development.

Usually around this stage the baby can sit with support, and it will be tempting to prop them up in a sitting position. We encourage waiting until the baby can put themselves in a sitting position. When we put the baby sitting upright before they are ready, we can put strain on the baby's bones and muscles and take away their sense of achievement when they manage it themselves. Some babies may like sitting so much that it becomes their preferred position, and this discourages crawling or other important transition positions and movements. Junnifa learned this after her first two children. When her third child came along, she did not sit her up before she could do it on her own, and Junnifa noticed a significant difference. First, her daughter crawled before sitting. Sitting was a natural transition from being on all fours. She could also get both into and out of the sitting position and did not fall back like her older sons had done. They would fall backward and couldn't get back into a sitting position without help. Junnifa also noticed that both her sons slouched or bent a little forward when she put them in a sitting position, but her daughter had, and still has, a straighter sitting posture.

Fine-motor skills

The rattles, balls, and other objects that we present to our baby to encourage gross-motor movements can also support the development of fine-motor skills.

As the baby's hand movements become more precise, they will begin to transfer objects from one hand to the other and use their two hands together. Around 7 months, wrist flexion becomes possible and our baby begins to use their palm and thumb. Often when our baby gets to a material, they might grasp it, move it from one hand to the other, and otherwise explore it using their hands and mouths. They will eventually move to what is sometimes called a monkey grasp, where the thumb is almost side by side with the fingers instead of facing the forefinger when the baby is picking up an object. We continue to offer various objects of different shapes, sizes, weights, and textures for the baby's manipulation. We can offer some rattles and objects with thinner circumferences, like a thin bracelet, to strengthen the use of the thumb.

Once the baby starts sitting, their hands become free to use for exploration. We can start providing more opportunities for exploration, like **treasure or discovery baskets**. These can provide rich sensorial experiences, extended periods of concentration, and entertainment. They are baskets with three to six items for the baby to explore. The baskets can hold random objects, and the baby learns to choose which one to explore. The basket could also contain objects that belong to a category. For example, a wooden spoon, a metal whisk, and a rubber spatula are all items used in a kitchen. They are different shapes and made of different materials that will provide unique sensorial experiences for the baby. Each of the objects and the baby's interactions with them provide opportunities for the baby to use and improve their fine-motor skills.

Here are some examples of category-themed baskets:

- Fabric basket (different fabrics with different textures, e.g., cotton, linen, felt, satin, wool, tulle; ideally, they would be of the same color with the only difference being the texture)
- Kitchen items (wooden spoon, metal spoon, cup, whisk, etc.)
- Bathroom items (hairbrush, toothbrush, comb, washcloth, etc.)
- Color-themed baskets would contain different items of the same color. (The balls from the Gobbi mobile would be great here.) These baskets also support the development of gross-motor skills because they often invite the baby to slither or crawl.

These baskets can be kept in different areas of the house for the baby to use while spending time there. For example, we might have the kitchen-themed basket available for our baby to explore on a blanket or mat in a corner while we cook.

Tip: While they are exploring the treasure basket, we could use it as a language opportunity to name what they are exploring. Not all the time. It's lovely for them to simply concentrate on exploring. But from time to time.

A favorite with babies from this age is the **glitter drum**. It's a wooden rotating barrel that spins when the baby's hand strikes it to make it turn. The balls inside provide a soothing sound as additional feedback, too.

Introducing solids provides a practical opportunity for the baby to work with and develop their fine-motor skills. The baby gets to use child-sized cups and utensils, which they pick up and manipulate using their hands. They can also manipulate the food with their hands using different grasps, depending on the size and their ability. A meal containing sliced carrots and peas, for example, will involve a whole hand grasp as well as a pincer grip. Often the baby will transfer food from hand to hand. While we don't want the baby to view the food as a toy, we can give time and opportunity for the baby to purposefully use their hands while eating.

We can also use a mobile for a sitting baby. Even when the baby has more control of their hands, their coordination can still be limited. While sitting, they will get a different perspective from when they were lying down and trying to catch the mobile by reaching up. Now they are sitting, and they are reaching forward to grasp the mobile. This requires different skills. Trying to catch the balls provides opportunities for hand-eye coordination and refined control of movement. The *takane* (or patchwork) **kicking ball** is a great one to hang for a sitting baby.

During this time, children also get interested in items used in their environment and can be provided with opportunities to explore them. Empty water bottles with screw tops can encourage newly acquired fine-motor skills. Or exploring the baskets or trays that hold their toys, or perhaps a toy with wheels. Being able to move gives the baby freedom to follow their interests. As long as it is safe, we do not interfere with such exploration and instead observe to see what draws our baby's attention and then provide similar opportunities for exploration.

OBSERVE 6 TO 9 MONTHS

- Observe how our baby moves. Watch their chest and stomach and then their knees and feet. Notice how they work together.

- Observe how they manipulate objects. What is each hand doing? What are the fingers doing? What is the thumb doing?

- Observe for intention. Do they decide what they want to reach for on their shelf and then move toward it, or do they get to their shelf and then look around to decide?

- Notice how they react when they struggle with an activity.

- Notice the difference between struggle and frustration.

- Observe how they change direction when slithering or crawling.

- How do they transition from crawling to sitting and vice versa? From standing to sitting and vice versa?

- Observe how they climb onto and off their bed. Do they go forward or backward?

- Observe how they explore objects. Notice when they start to explore less with their mouths and more with their hands and eyes.

- When they pull up and are exploring while standing, where are they putting their weight?

- Notice their preferences. Do they have preferred areas of the home? Preferred objects?

- What is their cycle of activity? How do they start their exploration and what do they do when they are done? Notice gestures.

From these observations, is there something new we learned about our baby?
Is there anything we would like to change as a result? Something in the environment?
Another way we can support them? Obstacles we can be removing? Including our own
intervention? Observe joy!

9 TO 12 MONTHS

Nine months is an important point in the baby's development. It is often considered the end of the external pregnancy. In 9 months, our baby went from a fertilized egg to a fully formed human ready to be birthed. And in another 9 months, they go from helpless uncoordinated newborn to capable (more) coordinated human. By 9 months old, if we have provided the right environment and opportunities, our baby will have acquired a basic trust in their environment and in themselves. The signs of this are observable. We will see signs that they feel capable—capable of movement, communication, and some independence, such as feeding and entertaining themselves. They can make simple choices, communicate beyond crying, set and achieve small goals, and solve simple problems by themselves. Most important, they will begin to build and show their personality.

Gross-motor development

At around 9 months, our baby may begin crawling. After some weeks of pulling up to a stand and cruising along furniture, the baby may attempt to stand without support. It is important to allow this process and not step in too quickly to help. As they learn to sit and stand, children also learn how to fall. Initially they might fall backward and hit the back of their head. Hopefully this happens on their movement mat and there is some cushioning. If we try not to react with too much shock, often they will go back to playing. We have observed that after the second or third time they fall, babies will learn to hold up their heads, and this is a skill that will help them as they grow through toddlerhood and childhood. So we can allow this process when they practice pulling themselves up to stand, cruising along a low surface, and one day find that they are able to stand without support, perhaps as they attempt to work at their shelf.

The activities to support the development of gross-motor movement are the same as in the last stage. **Low furniture** that they can pull up on and cruise along is very important. We could also add a **walker wagon** as the baby gets more efficient with cruising. A walker wagon has a handle they can use to pull up on and then push the wagon around. (It is not a baby walker, where the baby is placed in a "saucer," which puts a lot of pressure on their hips and places them in a position they may not yet be ready for.) We can put the walker wagon within view of the baby once they start cruising along furniture. One day when they are ready, they will crawl to it, pull up, and start to walk with it. For a baby starting to walk, we may need to place some heavy books in the wagon to slow it down until they are steadier on their feet as it moves. Enjoy watching them climb in and out of the wagon part. We have seen children in our classes come to stand in a wagon and balance as if they were surfing. It's amazing how babies challenge their bodies if we allow them to.

A large stable **ball tracker** that the baby can pull up on, drop a ball into, bend down to retrieve, and repeat is another popular activity at this age. The cycle of standing, bending, and repeating provides a lot of muscle- and coordination-building opportunities. The baby also benefits from tracking the ball with their eyes and crossing the mid-line (when their right arm moves across to the left side of their body, or their left arm to their right side).

Babies really enjoy crawling up stairs around this stage. If we have stairs in our house, we might provide opportunities for our baby to crawl up them with supervision. Often they can climb up unassisted but might need extra time to explore or guidance through modeling to figure out how to climb down. Babies in this stage also enjoy climbing equipment that incorporates stairs or a Pikler triangle.

One of the favorite activities in Simone's baby class is a **basket of soft balls** of various sizes and textures. Since the balls are soft, the babies are able to grab them with one hand and roll them, catch them, and, best of all, crawl after them.

Around 12 months, just like they did with standing, our baby will start to let go of their support object while cruising and will attempt to walk unsupported. Allow this process to follow its natural course and one day, the child will be walking! This milestone can be reached around 9 months, and sometimes it's closer to 16 months or even later. Remember that each child is different. Some babies will take a step or two and fall down. Other babies will wait until they are completely steady and able to walk across the room.

One important thing to note is that it takes an enormous amount of neurological effort to walk or to talk. So what we often see is that one of these—either the movement or language acquisition—plateaus as the other takes off.

It is always exciting when we notice the baby is close to acquiring a new skill or reaching a new level of independence. It can be tempting to help or see how to speed up the process, but by doing this, we can interfere with the process and also take away the baby's joy in having achieved something by themselves. So instead we can sit back and observe—our role is to prepare the environment and remove any obstacles. And when they walk, we can say, "You look so pleased. You walked all by yourself!"

If we do want to walk with our baby before they are very stable, we can offer a finger and let them take the lead. If they are not able to, then they are probably not ready. Offering one finger and letting them lead is different from taking both their hands over their head

GROSS-MOTOR DEVELOPMENT

0 TO 3 MONTHS

On the back

Head up

Chest up

3 TO 6 MONTHS

Roll over

Sit

Slither

6 TO 9 MONTHS

Crawl

Pull up

Stand

9 TO 12 MONTHS

Cruise

Walk

WHAT TO DO WHEN OUR BABY FALLS

As the baby builds their coordination and learns to control their body, there will inevitably be many falls. They might fall back while sitting, while standing, or while cruising or climbing. It can be so hard as a parent to watch our little baby fall, and this might lead us to react strongly by shouting, looking terrified, or running toward the baby to quickly pick them up. Often our reaction has a stronger effect on the baby than the actual fall. Babies are close to the ground, so these falls are usually not as terrible as they may look or sound.

So first, what not to do:

Do not follow the baby around to catch them when they fall or prevent them from falling. By not preventing every fall, we allow children to encounter, assess, and solve problems. As they do this, they will learn to discern what they can and cannot do. They will learn the limits of their bodies and how to read their environment. They will develop a positive attitude to risk that they will take with them for the rest of their lives.

Do not shout, look horrified, or run toward the baby when they fall.

Instead, prepare the environment for safety. We could have a large rug in the space where the baby spends most of their time during the first year. This will reduce the impact of falls.

When they do fall, take a deep breath, pause, and try to respond calmly with the most relaxed facial expression we can muster. This allows us to see the baby's authentic reaction to the fall instead of their reaction to our fear or shock. Mirror neurons in our baby's brain can pick up the sense of danger or calmness, safety, and well-being from our expressions and mimic them.

Often, if we pause and react calmly, they will get up and just continue what they were doing. The pause allows this to happen. By reacting in this way, we are helping the baby regulate their emotions and comfort themselves not just physically but emotionally. They will learn to react graciously and calmly to setbacks and will take this with them into adulthood.

If the baby is crying, pick them up and talk to them calmly to console them. If we rush in to save them every time they fall and immediately pick them up, we give them the message that they always need someone to rescue them. We also take away the opportunity for the baby to try again, and this interferes with their cycle of activity. Learning to fall, get up, and move again is an important preparation for life.

A last note: We often heard our parents say, "Don't worry" or "It's okay." If the baby is very upset, instead of brushing away their feelings, we can ask them if it was a shock. This often calms them faster too.

and walking with them. In that case, the adult is mostly taking the baby's weight and putting them into a position they are not yet ready for. This is similar to a ballet dancer who goes into pointe shoes too early and hurts their feet. Be patient. They will walk when their body has developed and is ready.

Fine-motor development

The baby's grasp is becoming more refined. The thumb is working in opposition to the fingers, and the baby begins to be able to voluntarily release and to coordinate eye and hand movements. They are able to retrieve hidden objects, and they are starting to explore cause and effect.

Children at this stage enjoy materials like the **object permanence box**, where they can put objects, perhaps a ball, through a hole and wait for it to roll out. They could also put pegs in holes or straws in bottles. Initially, the holes are big, but they can gradually become smaller as the baby's coordination and fine-motor skills improve. Older babies are able to manipulate a poker chip–sized coin to fit into a narrow slot.

We can continue providing **different kinds (size, texture, material, etc.) of balls, rattles, spoons, and other objects**, which allow the baby to explore the capacities of their hands. At this stage, we can also introduce play dough, tissue paper to tear, squeezable bath toys, and other pliable materials that encourage the use of the thumb. We are building strength in their hands that they will later be using to cut things with scissors and hold a pencil. If the baby is more interested in eating the play dough, then we can say, "Look!" and show them how we flatten it on the table with our hands or squeeze it in our fists. If the baby continues to eat it, we can try again in a few weeks.

We continue to provide activities that allow the baby to **use their hands in different ways**, build their hand-eye coordination, and build cognition and problem-solving skills. As the baby's grip evolves, they will enjoy:

- Activities where an object fits in a precise space; some examples include a wooden egg or peg in a matching cup. Nesting toys also provide this opportunity to put things in a precise space and invite the use of the baby's developing grip and grasps.

- Putting things onto a holder, like threading a ring onto a horizontal or serpentine dowel. This can even be done with bracelets and a mug hanger. We can offer smaller rings as the baby becomes more proficient. A stacker with rings will also be fun for them to explore, first taking off the rings, then putting them back on—we can adjust the number of rings and add more as they become more proficient.

- Some simple one-piece or three-piece knobbed puzzles. Between 9 and 12 months, they will mostly be taking the pieces out, practicing their pincer grip in different ways (as well as exploring with their mouth). We can put the pieces back in for them to pull out again.

- Rings on three colored pegs. This activity allows the baby to thread and adds the opportunity to begin sorting by color.

- Drawers to open. As our babies become more stable on their feet, they will enjoy opening drawers and emptying them. This supports both gross- and fine-motor skills. We could choose a drawer in our home that is at our baby's level and put in a few items that we don't mind being dumped out. There are also commercially available materials that allow the baby to drop an object in the hole and pull out the drawer to take out the object. This activity provides an opportunity for our baby's hands to work together, each doing different things, for example, pulling open a drawer with one hand and retrieving an object with the other hand.

The **introduction of solids** will also be an opportunity for our baby to develop their fine-motor skills. In chapter 7 (see page 173), we'll provide more information about this, including introducing a fork and a glass.

Remember that it is through repetition that the baby masters and perfects movement.

OBSERVE 9 TO 12 MONTHS

- What is our baby's preferred way of moving around? Do they prefer cruising or crawling? Do they switch modes when they want to move faster?

- When they stand, how are their feet? Do they stand on tiptoes or flat-footed? Are their feet facing forward or facing outward? Notice when this changes.

- Do they move differently when wearing socks versus being barefoot? When their knees are exposed versus not?

- How do they react when they fall?

- Do they squat, and how?

- When they are trying to balance with their hands free, how high are their arms and how far apart are their feet?

- How has the use of their hands changed? When picking up an object, what is their thumb doing?

- Are they crossing the midline?

- Is their wrist moving?

- Do they drop to the floor from standing or do they lower themselves carefully?

- Do they crawl, cruise, or walk while holding objects? Are they holding objects with one hand or two?

- How do they, hold thin objects?

From these observations, is there something new we learned about our baby? Is there anything we would like to change as a result? Something in the environment? Another way we can support them? Obstacles we can be removing? Including our own intervention? Observe joy!

PART FOUR

OTHER ACTIVITIES

MUSIC

Music can support our baby's development of language and fine- and gross-motor skills.

When listening to music, our baby hears rhythm, which is important for understanding spoken language. Often we can observe our babies responding to the rhythm of music by moving their heads, hands, or feet. We can also hold them and move with them to the music. In these ways, music provides a sensorimotor experience even before the baby is mobile.

We can offer it as an independent activity for our baby to choose. When Junnifa's babies were around 8 or 9 months old, she placed a sticker on the play button of a small CD player that she had placed at their level, and they could crawl over to it and press play, pull up, and move with the music. This supports the development of coordination. When they were tired, they could just press the same button to pause. There are also CD players that are operated by pulling a string that would be ideal for a baby.

Instruments to explore: Babies will enjoy maracas or other shakers as activities for developing their grasp. Junnifa's babies enjoyed drumming on a tom-tom once they could sit and kneel, and blowing into a harmonica. These instruments can be used by themselves or as an accompaniment to music being listened to. When Simone's son was around 9 months old, she put on some music to listen to with him. He immediately crawled off to the other room with some determination. He came back with two maracas and, indeed, they usually played along to the music while shaking the maracas.

We would gently caution against having music playing nonstop. Not only is it extra stimuli for the baby to take in, but babies adapt to their conditions and might begin to view it as background noise and block it out instead of enjoying it.

THE OUTDOORS

From as early as the first month, the outdoors provides activities that support the baby's development of both movement and language, in addition to giving the baby fresh air and other health benefits.

Trees, leaves, and flowers are nature's own mobiles. We can lay the baby in a *cestina* (a Montessori Moses basket) under a tree in the early weeks. They can watch the leaves, insects, and birds.

They can be placed either on their back or tummy on a blanket in the grass. If possible, make sure the grass is safe and has not been sprayed with pesticides.

When the baby starts to reach and grasp, they might enjoy trying to grab leaves, blades of grass, twigs, rocks, etc. Nature provides many natural grasping materials.

Grass provides a great cushion for a baby that is learning to stand or walk and who will fall many times. It also provides a different experience from walking on tiles, wood, rugs, or other indoor flooring.

As the baby practices walking, it is helpful for them to experience movement on different surfaces and textures—paved, rocky and uneven, smooth, etc. The outdoors offers variety to our baby. We can bring their walker wagon outside or to the market for them to practice pushing it along as they walk on different surfaces.

There is also rich vocabulary outside to give the baby—names of trees, birds, dogs, vehicles, shops, items at the market, etc.

TO PRACTICE

- Can we have conversations with our baby?
- Can we observe to find the ideal times for our baby to spend time in their movement area and build it into their routine? Can we make time to observe them daily to see what our baby is working on?
- Can we provide activities that support them?
- Can we check and remove obstacles like restrictive clothing and unsafe objects?
- Can we trust in our baby's abilities and allow them freedom to move, explore, and discover?

MOVEMENT IN THE FIRST YEAR

- Prepare movement area where the baby can spend time—make it a "yes" space.
- Enlarge this space when the baby starts to slither, creep, and crawl.
- Provide opportunity and freedom to move.
- Remove obstacles to movement, like swaddles or props.
- Do not put the baby in containers (like playpens, and limit time in car seats, etc.).
- Dress the baby appropriately to allow for comfortable movement.
- Observe the baby and provide activities that support the development of movement.
- Provide appropriate simple toys that the baby can interact with.
- Do not interrupt or interfere with the baby's activity.
- Don't hurry or encourage any kind of movement before the baby comes to it on their own.
- Ensure the space is safe and childproof.
- Allow the baby time.

NEWBORN

- Gross-Motor Skills
  - Arms and legs are bent and usually symmetrical
  - Moro, fencing, walking reflexes
- Fine-Motor Skills
  - Grasping reflex
  - Hand is usually fisted

MONTH 2

- Gross-Motor Skills
  - Starts to gain head control: can turn neck left or right
  - Eyes start to follow dangling objects
  - Can tilt head back to look at something above
  - Holds head up when on tummy
- Fine-Motor Skills
  - Hand starts to open loosely when lying down
  - Grasp reflex still present
  - Can bring hands to midline
  - Reaching still largely ineffective

MONTH 3

- Gross-Motor Skills
  - Holds head and upper chest up when lying on tummy and also when tilted up on back
- Fine-Motor Skills
  - Hand starts to open loosely when lying down
  - Grasp reflex starts to disappear
  - Can bring hands to midline
  - Observes hands

MONTH 4

- Gross-Motor Skills
  - Holds head and upper chest up when lying on tummy and also when tilted up on back
  - Rolls from back to tummy
  - Slithers slowly
- Fine-Motor Skills
  - Efficient reaching
  - Palmar (squeeze) grasp with no thumb participation

MONTH 5

- Gross-Motor Skills
  - Rolls from tummy to back
  - Slithers slowly
  - Stepping reflex
    (when baby is held upright)
    disappears
- Fine-Motor Skills
  - Efficient reaching
  - Raking grasp fingers only

MONTH 6

- Gross-Motor Skills
  - Uses hands to slither faster
  - Begins to bear weight on feet
  - Can sit with support
- Fine-Motor Skills
  - Efficient reaching
  - Precise pincer with no thumb
    participation
  - Eyes and hands start to work together

MONTH 7

- Gross-Motor Skills
  - Begins to crawl
  - Pulls up to a stand while holding
    on to something
  - Begins to bend
- Fine-Motor Skills
  - Whole-hand grasp
  - Can transfer objects from one hand
    to the other
  - Can wave

MONTH 8

- Gross-Motor Skills
  - Cruising
  - Stepping reflex disappears
  - Begins to bear weight on feet
- Fine-Motor Skills
  - Monkey grasp with thumb and next
    two fingers but not yet opposite
    fingers

MONTH 9

- Gross-Motor Skills
  - Standing against a shelf
  - Stepping reflex is gone
  - Bears weight on feet
- Fine-Motor Skills
  - Inferior pincer—grasps with thumb
    and index finger
  - Points with index finger
  - Begins voluntary release

MONTH 10

- Gross-Motor Skills
  - Pulls up to a stand
    (maybe without support)
- Fine-Motor Skills
  - Precise pincer using tips of thumb and
    index finger
  - Throwing

MONTH 11

- Gross-Motor Skills
  - Takes uneven steps
- Fine-Motor Skills
  - Precise pincer
  - Throwing

MONTH 12

- Gross-Motor Skills
  - Walking
- Fine-Motor Skills
  - Smooth release for large objects

MOVEMENT ACTIVITIES

0 TO 3 MONTHS

Munari mobile

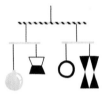

Octahedron mobile

Gobbi mobile

Rattle

Interlocking rings

Mirror

3 TO 6 MONTHS

Ring on ribbon/ Bell on ribbon

Ball with protrusions

Patchwork ball

Balls

Pop-up toy

Wooden book

6 TO 9 MONTHS

Glitter drum

Object permanence box

Wooden egg and cup

Basket of balls

Knobbed puzzle

Drawers

9 TO 12 MONTHS

Push balls with hands

Object permanence
box with drawer

Imbucare peg box

Walker wagon

Stacker

Cubes on dowel

PUTTING IT
INTO PRACTICE

7

DAILY LIFE

DAILY RHYTHM

Babies do not always show a daily regular rhythm, and it can be difficult to read their cues. Are they hungry again? Are they tired? If they didn't sleep well, should we try to get them to sleep again? It can get so confusing.

To avoid the confusion, remember that a usual cycle goes **wake, feed, play, sleep**. Using observation we can notice our baby's unique rhythm through this cycle and start to detect signs that our baby is transitioning from one part of the cycle to the next. We fall into a natural rhythm with our baby.

We can pay attention to signs that the baby is ready to feed (for example, opening their mouth or making certain faces or giving a warning cry); signs they are ready to play (for example, being alert, having burped, and becoming active); or signs they are ready to sleep (maybe starting to look away from an activity, touching their ears, getting restless, making jerky movements, or rubbing eyes).

It can be difficult to tell the differences between cries. If our baby starts becoming unsettled and we know they have already had a good feed and some awake time to play, then we can start to help them transition to sleep. Simone's son got into a crazy cycle of falling asleep while feeding, then waking soon after. He'd be crying, so Simone would end up feeding him again. It was all guesswork, and he wasn't super settled when he was awake. Simone learned from her mistakes and did things differently with her second child. Simone chose not to feed her daughter to sleep. Instead, her daughter would feed upon waking, then play a little, and then she was ready to go to sleep again. Simone observed to determine if she needed any help to fall asleep, for example, sitting next to her, a hand on her, or to pop in and check on her if she was happily chatting to herself.

- A newborn baby will wake from sleeping, feed upon waking, have some short cuddle time or stretch on a mat and diaper change (play), and be ready to sleep again.
- As they get a little older, they'll wake, then feed, have a little longer time to play and cuddle, before, again, a diaper change and sleep time.
- After a few months, we may find our baby wakes without desperately crying of hunger—they will then be able to play a little first, then back to the usual rhythm of wake, feed, play (plus a diaper change), and sleep.

While this is the general rhythm, through observation we can find our baby's specific rhythm and begin to predict and follow it. This is not a schedule—it is simply following our baby's rhythm to aid their orientation and sense of order.

Once we understand their rhythm, we can respect it as much as possible, for example, arranging to meet a friend after the baby wakes or planning for the baby to sleep in the car or stroller or carrier while we drop an older sibling off at school.

Things like growth spurts, teething, travel, and changes in the home or larger environment can affect the baby's rhythm. So we keep observing and make small adjustments if necessary. We don't need to make big changes at once—small modifications help the baby make such transitions more smoothly.

In our daily rhythm, we can also help our baby recognize transition times by having cues like a song, or saying the same thing every time, or having a regular process, for example, bath before bed or wiping their hands before meals. Again, they predict and come to know what to expect.

Similarly, if there is some predictability in the week—a weekly rhythm—this makes it easier for the baby to begin to follow what comes next, for example, with outings, bath times, time with sitters, etc. For those of us working, our baby will learn the rhythm of our week—when we are together as a family and when they are with other family members or a caregiver. As much as possible, we can coordinate with others so that their daily rhythm can be similar in all environments for some consistency for our baby. By the time they are a young toddler, this predictability becomes enormously important as they begin to develop a very strong sense of order and begin to know what comes next in the flow of their daily and weekly rhythms. There is an abundance of research to show that children who grow up in homes with regular routines and rituals are healthier and happier. For more information, we recommend reading *Montessori: The Science Behind the Genius* by Angeline Stoll Lillard.

RITUALS

It's never too early to introduce rituals for special moments throughout the year, or even the week. These rituals can include special elements that are unique to our family or culture.

- birthdays, holiday seasons—making crafts, preparing food, and going on special outings
- annual vacations
- regular weekly rituals such as going to the park on Friday afternoons or making a special Sunday morning breakfast

Our baby will absorb these rituals and, as they get older, look forward to celebrating them with us. It is an opportunity to create family rituals of our very own, for instance, incorporating different cultures into our family.

When there are older children in the family, the baby will enjoy being included in rituals that have already been established and they are sure, with time, to make their own contributions to these rituals too.

EATING

In the first year of the baby's life, the baby will move from being 100 percent reliant on the adult for feeding to taking over more and more steps for themselves. It's the process of moving from dependence, to collaboration, to the beginning of independence.

A baby of around 1 year old who can choose something from their plate, bring it to their mouth, chew and swallow it, and repeat, is a young child in control of their own food intake—they have learned to listen to signs from their body that tell them they are hungry or full and have acquired the physical coordination to feed themselves (albeit not with 100% accuracy). In addition to the independence, they are developing a healthy relationship with food.

Breastfeeding and bottle-feeding

Traditionally, the Montessori approach recommends breastfeeding when possible and that the mother be the primary one to offer milk to the baby, especially in the early weeks. But these days, we also welcome having the primary caregivers offer milk to the baby. This is to help the baby associate their primary caregivers with feeding. In day care, it's ideal to have the same caregiver feed the baby. However, once a baby is introduced to a bottle, feeding can be shared with a partner. Involving both parents in the feeding of the baby provides additional opportunities for bonding.

The production of colostrum in the first days after birth and breast milk thereafter is human biology at its finest: being able to produce the perfect food for the baby, which is (nearly always) available when the baby is hungry, is portable even when we are out of the home, and does not require any extra labor in the kitchen. Breast milk contains all the nutrition our baby needs, including important antibodies passed from mother to baby to help fight against any incoming illnesses.

There are also benefits for the mother: Breastfeeding helps shrink the uterus; studies show that it can lower the risk of breast and ovarian cancers, type 2 diabetes, and postpartum depression; and when there is a feeling of loss or emptiness after carrying the baby in the uterus, holding the baby for extended periods while breastfeeding can help.

Breastfeeding is considered more than simply food; it establishes a very important connection between mother and baby.

> "An infant suckling at his or her mother's breast is not simply receiving a meal, but is intensely engaged in a dynamic, bidirectional, biological dialogue. It is a process in which physical, biochemical, hormonal, and psychosocial exchange takes place."
>
> —Diane Wiessinger, Diana West, and Therea Pitman,
> *The Womanly Art of Breastfeeding*

When we nurse, we can use a relaxed position (reclined and nested in cushions for support). We can have full contact along the baby's belly and legs and some contact on their feet. This position allows the baby to lie with very little support and triggers their latching reflexes. Rather than bringing the nipple to the baby, we first adjust ourselves, then the baby, and then the breast if needed. For more information, look up "natural breastfeeding positions."

Some women may choose not to breastfeed. And for others, breastfeeding may not come easily. There can be problems with a baby latching on; or a tongue tie (when the tongue is held down in the floor of the mouth by a membrane) can make it difficult for the baby to attach; or the mother's milk production may be affected by her hormonal levels or she may have fewer breast ducts in the breast tissue. Early intervention by a specialist can be effective in many of these situations.

Mothers who work outside the home are often able to successfully continue to breastfeed by pumping milk while they are away from the baby. This puts an extra demand on the parent, but it allows all the benefits of breast milk to be passed on to the baby and to maintain breastfeeding when together.

Sometimes breastfeeding doesn't work out. If that happens, we may feel grief that we weren't able to offer our baby breast milk as we had hoped, that our bodies failed us, or that we let our baby down in some way. We can allow these feelings, perhaps find someone to help us process them, and do what we need to do for our baby to thrive. Regardless if we breastfeed or not, we can provide the care, connection, and nutrition for our baby by holding our baby while they feed, gazing into their eyes.

There are organizations that can match us to people with excess milk and supply breast milk for our baby. And there are now lots of formula products available that are as close as possible to breast milk. Whether we feed with breast or bottle, we can remember that holding our baby, looking into their eyes, and having a communication during feeding meets the needs of the baby and parent.

Tips for breastfeeding or bottle-feeding

- Make eye contact with the baby (rather than reading, talking on the phone, or watching a screen)—it is a built-in time for connection and rest with our baby.

- Observe our baby to learn about them in every way—what movements do they make with their hands, their head, their feet? What sounds do they make? What are they looking at? How do they respond to noises around them?

- Sit in a comfortable position with good posture because we will be sitting in this position for many hours in the first months after birth—keep shoulders relaxed and not hunched forward, and use extra pillows for support if needed, at least initially. Or use the reclining method as described on page 167.

- In the days just after birth, the baby may fall asleep while feeding and we can allow this. After these first days have passed, a slightly cool cloth can be used to help them stay awake until the feeding is finished. If they fall asleep while feeding, they will likely wake up again soon after, wanting to finish their feed, and it can feel like the baby is constantly feeding (affectionately referred to as "snacking").

How can we tell if the baby is hungry?

We will learn to observe the signs our baby makes if they are hungry. These could include:
- mouth gaping
- whimpering or squeaking
- body and mouth tensing
- breathing becoming faster
- starting to cry

How often will the baby feed?

A newborn feeds for around 30 to 40 minutes, 8 to 12 times a day. The baby will eventually become more efficient at feeding, so feeding times will become shorter.

After feeding, we can burp them, change their diaper, and give them cuddles and time to kick on the floor. Soon after, they will show signs of feeling tired, and it will be time to start a short sleep-time routine.

During the night, this rhythm will be simplified to feeding, burping, changing their diaper if needed, and then going right back to sleep. Keep the light dim or use a night-light. Note that night waking is quite normal in the first year—though not always to feed.

When we feed a newborn on demand, over time they will gradually establish their own rhythm with a few hours between feeds. They will go from dependence, to collaboration, to increasing independence. Not every cry means that they are hungry. They may be cold or experiencing some other discomfort so we can see if there is something else they may want before offering them the breast or bottle.

Burping

Burping helps to get rid of some of the air that babies tend to swallow during feeding. Burping the baby can be done over our shoulder, holding the back of their head and rubbing or patting gently on their back. Some babies burp more easily seated on our lap in a (very gentle) sandwich-type hold—one of our arms is placed vertically along their stomach with their chin resting on our hand, and our other arm running vertically along their back with their head resting on the hand.

Burping does not need to be rushed. We can use this moment to connect with our baby.

Some common problems while breastfeeding

Allergies. Allergic reactions often appear as diarrhea, sore bottoms, runny noses and eyes, rashes and eczema, or a crying, sleepless baby. Some babies have an intolerance to cow's milk protein and will present colic-like symptoms, wheezing, vomiting, diarrhea, constipation, a rash, eczema, or a stuffy nose. If breastfeeding, we can remove suspected sources of allergies from our diet to see if it helps—though keep in mind that it can take up to 21 days for all traces to leave our system. If bottle-feeding, we could try a different formula.

Biting during nursing. We do not have to stop if our baby bites us while nursing— though it might come as a shock! We can remove the baby from our breast by inserting a clean finger (usually the pinky) between the breast and baby's mouth to release the suction and their jaw. We can give a clear message that it hurts: "Ow. I'm taking you off the breast. Biting hurts me." When we continue to give this kind and clear message that biting hurts and we remove them, our baby learns not to bite us.

Nipple confusion. If we are hoping to exclusively breastfeed our baby, it is generally recommended to wait until the end of the first month to offer bottle-feeding to avoid nipple confusion (when the baby has difficulty switching between the breast and the bottle as they require different ways of sucking).

Introducing solid food: The Montessori approach

Around 6 months of age (and sometimes earlier), our baby will start to show increasing interest in solid food, watching intently as we eat or tracking the food from our plate to our mouth. At this age our baby's prenatal iron supply is depleting, they can usually sit (maybe with a little support), some teeth may be coming through, they can support their own head weight, and they start producing ptyalin (an enzyme that breaks down complex carbohydrates). These are signs our baby is getting ready to start eating some solid food. The current recommendation is to wait until our baby is 6 months old and showing signs of readiness before offering any solid food.

Introducing solids is an important milestone:

- Our baby is starting to see themselves as separate from their parent, and learns that food can come from another source.
- Early food experiences are explorations for the baby. Food from ages 6 months to 1 year is less about the intake of nutrition than the experience of food. We can remember this if we start to worry about how much (or how little) they are eating.
- We are helping them experience food in its natural form and learn more about it. For example, we can show them the fruit we are going to give them and let them feel its texture, smell it. Then they see it being prepared, and they get to taste it.
- They learn skills to feed themselves, and as young toddlers they will be involved in preparing food too.
- We expand their vocabulary around food—the food, the utensils, the actions we are doing.

> "Sitting at a table brings about a change in the child's ego and the start of a new human relationship that will recur throughout life. . . . He begins his separation with food which becomes the external agent of a much more important internal process; the building of a personal identity. The different food and the different way of receiving it is strictly correlated to detachment, independence and development of the ego."
>
> —Dr. Silvana Montanaro, *Understanding the Human Being*

We don't need to wean our baby onto bland baby food or rice cereal, or plain pureed vegetables or fruit. For our baby's first solid food, we can offer them a meal that includes all food types and is food that we would want to eat ourselves (rice with vegetables, a little cheese, some oil and seasoning).

Instead of spoon-feeding the baby, where they open their mouth to our rhythm, we can look for ways they can feed themselves at their own pace. It will be messy and it won't be quick, so we may need to prepare ourselves—but it encourages the baby to manage as independently as possible and follow their own rhythm.

Baby-led weaning aligns well with the Montessori approach to introducing solids. The food that is offered is cut into large pieces that a chubby-fisted 6-month-old can hold, bring to their mouth, and taste. Vegetables do not have to be pureed, but instead cooked until soft so that they fall apart in the baby's mouth. And small amounts are placed in front of the baby for them to pick up, bring to their mouth, and taste. This method is also great for refining their fine-motor skills.

Solid foods that are popular with young babies include:
- well-cooked sticks of carrot, broccoli, or other vegetable around 4 inches in length
- strips of toasted bread
- soft fruits first, building up to pieces of harder fruits that they can hold in their hand and nibble off small pieces
- whatever the family is eating, in a form they can manage themselves

CHOKING SAFETY

Babies have a gag reflex at this age. This is not a sign they are choking; this is a perfect reflex by the body to remove something going the wrong way. Choking signs to watch for are loss of color in face and the absence of sounds. If that happens, we can place the baby stomach-down along our arm horizontally with their chin in our hand. Strike between the shoulder blades with the heel of the opposite hand, and see if anything comes out. Repeat four more times. If the food has not dislodged, sandwich-hold the baby between our forearms (their chin and neck supported gently by our hands) to turn them onto their back for five breast compressions. Take a first aid course to practice this and learn of any updates to these protocols.

Where to eat

In Montessori we want to give our baby a sense of independence. So rather than using a high chair, we introduce a low table and chair called a *weaning table and chair*. The child can sit by themselves and get out of the chair when they are done, be an active participant in feeding, and feel more capable.

We can use this from the time the baby is able to sit steadily (around 6 to 8 months). The height of the table and chair allows them to reach their feet to the floor for stability. We can set the table with a small vase of flowers and can use a placemat for their meals to show where the bowl and cutlery goes. Sometimes the baby throws the placemat to the floor, so it's something we can keep introducing until they become less interested in removing it. This table can be used for all the baby's meals or only for snacks.

Our baby can join us at the family table in a tray-less high chair. This allows us to eat together rather than feed the baby separately. Our baby is learning that mealtimes are social occasions, and they can feel less pressure to eat when we aren't solely focused on them or rushing them to finish eating. Instead, they are learning cues from their own bodies about when they are hungry and when they are full, and they are taking part in the family meal.

Tools for eating

Rather controversially, in Montessori we like to use real plates, glasses, and metal cutlery rather than plastic ones. Not only are these choices more sustainable and made from more natural materials, but the food and drink generally taste better, and the baby can learn the logical consequence that plates and glasses will break if they fall. There are bowls and glasses that don't break too easily (for example, bamboo or enamel), that we can use when they are busy experimenting with letting things fall to the ground.

We can start first with a fork, which is easiest for the baby to coordinate. There are lovely videos online of babies feeding themselves with a fork from around 8 months. The parent spears one piece of food onto the fork and lays the fork on the plate in front of the baby with the handle pointing toward the baby. The baby chooses which hand to use to pick up the fork and brings the food to their mouth. Then the parent fills the fork again and waits until the baby is ready to continue.

It takes our baby more coordination to keep food on their spoon, so we can offer thicker foods to master at first, like oatmeal or thick yogurt.

As young babies are still refining their fine- and gross-motor coordination, we are available to assist them when needed, for example, offering a gentle hand to support the glass to their mouth and then giving less and less support as they develop, and only filling their glass with a small amount of water.

We don't need to use bottles or sippy cups for water. It might take a few days of wet clothes, but babies learn quickly. If we would like to use a water bottle for outside of the home, we can look for bottles with straws as the teats on sippy cups keep the tongue in the sucking part of the mouth.

With any of these tools, look for metal cutlery that is baby-sized, small enough to fit in their hand with a shorter handle. In Simone's classes, she uses cake forks with prongs that are not too sharp and small teaspoons. She uses the smallest Duralex glasses (which hold 3 oz/90 mL) or shot glasses as baby's first drinking cup. Small bowls with low sides make it easier for the babies to serve themselves and get the food out by themselves. Size does matter. In this case, often the smaller the better.

Learning to handle a fork and glass are the first practical life activities we introduce to our baby. Practical life activities are also known as activities in daily life. As a toddler and preschooler, these daily activities will include preparing, serving and cleaning up after meals as well as sweeping, cleaning windows, and taking care of plants and of themselves.

We can also offer them a cloth to wipe their hands and mouth before, during, and after meals. These are the first self-care activities they learn. A small mirror by their snack table can be useful for this.

It's not a perfect process, and we will have to clean up, but practice makes perfect. And we can involve them in the cleanup—an 8-month-old can wipe the table, albeit imperfectly. And when they are done, they can place their cutlery into a small basket that is sitting on their table.

More tips

1. **The adult is in charge of what their baby eats, where they eat, and eventually when they eat. How much they eat is up to the child.** Trust that they are learning to listen to their bodies. We do not have to force in one more spoon, pretend an airplane full of food is flying in their mouth, or distract them with a screen.

2. **In Montessori, breastfeeding and food aren't usually used to help calm a child or help the child fall asleep.** We are available to offer comfort to our child in other ways—cuddling, listening, wiping away tears, and with understanding.

3. **Role of the father or partner.** The father or partner can be involved in feeding from time to time as a way for them to feel involved and bond with baby. If breastfeeding, the mother can pump milk for their partner to offer in a bottle.

4. **Some adoptive mothers and non-gestational mothers can breastfeed their baby.** It is possible to begin lactating even if we have never been pregnant. Supplemental nursing systems are also available, which can be used to induce lactation. Even if no milk production is possible, holding the baby while feeding will help attachment and bonding with the adopted parents.

5. **If they throw food.** If a baby throws food, they are generally all done. When they are hungry, they sit to eat and may take in all they will eat in 5 to 10 minutes. If they then start to throw food, we can ask them, "Are you all done?" Then we can show them how we take the plate to the kitchen and offer to help them get down from the table. They will soon learn that food is for eating.

TO OBSERVE

Observe our baby to learn about them in every way while feeding and eating:

- What movements do they make with their hands, their head, their feet?
- What sounds do they make?
- What are they looking at?
- How do they respond to noises around them?
- When do they feed/eat? How long do they feed/eat for?
- Are they a passive or active eater?
- If nursing, how do they detach?
- How is food presented? What are they eating?
- How is self-feeding encouraged?
- How do we feel about the baby's feeding attempts? Are we bringing any fears to feeding/eating?

From these observations, is there something new we learned about our baby? Is there anything we would like to change as a result? Something in the environment? Another way we can support them? Obstacles we can be removing? Including our own intervention? Observe joy!

Weaning baby from the breast

Deciding when to stop nursing is a very personal decision.

Exclusive breastfeeding has been recommended by the WHO for the first 6 months of the baby's life (this means without giving extra water or solid food) and then with complementary feeding (giving nutrition from food in addition to breastfeeding) from 6 months to 24 months and beyond.

Some Montessori sources, like Dr. Montanaro's *Understanding the Human Being*, suggest weaning around 10 months, when the baby starts to have increasing independence and is beginning to separate more from the parents as they begin crawling and soon walking.

For others, there may be personal reasons for wanting to stop breastfeeding in the first year. If we are no longer enjoying it and beginning to resent it, stopping might be a better decision than continuing longer than we are comfortable with, as our attitudes will also be absorbed by the baby.

Whenever we choose to wean from breastfeeding, we can tell our baby that we will wean in a couple of weeks. That it has been a special time. And that we will enjoy the last weeks feeding together in this way. This gives closure to us and to the baby in a positive way, and acknowledges the special feeding relationship we enjoyed together.

BOOK RECOMMENDATIONS

For more information on breastfeeding, we recommend La Leche League International's *The Womanly Art of Breastfeeding* and *Breastfeeding Made Simple: Seven Natural Laws for Nursing Mothers* by Nancy Mohrbacher.

SLEEPING

The most common questions Simone receives in her parent–baby classes are about sleep: learning to settle the baby in a Montessori way, night waking, using a floor bed, and (mostly) how everyone can get more sleep.

The only problem is, what works for one baby doesn't work for another. Or for every family.

And what exhausted parent wants to even read the words "consistency," "sleep routine," or "make sure the room is dark," one more time?

So how can we give some practical advice on sleep that aligns with the Montessori approach and will be helpful to tired parents?

The best we can really offer is to go back to the principle of **observation**, which has guided us through every step of raising and working with newborns, babies, toddlers, and children.

Every child is unique. Let's look to our baby and observe like a scientist—how many minutes they took to fall asleep, what they ate, how and why they woke up, and more. Then, armed with information about our child, we can help them have a good relationship with sleep and make small adjustments when needed.

The Montessori principles that follow can work whether we have our baby in our bedroom, in their own room, or choose to co-sleep.

Remember that we are our child's guide. We cannot make them close their eyes and fall asleep. But we can nurture beautiful infant sleep by observing, responding, and preparing a safe and comfortable sleeping environment.

> "A great deal of mental work goes on during sleeping and dreaming. All daily experiences must be integrated and all personal 'programs' must be reviewed on the basis of the new information received during the day."
>
> —Dr. Silvana Montanaro, *The Joyful Child* by Susan Stephenson

We can apply the following Montessori principles to sleep.

1. Observe our baby and learn their sleep/wake rhythms

A baby has their own sleep rhythms. We can meet their needs for sleep by observing them to learn:

- when they show us they are ready to sleep (tired signs)
- how much (or little) help they need to fall asleep
- their activity during sleep (yes, they are active even while they sleep)
- how long they sleep for, and
- how they wake up

Because it can be difficult to always differentiate among the baby's cries, remember the rhythm—new babies wake, feed, play, then sleep. After a good feed, they enjoy some playtime—on a movement mat, perhaps watching a mobile, having some cuddles—with enough stimulation (but not too much). And then, by observing the baby, we will see their tired signs. These may be:

- jerky movements in their arms and legs
- rubbing their eyes or yawning
- other signs unique to our baby (we are always observing to learn our baby's signs)

When we see these tired signs, we can begin a slow sleep-time routine. A simple, short routine for each sleep time may include:

- telling the baby that we see they are getting tired and that we are going to bring them to bed
- waiting until they respond, for example, by raising their head
- using gentle hands to pick them up, change their diaper, and carry them to their bed
- singing to them, reading a short book, or doing another connecting activity
- laying them down on their back while they are awake, so they can sleep in their consistent sleeping place
- providing calm reassurance that we are there if they need us

Enjoy this process of observing them. It is much more relaxing to observe and assist them than to feel like we have to "put them to sleep." Remember, we are their guides. They generally know when they are tired; it is up to us to read their cues. Then they are the ones who will close their eyes and fall into sleep, with us as their guides to support them if needed.

Tip: Young infants will still be adjusting their circadian rhythms, so lots of sunlight and fresh air during the day help them begin to adjust to day and night over the first months.

TO OBSERVE

It can be helpful and even fascinating to make and review observation notes in a dedicated notebook like a scientist. We can note the following:

When they are getting tired:
- What signs do they have that show they are tired?
- Have their wake windows gotten longer?

While falling asleep:
- What are the movements they make with their arms and legs?
- Are their hands in fists or open?
- Do they make any cries or sounds?
- What are their facial expressions?
- Do they continue to move right up until the moment they fall asleep? Or do they fall asleep gradually?
- How much help do they need to fall asleep? Are they ready to move to the next stage, going from dependence, to collaboration, to increasing independence?

During sleep:
- What is the quality of their sleep—fitful, peaceful, etc.?
- How is their body positioned?

- Do they make any movements with their limbs or head?
- Can they resettle themselves from light sleep back to deep sleep? If not, why do they wake up? Are they looking for us to reestablish a condition from when they fell asleep?

Upon waking:
- How long does it take them to wake up?
- What is their temperament on waking?
- How do they communicate to let us know they are awake?
- What is their body position?

Wake/sleep patterns:
- How long are they awake between naps? How long are their naps?
- Is there a pattern developing? (how long they can stay awake or if they have a regular bedtime.)
- Are they affected by light entering the bedroom?

From these observations, is there something new we learned about our baby? Is there anything we would like to change as a result? Something in the environment? Another way we can support them? Obstacles we can be removing? Including our own intervention? Observe joy!

2. Give as much help as necessary, and as little as possible

When a child is learning to crawl or walk, we can set up a supportive environment and offer help when it is needed—as much help as necessary and as little as possible. Then we let our baby master these skills.

Similarly with sleep, we set up a safe environment and support them, giving just as much help as is needed and as little as possible. This might be sitting with them until they fall asleep, placing a hand on their belly, rubbing their back, or offering a soothing sound.

They may fuss a little as they transition to sleep—this is normal, and we can be there to perhaps place a hand on them and provide a few comforting words. If they have not settled after some time (say around 20 minutes), we can offer them a bit more milk or, if they are an older baby who is thirsty but not hungry, some water.

Sometimes the baby will not settle at all—we can still give them "rest time" by placing them in a baby carrier or taking them for a walk.

3. Move from dependence, to collaboration, to increasing independence

As we have mentioned more than once in this book, in the first year, the baby will move from dependence, to collaboration, to increasing independence. This also applies to sleeping.

In the early days, our baby depends on us noticing when they are tired, giving them a short sleep-time routine that they will come to recognize, and consistently putting them in the same place to sleep. We learn to observe our baby and then provide as much help as necessary and as little as possible (*dependence*).

This will create a foundational pattern from which the baby will gradually pull away in the first year. Some babies will crawl to their floor bed when they are tired. Others will need us to observe their tired signs, follow their sleep-time routine, and come to sit next to them until they sleep (*collaboration*).

Toward the end of the first year, babies sleeping in their own room may come to find us upon waking— indicating that we have supported them to build a good relationship with sleep (*increasing independence*).

If our baby becomes dependent on us to sleep, rocking them or feeding them to sleep, for example, become sleep crutches. When the baby gets into a light sleep during the night, they can find it difficult to resettle without this rocking or feeding. As an adult, if our pillow moves during the night, when we get into a light sleep, we will wake to find it and put it back, unable to sleep until we're comfortable again. Similarly, when a baby gets into a light sleep, they will wake to look around for the arms that were rocking them or breast they were sucking on.

If we are currently rocking them or feeding them to sleep, it's okay. But at some point this will need to change for them to fall asleep by themselves and stay asleep—when we and our baby are ready.

As the baby gets older, we can continue to observe them to see how much (or little) assistance they need to sleep. We may be able to sit farther away from them, then sit by the door, then leave them to sleep by themselves, gradually moving from dependence, to collaboration, to increasing independence.

4. A consistent sleeping area, ideally with a floor bed

As we discussed in chapter 3, having a consistent sleeping area is so important for the baby's points of reference.

We like to use a low mattress that is around 6 inches (15 cm) high on the floor for sleeping—a floor bed. This gives the baby the freedom to eventually crawl into and out of the bed independently, and they are able to see the whole room, without bars blocking their view of the space. It can be relaxing for the adult to be able to sit or lie next to our baby as they settle, rather than standing while leaning over into a crib.

At birth, we like to use a cestina (a Moses-style basket) for them to sleep in. It gives a feeling of security to be in a smaller bed. The cestina can be placed on top of their floor bed from birth to orient the baby to their sleeping place, a point of reference they will remember. Following SIDS guidelines, this may be in the parent's bedroom.

Cribs were designed to be convenient for adults, not babies. It can be difficult to drop these ideas that have always been used in the past. If we are uncomfortable with using a floor bed, we can transition the baby from a crib to a toddler bed at around 12 to 16 months, when they are able to climb in and out of bed by themselves. They will then get to experience the benefits of a floor bed before they are (likely) going through the "no" stage of development, which commonly happens around 2 years old.

Note: It's important that the room is thoroughly checked for babyproofing, because the baby will soon be able to wake, wriggle off the bed, and begin to explore the whole space. If we cannot make it safe for our baby to leave the bedroom independently, a baby gate may be put across the doorway so they are free to crawl out of their bed to play.

5. *Allow free movement*

We like to offer the baby as much opportunity for movement as possible—even in sleep. During Simone's Montessori training, she participated in 50 hours of newborn observation (from birth to 8 weeks). She couldn't believe how much there was to observe while a baby was sleeping. During sleep, their hands constantly move, their arms rise and lower, their legs kick and straighten, their head can move from side to side, and their mouth makes movements too.

We can look for sleep clothes that are soft on the baby's skin, with few labels or seams to irritate them, that will also allow free movement of their legs and feet. If it's cooler outside, consider using socks rather than all-in-one suits to allow the feet more movement.

Swaddling can limit the baby's free movement. However, swaddling can also provide comfort for some babies, giving them a feeling of safety like being back in the womb or to keep them from being startled by their Moro reflex. In these cases, the upper body might be swaddled, while the legs are left loose to allow for free movement.

Sleeping bags or sleep sacks have become popular in recent years as the American Academy of Pediatrics recommends no blankets until 12–18 months. Look for one that enables the baby to move freely while keeping in mind that it may limit their ability to crawl, stand, and walk upon waking.

6. *Topponcino*

A topponcino is a soft, quilted cushion that we can lay the baby on from their first days. We have mentioned that the toppocino is often used during the day to limit the stimulation the baby experiences when we hold them, or give them to someone else to hold. The toppocino has a familiar smell to it, a consistent warmth, and becomes one of the baby's points of reference.

It is useful for sleeping time too. Imagine we are holding our baby and they become sleepy. Without the topponcino, most babies do not like to be transitioned from our arms to their bed. Using the topponcino, we can lay them down in their bed or cestina (Moses basket) with their topponcino under them and they rarely startle. The temperature, scent, and cushioning remain the same.

Junnifa was so fond of the topponcino, she brought it everywhere—when they were visiting Grandma's house or if they were out for the day—and she used it for the first few months at sleep time, while she and her baby were co-sleeping. The topponcino became a point of reference for her babies when they eventually transitioned into their own beds.

Consider going pacifier-free

Most Montessori sources do not recommend the use of pacifiers. A young infant cannot easily put a pacifier back in by themselves in the night, and pacifiers can be overused by the adult when a baby is attempting to communicate their needs. So we may wish to go pacifier-free. See more on pacifiers on page 195.

WAKE WINDOWS AND NUMBER OF SLEEPS A DAY

While every baby is different, it can be useful to know how long on average a baby stays awake between sleeps so that we can keep an eye out for tired signs.

0–12 weeks	1–1.5 hours (many naps)
3–5 months	1.25–2 hours (3–4 naps a day)
5–6 months	2–3 hours (3–4 naps a day)
7–14 months	3–4 hours (2–3 naps a day)

*Source: TakingCaraBabies.com

Around 12 to 16 months they will start to stay awake all morning, with one nap a day in the middle of the day, and they are able to stay awake until bedtime.

Co-sleeping

Co-sleeping and Montessori can coexist.

Some families choose to co-sleep with their baby. Sleeping arrangements are a personal decision, and each family must decide what works for them. Even with co-sleeping, we can provide a consistent sleeping area for our baby.

Junnifa co-slept with her children for the first few months. She would put them to bed in their floor bed and then when she herself was ready to sleep, she would transfer them to her bed so she could feed them easily during the night. She would lay them on their floor bed for daytime naps, and once they were no longer breastfeeding, they transitioned to spending the whole night in their own bed. Junnifa felt that the co-sleeping arrangement was more for her than for her babies, and they peacefully transitioned to their own bed at their family's pace.

Whatever the sleep arrangements, we are always observing to see when the baby is ready to move to the next step from dependence, to collaboration, to increasing independence. And we can consider if it is our need or theirs we are meeting.

Note: Please refer to page 63 for SIDS guidelines.

THINGS THAT CAN HELP NURTURE BABY'S SLEEP

- observe our child's sleep/wake rhythm and how it changes
- note how much assistance we give them to sleep
- be consistent—do not try three things one night; if we make a change, keep it the same for a week and record it objectively in a notebook
- provide a safe, comfortable place for sleep
- have realistic expectations around sleep—most babies are not sleeping through the night in the first year
- note sleep crutches and remove them when we are ready
- nap when baby naps—take care of our sleep and well-being; do our chores when the baby is awake and allow them to observe, talk to them about what we are doing, and involve them

COMMON SLEEP QUESTIONS

The first answer we usually give when it comes to questions about sleep is, of course, to observe the baby. However, here are some more specific answers to the most frequently asked questions about sleep.

Why does my baby wake up at night?

- From 0 to 3 months, our baby will be waking at night to feed. Their bodies will still be adjusting their circadian rhythms, so lots of sunlight and fresh air during the day helps their bodies begin to adjust to day and night over the first months. When nursing at night, try to keep the lights dim and move the baby as little as possible, ideally feeding in the room where they are sleeping. After feeding, burp them, change the diaper if necessary, and put them right back to sleep.

- Are they teething or sick? They may need some extra comfort at this time. Once the tooth is through or they are better, we can try not to let this extra comfort become a new crutch, by helping them go back to how they slept before the teething or sickness.

- Do they have a wet or soiled diaper? Is there a noise? A crease in their sheets that is bothering them? Are they too hot/cold? Are they going through a lot of developmental changes that they are processing? Are they checking that we are still there?

- For an older baby who is feeding and growing well, we may wish to first offer some water in the night. Sometimes this is enough and they will go back to sleep. Many families find that the baby then becomes less interested in waking and will sleep for longer periods. We can also gradually offer less milk at night if the baby drinks from a bottle by diluting the milk with water at a proportion of 75/25, then 50/50, then 25/75, until they are drinking water.

- Is our baby smelling the mother's milk and waking up? We may wish to have them sleep in their own room if space allows.

- When in doubt, take notes—objective observations can be very helpful. What time do they wake? For crying, what is the intensity, duration? How do they respond to our efforts to soothe them? What do we do when baby wakes? Is this the same every night? If we bring them to our bed in the middle of the night, may this be a reason our baby wakes?

- Be consistent—we can make a plan (not in the middle of the night when we are tired and can't think) and respond in the same way to our child for at least seven nights before changing. New patterns take time.

How can I get my baby to resettle when they wake during their nap or during the night?

- Babies enter into light sleep at the end of their sleep cycle—often after around 40 to 45 minutes. They may stir or completely wake up. When this happens, they will look for any conditions that existed when they were asleep, for example, if they were sucking a pacifier, being rocked, or fed. So when we help them gradually learn to fall asleep in their bed, it will be easier for them to resettle. We give them as little help as possible and as much as necessary— maybe sitting next to them, or placing a hand on their belly, or saying some comforting words.

- We can use observation to help us understand why our baby is waking up. Revisit Junnifa's story in chapter 2 about observing her son when he was waking up 40 minutes into his nap. He was looking for her in his new space.

Is it okay to wake a sleeping baby?

- We like to follow their rhythms as much as possible. If they sleep late, they are likely tired. It requires some flexibility on the adult's behalf and some creativity. Try to make plans around your baby's naptimes. Or try to leave the house when they are getting sleepy so they can sleep in a carrier, stroller, or in the car.

Should I use a night-light?

- Most babies under 12 months old are not yet scared of the dark. So it can be preferable to keep the room completely dark if possible.

- We could use a night-light as we are getting them ready for sleep, or during night feeds.

- If using a night-light, look for a red-based night-light and avoid white- and blue-based ones, which can suppress melatonin and affect the baby's sleep.

What can I do about early waking?

- If they wake early, some babies will feed and go back to sleep. Many will already have had most of their sleep, so they will have difficulty going back to sleep.

- Check for any light coming in through their blinds or around the edges.

- Are they having long daytime sleeps? Is it possible to delay their first nap a little?

- Many sleep experts suggest an earlier bedtime can help, even though this may seem counterintuitive.

- Does baby associate coming into our bed with waking up early?

Why won't my baby settle?	• We can take them to their room, sit by their bed to observe them, and let them crawl and babble until they show tired signs (e.g., yawning, rubbing eyes). Then lay them in their bed. This can also work when they are overtired and become very busy. Let them explore until they are tired, then change their diaper and lay them on their bed.
	• It is fairly common for younger babies to have a period during the day when they won't be able to settle. If they haven't fallen asleep after around 20 minutes, we can take them for a walk in a carrier or stroller or have them in a carrier while we do some things around the house. If they don't fall asleep, at least they will have had some rest and will be ready to begin the next cycle of feed, play, sleep.
Help! My baby is going through a sleep regression.	• A sleep regression is when our baby was sleeping well and then it changes. At these times, our baby is going through some transitions. We don't love the word "regression," as these phases generally mean that our baby is making a "progression." Our baby's sleep is changing to something different.
	• At around 4 months they become more wakeful and alert, have increasing awareness, and may find it more difficult to fall asleep.
	• At around 8 months they are going through enormous developmental changes, now able to slither or crawl and sometimes pull up—they are busy with these newfound skills.
	• At around 12 months they have developed more gross-motor skills, like crawling and coming to a stand, and are gaining new understanding about object permanence (that when something goes away, they can bring it back with their own actions). These motor changes bring on a host of psychological ones. They can also be transitioning to one nap a day.
	• We may need to move back to some collaboration until it passes. Then remember to observe when our baby is ready to move back to increasing their independence.
	• Hang in there. Give it some time and try again.
Questions about using a floor bed	• See chapter 4, page 64

How can I move my baby out of our room?

- If our baby has been sleeping in our room and we are ready to move them into their own room, we can spend time with them in their room during the day for them to get used to the space.

- We can place them in their room for their daytime naps. Then they begin to have their night sleep in their room too.

- Be confident with the change. Bring them to their bed, explain, "This is your own bed," and have limited choices available—they can explore quietly in their room while we sit by their bed to observe until they are ready to sleep.

- Set up points of reference that are familiar to them, e.g., using a topponcino, a familiar picture of the family, a blanket.

- We may need to sit with them while they fall asleep. Once they have adjusted to their new space, little by little we won't need to be there anymore for them to fall asleep.

I'm stressed— my baby won't sleep.

- Consider offering the baby the opportunity to "rest" rather than "sleep." Then we can let go of the idea that they need to sleep; they will at least have some quiet time. The baby will not feel pressure from us to sleep. And often they do fall asleep.

- We can examine our own fears around their not sleeping. We may be worried they will be cranky or not in a good mood for some visitors. What are we bringing to the situation?

- Keep our sleep-time routines consistent for a week. Instead of trying something different every time, we can do our best to respond in the same way when baby wakes in the night.

- If we are feeling stressed or burned out, we can also get some support with sleeping from an early childhood nurse or sleep consultant.

- We also need to consider the adult's needs. If our baby's sleep is affecting the whole family, then we need to look at a way that everyone's sleep needs can be met.

BOOK RECOMMENDATION

For more information on sleep, we suggest *The Sleep Lady's Good Night, Sleep Tight* by Kim West.

PART TWO

PHYSICAL CARE

CLOTHING

Giving our baby freedom of movement is an important part of the Montessori approach. We can select clothing for them that is comfortable, soft against the skin, and allows for easy movement.

We can look for:

- clothing that is easy to get over the baby's head—look for tops that wrap (for example, kimono tops) or that have buttons on the shoulder to create a wider opening when dressing
- natural materials like organic cotton, silk, or wool
- clothing that is not too tight (which can restrict movement) nor too loose (which can create uncomfortable creases for them to lie on or get tangled in)
- a top that is separate from the trousers and without feet attached, which will enable the most freedom of movement
- socks to cover feet, if needed
- we can save party dresses, denim jeans, and baby sneakers for special occasions (if at all)

When dressing

Dressing our baby is a perfect opportunity for connection with them. We use gentle hands, tell them what we are planning to do, and wait for their reaction first before picking them up. We talk about the clothes we are going to put on, we ask for their assistance to raise their arm or leg, and we are careful yet confident when putting clothing over their head. And we move them as little as possible. The idea of using our gentle hands, which we talk about a lot in this chapter and in this book, Junnifa learned in her RIE training based on the work of Emmi Pikler.

We can also start offering choices—even with a young baby. For example, we can offer two T-shirts of different colors and observe to see which one the baby's gaze lingers on or which one they reach for. Over time they will be a more active participant, sliding an arm into their T-shirt sleeve, possibly managing to take off their socks by themselves, or pointing to the trousers they would like to wear.

Simone still remembers the shocked faces from parents in her class when she helped ready a baby for class while the mom visited the bathroom. Simone asked the baby if it was okay to take their coat off for them. There was no objection from the baby, so she told them she was going to undo the jacket first and sat the baby in such a way that they could see Simone as she carefully unzipped it. Then she asked the baby to help her take their left arm out of the jacket. While she was handling the baby, she asked, "Is that okay?" using as gentle hands as possible. She continued with the other arm until the coat was removed.

The other parents were surprised because it's so different from the way we unconsciously dress and undress our babies.

So let's slow down. Let's make it a special moment with our baby. Let's look into their eyes. And let's always be respectful and gentle with our touch.

DIAPERING

Rather than rushing through diapering, we can use this time for conversation and connection with our baby. And we we can show them respect.

When changing a diaper, we can:

- Watch our language and gestures, for example, not scrunching our nose or saying things like "You stinky baby" or reacting negatively. Instead, we can say, "I see your diaper is soiled" or "I see you pooped. Let's go change." Wait for the baby's response and then pick them up.
- Give the child some privacy when we change them, ideally a changing table or area.
- Communicate what we are doing while changing them: "I am going to take off your diaper." We wait again for a response from the baby and then begin to change them, talking through the process and collaborating with them as much as possible: "First this snap and now this one. I will help you lift up your leg."
- Describe bodily functions and parts with their correct names.

- Use gentle hands during diaper changes. Be careful and respectful in the way that we lift up their legs when changing them. If we pause and touch gently, we will find that they collaborate and actually lift their legs by themselves from very early on.

- Change the diaper in the same way and in the same place as much as possible each time—babies thrive on predictability.

- Once the baby is pulling up to standing, they may resist being laid down to be changed. We can understand how vulnerable this position must feel. Instead, we can sit on a low stool while they stay standing during the change. This takes some practice but reduces their resistance to being changed. For a bowel movement, we can have them lean forward to place their hands maybe on the side of the bathtub while we clean them.

- A general note, when cleaning them during diapering, it is more hygienic to wipe from front to back, especially for girls, to prevent infections.

Even in the first 12 months, we are laying the foundation for their later toilet independence. That doesn't mean that our baby will be using the potty or toilet by themselves yet, but:

- By using cloth diapers or thick underwear (sometimes called "training pants"), our baby will feel wet, have freedom of movement, and gain increasing awareness when they pee or poop. These days disposable diapers are so effective at keeping the baby feeling dry that the baby misses the feeling of wetness when they urinate, which they will need later when they learn to use the toilet independently.

- By using proper vocabulary when changing them, we are teaching them about how their body works and to not feel shame about their bodily functions.

When they refuse to get dressed or have a diaper changed

There are several things to consider if our baby is resisting getting dressed or getting a diaper change:

1. Are they telling us they are ready for the next step? For example, an older baby may want to take over more control in the process. A baby who is trying to wiggle away while having their diaper changed may want to stand to be changed or may show interest in the potty.

2. Involve them in the process, for example, giving them time to allow them to pull the shirt over their head, choosing the T-shirt from a limited selection, or, once they are walking, carrying the pants while we carry the rest.

3. Are we interrupting their play to get them dressed or change their diaper? Instead, we can allow them time to finish what they are doing and let them know that when they are finished we will change them.

4. Don't underestimate humor and singing silly songs—not as distraction but as a form of connection.

5. Seek to understand them and guess how they might feel: "Are you feeling frustrated?" or "You don't want to be touched?"

Sometimes they may not be willing to be dressed or changed, meanwhile we need them to be ready to leave the house. If this happens and we have done everything outlined above, we can be as gentle as possible getting them dressed or changing their diaper. "Sportscasting" can be useful at these times too—we describe aloud and in an objective way to the baby what is happening, just as a sportscaster might give a detailed account of a sports event.

Using as gentle hands as possible, we can tell them what we are going to do, pausing for them to process it, and seeking to understand. "I can see that you are pulling away from me. It's important for me to give you a clean diaper. Are you saying you don't like that? And I'm lifting you with my gentle hands. . . . That was a tough one, wasn't it?"

They see that we are respectful, gentle, and taking care of their physical needs as well. And by saying "I'm using my gentle hands," it's a reminder to use softness at all times, especially when there is resistance.

BATHING THE BABY

As with dressing and diapering our baby, when bathing the baby we want to be as gentle, calm, and confident as possible, and use it as a moment of connection. Most babies are very relaxed in the bath and enjoy it a lot.

With a newborn in particular, we want to limit any unexpected movements, make our movements as minimal and efficient as possible, and support their head at all times. In our Montessori training, we practiced bathing the baby with the same sequence of movements each time. This can make us more confident to find ways to handle the baby as gently as possible and with adequate support for the baby.

Make the temperature of the room where the baby will be bathed a little warmer, and run the bath to around 2 to 4 inches (5 to 10 cm) deep, with water at body temperature (check the temperature with your wrist to get the most accurate read). There is enough water in the bath so the baby can float, with our gentle hands for support. Have everything we'll need at the ready, including a towel open to receive the baby.

When bathing the baby, move slowly and use equal pressure on all body parts, including their genitals, to give the baby a full sense of their body schema (how their body is made up). Talk to the baby during the bath, smile, and make eye contact.

The WHO now recommends waiting at least 24 hours before baby's first bath. Also, our baby does not have to be bathed every day—instead maybe three times a week.

RECOMMENDED WATCHING

To see how gently we can bathe a baby, watch Thalasso Bain Bébé's videos online.

There is also one with twins holding each other while being bathed.

TRAVELING IN THE CAR

Car seats limit both a baby's movement and what they can see around them. However, car seats are essential for safety, so we can be respectful, understanding, and use our gentle hands as we place the baby into the car seat.

Make sure the baby is not hungry and their diaper is clean before getting in the car. We can tell them that we are going to place them in the seat and allow them to collaborate as much as possible for their age, for example, asking them to give us their arm so we can pass it through the seatbelt.

Being confident also helps as the baby picks up any sense of unease we may have. If there is a period where our baby is not enjoying being in the car, we may start to become anxious before any car trips—anxiety that our baby will pick up on and share.

Once in their seat, we can have something for them to look at in the car, like a black-and-white picture board, something from nature hung up for them to look at, or a board book, which can be attached for them to pull at, teethe on, and look through. Music that we enjoy or classical music can be relaxing for some babies, and longer audio books become interesting when they are a little older.

BABY WEARING

Most babies feel secure and soothed by the movement in a baby carrier or sling, and they love being close enough to smell their special people. Using baby carriers gives us flexibility in places like public transportation, the supermarket, or around the house when we need both arms free. An unsettled baby can be worn close to our chest and have a rest even if they don't fall asleep. During symbiosis in particular, baby wearing can help the transition for the baby from womb to the outside world.

The variety of baby carriers has grown enormously, so look for one that gives you enough support for your back and can grow with your baby.

That said, we love giving babies an opportunity to move their bodies. So we can allow time for them to be on a mat on the floor as well. As our baby starts to crawl and take their first steps, also allow them to crawl and walk freely when outside, and keep the carrier for longer distances.

TEETHING

Some babies may never have trouble with teething. However, if you've ever had a baby that drools nonstop, starts night waking when they normally wouldn't, has poop that looks different, and sometimes has a red bottom, these are signs the baby is teething.

We can observe the baby and try to make them more comfortable with a natural teething gel or powder, have cloths on hand to wipe their chins, and perhaps have them wear a sweet bandana to catch the drool while it lasts. Some babies get a bit of relief from sucking on something cold, and so some natural teethers can be kept in the freezer.

Fortunately, once a tooth comes through, we can reestablish the baby's regular rhythms (until the next tooth is on its way).

We can also start to clean their newly emerged teeth with a soft cloth or toothbrush and some water.

USING A PACIFIER

Most Montessori educators do not encourage the use of a pacifier. If the baby has something in their mouth all the time, they cannot communicate their needs—all of baby's cries have meaning and shouldn't be stopped with a pacifier. And the youngest babies cannot put it in their mouth by themselves or take it out themselves.

Studies show that pacifiers may reduce the risk of SIDS. If using a pacifier helps an unsettled baby or it helps a baby to fall asleep instead of crying for a long time, then use it at these limited times. It can be useful to keep the pacifier in a box by the bed so that it isn't tempting to use during the day, when we feel like we want some quiet.

The earlier we are able to reduce use of and remove the pacifier, the easier it will be, before it becomes an attachment for the baby. Ideally, this would be in the first year.

We can explain that they are getting older and that we will help them to find a new way to calm themselves. Since sucking on a pacifier often helps to relax their nervous system, here are some other ways for them to relax:

- holding tightly onto a book or soft toy
- using a bottle with a straw
- getting a brisk towel rub after a bath
- getting deep-pressure bear hugs
- squeezing bath toys
- getting a slow, firm back rub

Usually the transition goes surprisingly easily, but understand that it may take some days for some babies. If we are clear on wanting to get rid of pacifiers, it can help to remove all of them from the house, because the more consistent we can be, the clearer it will be for our baby to understand the new way. It can also be helpful for our baby to see them being removed.

Some people ask if thumb- or finger-sucking is preferable to using a pacifier. This can be preferable because the baby is in control of putting their fingers or thumb in their mouth and how often they do it. And we can also observe to see when and why they suck and determine if we can meet this need in another way. For example, if we observe them sucking their thumb when they are bored, we can offer them something to manipulate with their hands.

SHARING

The concepts of sharing and toy ownership do not often present in babies until close to 12 to 16 months old. In the first year, a baby generally explores by playing with one thing and then releasing it to move on to the next object of exploration. If another young baby or child sees what they are playing with as interesting and takes it out of their hands, often a baby will turn around to find another object.

If there are older siblings who are often taking their things, a baby may learn to hold on tight and not let go. We can translate for them, explaining to their sibling, "It looks like the baby wants to finish playing with it first." This models to the baby that it's okay to finish playing with their toy and that eventually we'll share by taking turns.

If our baby is the one who is taking things from another child, it can be respectful to model that we ask before taking something. "Did you want to play with that? Let's ask the other baby if they are all done." If the other baby looks like they want to hold on to it for now, we can say to our baby, "It looks like they are playing with it right now. It will be available soon." Our baby will learn to watch and wait or to find something else to play with.

COLIC AND REFLUX

Colic is when a baby has "frequent, prolonged and intense crying or fussiness," and no reason for it can be found. Infant reflux "occurs when food backs up (refluxes) from a baby's stomach, causing the baby to spit up." (Mayo Clinic)

Both colic and reflux make for a very fussy baby. And most of the advice says that both will get better at around 3 to 4 months, once the baby's digestive system has matured a little more, so just hang in there. This is not very helpful for tired, stressed-out parents whose hearts are breaking seeing their child crying or in pain.

Like everything in Montessori, we suggest observing. We can write down what we have eaten if we are breastfeeding, the ingredients in our baby's formula, what time the crying occurs, how long the crying or symptoms last, if the baby is pulling up their legs or making uncomfortable faces, how they latch on when feeding, if they have a tongue tie or cleft lip and palate, whether they are overtired or overstimulated. We can look for any patterns and present them to our doctor or pediatrician.

We can also seek medical advice to see if there are any allergies, histamine sensitivities (in foods like strawberries), or a physical problem like an intestinal blockage, bacterial overgrowth, ulcers, or occasionally a narrow entry preventing food from entering the small intestine or the stomach pushing through the diaphragm. (Some research has also shown that birth trauma or a breach presentation may create colic symptoms.)

The good news is that many parents who follow their intuition that their baby's crying or pain is not normal are able to get to the root cause.

And, in the meantime, we can be present for our baby, make them feel as comfortable as possible with body contact and time together. Often, a little pressure on the belly helps, we can lay them, belly side down, on our own body or give them supervised tummy time on a softer surface like a bed or carpet. We also need to look after ourselves and get support if we can—perhaps someone to take over for some time each day—because hearing a baby crying constantly is tiring and emotionally challenging for parents.

SCREEN TIME

The Montessori approach is for the child to experience the world around them in real life. For a baby, this is with their bodies, their hands, and their mouths. This experience cannot be replicated on a screen, so we do not offer screens to babies. And we can be mindful of our own use of screens and put them away as much as possible in front of the baby.

If the baby gets bored at a café, rather than using a screen, we can walk around to show them what is happening, look out the window at passing vehicles and people, and bring a small pouch with a few favorite things for them to explore. And rather than distracting a baby with a screen if they are upset, we can provide loving arms, calming words, and patience.

PART THREE

COMMON QUESTIONS

WHAT SHOULD WE DO WHEN BEHAVIORS CHANGE? (HITTING/THROWING/BITING/PUSHING)

Some babies show strong preferences from birth. Others seem to be pretty relaxed, aside from telling us when they need to eat or sleep—then, at around 9 to 12 months, we start to see them show preferences. They may hit us, throw things, bite, or even push us or another child. They may seem to become strong-willed, not changing their mind regardless of what we say or do.

With their limited communication skills, our baby is telling us something important. Instead of thinking of them as "naughty," we can ask ourselves, "Why would my baby be doing this?"

- If they hit us, are they telling us they don't like what is happening? That we took something away? How we are holding them?
- If they throw something, is the toy too hard or too easy for them? Are they experimenting with how things fall down? Learning about cause and effect? Are there ways for them to try this in a way that is not dangerous or disruptive?
- If they bite us, are they hungry? Has something upset them? Are they teething?
- If they push us or another child, can we translate for them? Can we say, "Are you trying to get past here?" or "Were you wanting to play with that toy right now?"

So we first seek to understand.

Then we translate or make a guess: "Are you telling me . . . ?"

Then we kindly and clearly let them know that we won't let them hurt us/themselves/someone else/the environment. We may be able to find another way for them to meet their need, e.g., to hit a cushion. And, if necessary, we will remove them from the room or the situation and sit with them until they are calm.

Once they are calm, we can connect with them and model how to make amends if needed, for example, apologizing to a friend, offering a tissue or wet cloth if a child is hurt, or putting back things that have been thrown. As they become toddlers, they will learn to help us to repair any hurt feelings or mistakes.

Early tantrums

If our baby is crying uncontrollably, they won't be able to hear many of our words. We can offer a cuddle and our love. And stay nearby if they don't want to be touched. We first want to help them release whatever emotions need to come out, then help them calm down.

Once they are calm, we can give a short, age-appropriate explanation and tidy up with them and model apologizing if needed.

This also lays the foundation as our baby becomes a young toddler and they begin to exert their independence.

Tantrums and having a strong will are important phases of development, and we can be a supportive guide to help them through these—first giving them space to let out the feelings, then helping them calm down, and finally, helping them make amends if needed.

Observation

If this behavior continues, we can practice objective observation to see if there are any triggers causing the behavior. We can then use this information to limit these triggers. For example, we can note if the behavior happens before meals, in particular environments, around particular children, or if the space is very stimulating (which could be a trigger for sensitive children).

When there is difficult behavior, we can observe:

- **Time.** What time does the behavior happen? Is our baby hungry or tired?
- **Changes.** Are they teething? Are there any changes at home, such as a new house?
- **Activity.** What are they doing or playing with at the time of being triggered?
- **Other children.** How many children are around? Are the children the same age, younger, or older?

- **Emotion being expressed.** Just before it happens, how do they look? Playful? Frustrated? Confused?

- **Environment.** Look at the environment where the tantrums happen. Is it busy? Is it very colorful or otherwise too stimulating? Is there a lot of clutter? Is there a lot of children's artwork around the room, which is possibly too much sensory input? Or is it peaceful and serene?

- **Adults.** How do we, as adults, respond? Do we bring additional anxiety to the situation?

Preventing the Behavior

By observing, we may see patterns to their behavior and identify ways we can support our child. Here are some examples:

- **Just before mealtime.** Give them something hard like an apple they can bite into to snack on before they get too hungry (good for relaxing their nervous system).

- **Teething.** Offer a variety of (cold) teething toys.

- **Exploration.** Allow them to explore toys with their mouth.

- **Environment.** Reduce the amount of stimulation to make the surroundings calmer.

- **Noise.** Remove the baby when we start to notice that things are becoming too loud for them.

- **Sensitive to their personal space.** Help them avoid situations where they are cornered or do not have enough personal space.

- **Playful.** Some babies may bite to be playful or show love, perhaps misunderstanding games such as blowing raspberries on their tummies. Show them other ways to be affectionate, such as cuddles or mutual rough play.

- **Learning social interactions.** If they push another child, they may be wanting to say, "Can we play?" Model words that they will learn over time.

- **Check their hearing and eyesight.** A problem with either can feel disorienting for a baby, and they may react by being aggressive.

- **Transitions.** Is the structure of the day predictable enough? Are transitions difficult for them? Allow enough time for them to finish what they are doing. Make sure they get enough free, unstructured playtime.

- **Releasing their nervous system.** Refer to page 195 for ideas on relaxing their nervous system, such as deep massage or big bear hugs.

WHAT IF THE BABY IS CLINGY AND WON'T LET US PUT THEM DOWN? WHAT IF THEY HAVE SEPARATION ANXIETY?

Some babies are more independent, and some babies will cling to us. Sometimes we play with children a lot and they start to depend on us to entertain them. So it becomes a combination of their character (that may not necessarily change over time but where we can start to give them skills) and what we do as the adult (which we do have control over).

In a Montessori approach, we see babies as capable beings, if we let them be. We try to give the baby time to see their effect on the world, from the noises they make, to the movements of their arms and legs, to reaching out to touch or strike something.

First we can see if we are an obstacle to their development. Are we interfering in their play? Are we doing a lot to get them to eat and sleep, and entertaining them during waking hours?

Instead, can we observe them to see how much help they need (if any)? This can change every week, every day, and sometimes every hour, so we need to keep observing.

If we are used to entertaining them, can we gradually shift from entertaining to being together? From being together to following their lead?

If they always want to be held, can we gradually show them they can also be on the ground playing for short periods? We can lie down next to each other. Then, over time, we might move from being right beside them to maybe 4 inches (10 cm) farther away. To popping to the kitchen to put the kettle on, letting them know where we are going, and then coming right back. To letting them discover a newfound interest without interruption. They will also be experiencing the reality of object permanence—that when we go away, we come back again.

Babies pick up our own energy. If we are starting to feel frustrated about needing to hold them all day, the baby may sense we are uncomfortable and cling even tighter. If we have any doubts about letting them be on the floor to play or letting someone else care for them for us, the baby may also pick up on this and again cling more. We need to work on ourselves to help our children so that we can confidently show them they are already so capable, and find that fine balance between attachment and separation.

From around 6 months to 16 months, babies can experience separation anxiety. They are still learning that when we go away, we will come back again—and they are beginning to feel a preference for having us nearby. It is difficult to see our baby upset, but there are some ways we can help them get through this stage:

1. We can give them a verbal cue as we are leaving: "I'm going to the kitchen;" from the kitchen we can call out to them: "I'm in the kitchen;" and when we get back we can tell them: "I'm back from the kitchen. It's so nice to see you!"

2. We can be positive in our communication when we have to leave as the baby will pick up our feelings of concern or trepidation.

3. When introducing them to a new caregiver, we can first invite the caregiver to the home while we are still there so our baby can get to know them, and so they become a new point of reference for them. We can then practice being in another room while the caregiver is with our baby, building up to leaving the house for longer periods of time.

4. We can keep other points of reference consistent—the order of the room, their daily rhythm, their food, etc.

5. If they are starting at a new day care, we can sit on the side of the room with them between our legs until they are ready to crawl or walk away from us to explore.

6. We can leave something nearby that has our familiar scent.

When our baby has a secure attachment and we choose other caregivers we trust, our baby also learns trust in others and themselves. (See page 96 about secure attachment and page 235 about saying goodbye to our baby.)

HOW CAN I STOP THEM FROM TOUCHING THINGS? WHEN WILL THEY STOP PUTTING THINGS IN THEIR MOUTH?

We can't stop babies from touching things or putting things in their mouths. Babies are born explorers—they need to move and explore the world around them, and the best way for them to do this is by touching what they see and bringing it to the most sensitive part of their bodies: their mouths.

The nerves in their mouth are one of the earliest parts of the body to be *myelinated* (where the nerves are able to allow signals to pass through more effeciently) so that they can feed effectively from birth. This makes the mouth the most sensitive and most suitable body part for exploring everything in the baby's path.

At the end of the first year to around 16 months, the hands will become more sensitive as myelination extends to the peripheral parts of the body, and the oral phase of development usually starts to come to an end. If a 14-month-old brings a coin to their mouth, we can usually show them how it goes through the slot in the coin box, and then they become more interested in completing that activity than putting the coin into their mouth.

Some babies stay longer in the oral stage of development if they like to suck, for example, babies who use a pacifier a lot or suck on a bottle. So the oral stage of development will ease once the pacifier and bottle are no longer being used.

WHAT DO WE DO WHEN WE NEED TO GET THROUGH OUR DAILY TASKS?

Montessori is a child-focused approach to raising children. We treat them with respect, we try to follow their needs as much as possible—yet we also have things we need to get done like cooking, cleaning, running errands, and other things we need to do or simply enjoy doing.

In the symbiotic period (the first 6 to 8 weeks after birth), it can be useful to have our partner (if we have one) and some extra hands (family, friends, a cleaning person if that's available to us) to manage the daily tasks of the home and give us time to form the connection with our new baby, establish feeding, and to rest. We may have some pre-prepared food in the freezer if we are super organized too.

In the symbiotic period and beyond, even with the best of help, there will be many times when we need to do things around the home, like cooking and washing, as well as looking after the baby. We can get some of that done during nap times, although it is a good idea to spend a lot of these nap times to rest ourselves, something many of us have difficulty with. Rest assured, the tasks will wait for us, and these special days will speed by.

As the baby becomes more wakeful, they will enjoy absorbing aspects of our daily lives. In Montessori we like to involve children in our daily life, and this can start from birth by keeping them close by as we do our own things. At first they will watch from our arms, or play on a blanket on the floor nearby, or be carried in a baby carrier. Then they will reach out to touch and explore, and over time they will be able to participate in the process. Some examples:

- We can talk to our babies about what we are doing, show them everything, and let them touch.

- Preparing a meal is like we are preparing a gift for our family, and our baby will absorb our intention, our language, and our connection.
- On a trip to the supermarket, if they are awake, we can look for the items together, count things as they go into the shopping basket, and sing songs.

These tasks and errands can become times of connection, not just something to be rushed through or something we have to do.

HOW CAN YOU DO MONTESSORI ON A BUDGET?

Often people think that Montessori is synonymous with expensive wooden toys. However, it's less about the Montessori materials and more about seeing our baby as capable and finding ways to treat our baby with respect, love, and gentle hands.

We can involve our baby in daily life and use what we already have—no need for new toys. They love to be alongside us and perhaps explore what's inside the kitchen cupboards while we cook. Instead of buying an expensive set of stairs for climbing, we can practice on the stairs to a front porch. Instead of buying a set of swings, we can hang an old tire from a tree.

When we are looking for some Montessori materials, we can try making them ourselves, for example, the Montessori mobiles can be made with supplies found in a local craft store, or sometimes even with things we have around the home.

We can buy secondhand. Find local thrift stores where we can get some pre-loved wooden toys, baskets, and baby-friendly furniture.

We can repurpose furniture and some materials as our child grows, for example, a low shelf can become a bench to sit on, and a low cube chair can become a stool.

We can rent toys or buy them together in a community where we share more expensive materials.

We can get out into nature. We can take our baby for a walk in a baby carrier or stroller, we can lie on a blanket together in the park or on the beach or in the woods, and we can pass time watching the tree leaves and branches moving.

As we learn more about Montessori and its true principles, it becomes clear that it doesn't have to cost a lot of money to do Montessori at home.

PART FOUR

OTHER SITUATIONS

SIBLINGS

If there are older siblings in the family, the arrival of a new baby may make them feel like they have been replaced or that they are receiving less attention or love.

Adele Faber and Elaine Mazlish write in their book *Siblings Without Rivalry* that the arrival of a newborn in the family is the same as our partner telling us that they love us so much that they are getting another partner. And that the new partner will sleep in our old bed and wear our old clothes, and we have to make them feel welcome and help to look after them. No wonder having a new baby in the home can be quite a transition for some children.

Preparing an older sibling

Books with realistic pictures about a new baby in the home are especially helpful to prepare an older sibling. We can let them talk and sing to the baby in the belly and begin to build a connection. We can let them help prepare the baby's space. And we can make a point of enjoying our last days together in our current family configuration.

One tip for siblings is to have the older sibling sing to or talk to the baby while they are still in utero. They can sing the same song every time, and the baby will recognize it from birth and will find it soothing. The topponcino is also great for allowing older siblings to cuddle the new baby.

When it's time to introduce our older child to the new baby, if they have not been present at the birth, we can put down the baby before the older child enters the room so our attention is solely on them. This can be easier than walking in to see us holding the new baby in our arms.

As much as possible, keep the early weeks at home simple, and if possible, ask other adults for extra hands to help. We can ask them to help with the newborn for some of the time, so we can have time to be alone with the older child or children. Some older siblings like to be involved in caring for the new baby—fetching a clean diaper or getting soap for the baby's bath. Some won't be interested, and that's okay too.

We can keep a basket of books and some favorite toys on hand while we feed, so that our other children can be occupied while we feed the baby.

When the older one is playing and the baby is awake, it can be fun to talk to the baby about what their older sibling is doing. The baby will benefit from our conversation, and the child will like being the topic of discussion.

We also don't have to give the older sibling the role of being the "big kid in the family." This can be a lot of responsibility for a young child or toddler. Instead, we can give all the children in the family responsibility, for example, saying to them, "Can you look after each other while I go to the bathroom?"

Junnifa introduced the idea of her children caring for each other. If the new baby was crying, she'd ask one of the other children to go and check on their brother or sister. This taught them that they all look after each other, not by age, but as part of being a family.

Note: For tips for setting up the home with more than one child, see page 66.

If the older sibling is upset

Often our response to an older sibling saying "I hate the baby" is that we say, "No you don't. We love the baby." However, in that moment, the older sibling needs to express how they are feeling.

Instead, we could guess how they might be feeling: "Right now you look pretty angry/sad/frustrated with the baby. Is that right?" We can give a listening ear or a cuddle, so they feel understood. And we would also be okay with limiting any physical attacks on the baby, like hitting or biting. **Allow all feelings, not all behavior.**

Then, at another neutral time, we can show the older sibling how to handle the baby: "We are gentle with the baby." And we can translate for the baby: "The baby is crying. I think they are saying that is too rough. Let's use our gentle hands."

Make special time with each child

It's important to schedule some time with each child when we can. If the baby is napping and the older child is awake, this is a perfect moment to connect and do something special together. On the weekend, if there is a partner or family member to help, we can plan a small outing with the older child—to go to the playground, to go to the supermarket together, or for a short walk to chat.

By filling each child's emotional bucket, we can help reduce the cries for attention at other times during the week. And when tempers flare and things don't go their way, we can write down in a notebook what they wanted to do but wasn't possible right then, to remember for our special time together later in the week.

Adjusting to a bigger family

Sometimes we are the parent who needs to prepare for the growing family. Will we love the baby as much as the older sibling? How will we manage with more people to look after? How can we get rid of the guilt we feel that we're not spending as much time with the new baby as we did when their sibling was young?

In his book *Thriving!* Michael Grose suggests that we parent siblings as if we have a large family with four or more children. Parents of large families can't solve every argument and entertain every child. We are the leaders of the family. We lay the foundations of the family's values and oversee the running of the ship.

And love will grow just as a candle can light another candle or another five candles without losing its own light. So our love can be shared with ourselves, a partner, and any number of children. The love keeps growing.

One last thing: Feel free to use the phrase "happy handfuls" when people say we must have our hands full. A friendly reply can be very helpful to staying positive when times are indeed "full."

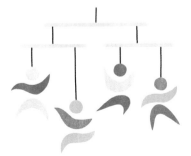

TWINS

There are very few resources about Montessori for twins. However, parents who have come to Simone's classes with twins have found that the Montessori approach is invaluable, with the biggest advantage being the children become more independent as they grow. With two of them at the same age, this is priceless.

Some suggestions for twins are:

- treating each child as unique, for example, looking at their needs individually and calling them by their names rather than "the twins"
- setting up the home so the babies can explore as independently as possible
- involving children in daily life and slowly building skills so they can manage steps for themselves
- sharing by taking turns—rather than having two of every toy in the home, the babies learn to take turns or become creative in finding a way to play together
- it's possible to breastfeed twins simultaneously, and it's okay if that is not manageable for us
- when we are busy with one twin, we can tell the other that we'll be available soon— they learn that when their turn comes, they will have their needs met
- after they can sit without support, they can enjoy sitting opposite each other while eating at a weaning table; look for chairs with arms that will keep them tucked in against the table and low seats so their feet can be flat on the floor

BOOK RECOMMENDATION

For those with twins, *Raising Your Twins: Real Life Tips on Parenting Your Children with Ease* by Stephanie Woo is written by a Montessori-trained parent of twins.

PREMATURE BABIES

We can still connect with babies who are born prematurely and need to be in an incubator in a neonatal intensive care unit.

We can pump milk to offer breast milk if possible. We can talk and sing to our baby when they are awake, and our scent will be familiar to them. We can place our hands on our baby in the incubator and, once our baby is strong enough, we can practice kangaroo care, where the baby is placed on us in an upright position, skin-to-skin. We can also learn special massage for a premature baby that is not too rough on their delicate skin. We observe to see if they are content or if it's too much for them.

And even through the sides of the incubator, we can make deep eye contact with our baby. We can let them know they are loved.

BEING AN ADOPTIVE PARENT

Adoptive parents will have a different experience. We don't have those nine months to get used to the idea of becoming a parent and being able to already connect and bond with the baby through points of reference from the womb (our voice, our heartbeat, our movements), and the baby may come into the family after a drawn-out process of adoption and at any age.

Imagine meeting a baby at, say, 6 months old. Already the baby is starting to move, wriggle, and slide. They may be interested in starting solids as well as milk feeds. And they may come to us feeling emotionally unstable from a difficult situation.

As adoptive parents, we become their rock when everything else in their world has been unstable.

We can create our own type of symbiotic period (see chapter 3), lasting for 6 to 8 weeks, when we limit our social responsibilities and focus on becoming a family. We can establish a home that feels safe, with predictable rhythms and reliable points of reference—places to sleep, feed, and play, as well as our smells, our voices, and our gentle way of handling them.

As mentioned previously in the section for feeding, supplemental nursing systems are available, which adoptive parents can use to induce lactation. If we cannot or choose not to breastfeed our baby, feeding with a bottle while holding the baby close and making eye contact is still a time to create strong bonds.

PHYSICAL DISABILITIES OR NEUROLOGICAL DIFFERENCES

People often ask if there is anything written in Montessori about children with special needs or who are differently wired. There are now Montessori training courses for children with special needs. While it's beyond the scope of this book, we have had children in our classes who have hearing difficulties or physical disabilities like cerebral palsy and children who have selective mutism, ADHD, or autism. We have family and friends whose babies have had heart surgeries, a hip brace in the first year, or needed helmets for head shaping and other reasons.

We treat every child as unique. We observe to see what they are capable of. We give them as much help as needed and allow them to challenge themselves. We look into their eyes with the same love and respect as every other child.

Their timeline may look different. But they are no less capable of being treated as the beautiful human they were put on Earth to be. Let's look at capability. Not disability.

BOOK RECOMMENDATION

For families of a baby with neurological differences, we recommend *Differently Wired* by Deborah Reber and her *TiLT Parenting* podcast.

TO PRACTICE

1. Is there a clear rhythm to our day for our baby?
2. Are we remembering to use moments of physical care as moments for connection?
3. How can we support our child's eating and sleeping? Can we let go of our anxiety in these areas? Can we help as little as possible and as much as necessary?
4. Do we want to make any changes to support our baby:
   - if they are hitting/biting/throwing/pushing?
   - when traveling in the car?
   - to limit or get rid of a pacifier?
   - when they are teething?
   - to learn early skills around sharing?
5. How can we help prepare an older sibling for the new baby?

PREPARATION
OF THE ADULT

8

OUR ROLE AS THE ADULT

One of the great things Montessori teaches parents is that we are not responsible for imparting every single piece of knowledge or idea to our child.

Children are not empty vessels needing to be filled. Dr. Montessori believed that children have the potential to learn most things if put in the right environment. This relieves parents of the responsibility of having to know everything and be everything for our children.

Children—even our tiny babies—are already capable of so much. All we do is prepare conditions that allow all that they carry to blossom. They are like seeds, and parents are like gardeners. We prepare the soil and provide nurturing, and they do the blossoming.

In many ways it is us adults who frame the way our children see and approach the world. The way we speak to them and to others, the opportunities we provide for them, and the environment we prepare for them all have a significant impact on the people they will become.

So even though we don't have to teach our babies everything, everything we do teaches them something, and this can feel like a huge responsibility. It is big work. The kind that we can be intentional about.

We start this work by first preparing ourselves.

> "Every generation of children is destined to change humanity—their mission is to transform humanity to ever greater levels of awareness and sensitivity of what is good for everyone. That is why all cultures see in their children the 'hope for tomorrow,' the expectation being that they will be able to make all things better—especially in how we treat each other. But that can never come about if children incorporate our hates, our prejudice, and our petty pride. We must help them adapt to the inherent goodness of humanity and not to the present evils of society."
>
> —Eduardo J. Cuevas G., 2007, "The Spiritual Preparation of the Adult,"
> Montessori Conference China

PREPARING OURSELVES

We talked about preparing the environment in chapter 4—our homes and our baby's space. But there is another very significant part of the environment that we also need to prepare: ourselves!

We need to prepare ourselves physically, intellectually, emotionally, and spiritually for this work of guiding our children. The airplane warning to put on your own oxygen mask first before helping others is such an apt analogy for parenting.

We have to care for ourselves in order to care for another human. Eating, resting, filling our emotional and spiritual tanks—this is what helps us to stay regulated and objective in dealing with our baby. Parenting, especially in the early days, can be very taxing and draining. Our babies are relying on us for so much, and if we do not make conscious efforts to meet our own needs, we might find ourselves so depleted that we go into survival mode. In this mode, we will be less able to respond positively to our babies. In this mode, our baby's cry, which once was just a cue, might become a frustration.

We want our baby to have a fulfilled parent, rather than a resentful parent (putting everyone else's needs first) or a selfish parent (ignoring the needs of others). We need to look after ourselves as well as our baby.

Intellectual preparation

We need to be knowledgable about our child's development, their needs, and how to support them.

This book is a start. We can continue to build on the knowledge by being open to new research and continuing education (such as podcasts, seminars, and workshops) related to parenting, positive discipline, and other related tools that improve our knowledge of the child and equip us with tools for parenting.

Observations are also a good way to increase our knowledge of our child.

With this comes a caveat though: There are so many options now and it can become overwhelming, so we can **be selective and limit our exposure to a few options that resonate with us.**

We can also be open to learning opportunities outside of parenting or Montessori. For example, learning to play an instrument, trying a new sport, or reading something that has nothing to do with parenting but fills our soul. Anything we learn and open our heart to is something that we can model for, or share with, our child.

Physical preparation

Caring for a baby involves a lot of energy, both physical and mental. We need to be in good physical condition to be able to optimally care for our babies.

Good nutrition is so important. Every day we can hydrate often and nourish our body with healthy meals, fruits, and vegetables. As we make this conscious effort for our children, but we need to do the same for ourselves. We can set reminders on our phone to make sure we don't miss a meal. Or we can prepare meals in advance or make sure to have simple ingredients on hand that we can easily throw together.

Exercise. It can be as simple as taking walks with our baby or setting aside time to stretch or work out. This can make all the difference for our well-being and mental health.

Rest. Get as much rest as we can. Lack of sleep can affect our immune systems and also our brains. We don't need to feel bad about asking for help or getting a nanny or babysitter to give ourselves a break.

If we are the child's primary caregiver, we may feel that we have to do everything ourselves or always be there. In the very beginning, it helps to be there as much as possible and form that strong attachment with our baby, but it is okay to take breaks and ask for help as needed. Once the child has formed that strong attachment and has begun trusting the environment, thanks to consistency of care and routines, breaks can be positive for both adult and baby.

Physical care of oneself is so important because it addresses our basic needs. When we are dehydrated, hungry, tired, or sick, it is almost impossible do our best as a parent. Most of the time our brain is in a survival state, so most of our reactions will be freeze, fight, or flee responses. We can monitor ourselves for the following kinds of reactions: feeling overwhelmed, wanting to abandon ship and run away, or anger toward the baby or to the whole situation. If we feel these things, we probably need some time to nurture ourselves physically.

The other advantage to caring for ourselves physically is that we are modeling it for our baby—remember, they absorb everything they see us do.

How do you relax? Find moments to enjoy. (See our list of suggestions on page 220.)

Emotional and spiritual preparation

A support system is so important when parenting. This journey is so much nicer when it is done while walking alongside another person, whether in the form of a partner or co-parent, grandparents, caregivers, or friends.

An extra set of hands is so helpful in the first few months—someone to help make meals, take care of other children, hold the baby, or give the parents a break. (See page 224 for more ways this person can support new parents.) This can be a family member or a friend or, if within our means, a postpartum doula or mother's helper who brings with them some experience of the needs of mother and new baby and understands how to support the family physically and emotionally. Dr. Montessori and Adelle Costa Gnocchi saw a need for this person and envisioned the Assistant to Infancy—a trained Montessori guide—as one who can serve in this role. (Professional help may not be attainable for all families, though in some countries the government will send a mother's helper to assist a new parent in the early weeks.)

Other parents with babies around the age of ours or a little older can also help. Talking to friends can remind us that we are not alone and that whatever we might be experiencing is normal or is a phase that will soon pass. Many parenting struggles are transitory, and we need someone who has gone through that stage to remind us of this.

We can take time to appreciate ourselves, count our blessings, and consciously acknowledge and document the things that are going well. One of the things that can lead to an emotional breakdown is not feeling appreciated for our efforts or not feeling loved. Babies are not using words, so after a day of poopy diapers, little sleep, and lots of crying, we can feel emotionally drained and unappreciated. We can be our own cheerleader and take time to pat ourselves on the back for every day. We can get a pedicure, go out with our friends, or find a simple way to take care of ourselves. It is hard work to be responsible for another human. We want that acknowledgment from others, but we can give ourselves the gift of acknowledging it first.

Taking pictures and documenting the stages is helpful. Review some of the pictures at the end of the day, and often; even seemingly insignificant moments can trigger a memory or a smile. Do remember to enjoy the moments though—we don't need to catch every single one on camera. Also remember to be in some of the pictures, not always behind the camera. Right now we might not feel like being in a photo, but we will look back and cherish these moments.

For those who may be struggling to find the joy in the baby days, there is help available. Postpartum depression is a dark place to be and is experienced by around one in seven mothers (sometimes only after a second or third child). Seek support from a doctor or a health professional we trust.

Self-trust and forgiveness

When we have a baby, there are so many voices telling us what to do and what not to do. Many times they can be conflicting. We believe that parents are gifted with an instinct that they can trust and follow.

We can forgive ourselves when we come up short and know that every one of us has these moments. We learn and grow from our mistakes. And there will be many mistakes—that's okay.

PREPARATION OF THE ADULT

OUR INTELLECTUAL PREPARATION helps us cultivate trust in our babies: We can trust that they know what they are doing and that they have all that they need. And that they will follow their unique paths and timelines given the best conditions, which we do our best to provide.

OUR PHYSICAL AND EMOTIONAL PREPARATION allows us to come to the child with a loving attitude. We can accept our baby unconditionally and love them in spite of any flaws, ours or theirs. Love is void of anger, pride, and ego.

OUR SPIRITUAL PREPARATION allows us to adopt a posture of humility. It is this humility that allows us to constantly work on preparing and improving ourselves for the baby. It allows us to see the baby's potential, to not see them as empty vessels or even as reflections of us or any ideas or aspirations we have for them, but instead as the unique, special beings that they are.

Our own childhood and the way we were parented can affect our parenting. For some of us, we may idolize the way we were raised and often feel like we don't measure up; for others, we may not like the way we were parented and want to do things differently, but we still often find ourselves repeating the patterns; or for some, the balance is just right. In preparing ourselves to be Montessori parents, it helps to take time to revisit what we liked or did not like about our own childhood. To make peace with it and let go as much as we can, knowing that we are starting our own journey.

Instead of feeling like we are falling short, we can acknowledge our efforts and commit to doing the best we can and let that be enough.

We have talked about observing our babies and the environment, but part of preparing ourselves is observing ourselves. Observing our needs, our feelings, our reactions or responses. Often this happens as reflection. Sitting back at the end of the day and thinking about our needs.

TO OBSERVE

Here are some questions we can use to observe and reflect on ourselves. Remember that this should be a growth tool and not a judgment of self.

Did I drink enough water?

Did I eat?

Did I take a break when I needed it?

How did I react to different events during the day?

How might I have reacted differently?

What drove or triggered my reaction?

Are my tanks full?

What did I do well?

What am I thankful for?

49 IDEAS FOR STAYING CALM

How we prepare ourselves physically, emotionally, and spiritually is a personal thing. Yet so many people ask how we can stay so calm in the classroom and at home.

So here are forty-nine ideas to inspire you. These are the things that have helped us show up as the best parents and teachers we can be, and we hope that they help you too.

1. Have a morning ritual for ourselves. Get up before our baby to have some "me" time.

2. Have an evening ritual for ourselves. Enjoy the quiet.

3. Exercise. Yoga. Running.

4. Meditation.

5. Nature. Head outside.

6. Dance.

7. Enjoy our cup of coffee/tea.

8. Meet up with friends with kids.

9. Meet up with friends without kids. Perhaps drink wine.

10. Practice presence.

11. Practice gratitude.

12. Journal.

13. Write down one thing today that would make us happy.

14. Write down one thing today we'd like to remember.

15. Cook (preferably alone while someone is looking after the baby).

16. Video-chat with a friend.

17. Invite friends for a meal.

18. Bake something.

19. Arrange a night out (by ourselves, with our partner, or with friends).

20. Do a babysitting swap with friends.

21. Travel. A weekend away. An overseas adventure.

22. Say "no" to things that don't light us up, or suggest something that you'd enjoy more.

23. Use observation as a tool for being objective about a situation.

24. Be our baby's guide. We are there to support, but cannot make them happy all the time. We can offer a hug though.

25. Set up our home in a way that helps relieve some of the work. A place for everything and everything in its place.

26. Have someone to care for us. An osteopath. Chiropractor. Doctor. Psychologist. Friend.

27. Sleep.

28. Own our choices. Change what we can (be creative), and accept what we can't.

29. See things from our baby's perspective. "Are you having a hard time?" "You're one year old, and you're probably hungry/tired/had a busy day."

30. Go to bed early. Take a nap.

31. Read a good book.

32. Be aware of our thoughts and feelings without judgment.

33. Laugh.

34. Eat cake.

35. Listen to music. 432hz or 528hz frequency music can be particularly healing.

36. Take the dog for a walk.

37. Schedule some alone time.

38. Count down in our head to create a pause and respond rather than immediately react.

39. Have a bath. Every night.

40. Listen to or play music.

41. Nourish ourselves. Notice when we are sluggish, scattered, or pushing ourselves too hard. Make adjustments to balance ourselves.

42. Slow down. Allow enough time. Stop overscheduling.

43. Forgive ourselves when we make mistakes. Model making amends.

44. Celebrate where we are. We are doing our best.

45. Be self-aware and notice when we are being triggered. Make a note to meditate on why. Work on healing.

46. If we feel depressed or burned out, see a doctor or talk to a friend.

47. Practice compassion for ourselves, others, our baby.

48. Stop taking ourselves so seriously.

49. Keep practicing.

DOING OUR BEST

The wisdom from the book *The Four Agreements* by don Miguel Ruiz sums it up so well:

1. **Be impeccable with our word.** Our baby is watching us. Let them see us speaking the truth. In a sensitive way.

2. **Don't take things personally.** Our baby will cry. They are telling us something. We are there to listen. But we don't need to blame ourselves.

3. **Don't make assumptions.** If we are not sure, check. It's amazing how many times we make assumptions about something someone said that was not their intention.

4. **Always do our best.** Even when we have had very little sleep, what is the best we can do today? Perhaps today we will parent from bed, put on some music, postpone some appointments, lie down next to our baby, and let go of everything else.

In the end it is not about perfection. It's about presence. So let's aim for connection over perfection.

TO PRACTICE

- Can we build time for a self-care activity into our daily routine?
- Can we start a daily gratitude routine where we celebrate one thing that we did?
- Can we do something that is just for ourselves at least once a week?
- Can we forgive ourselves for the moments that don't go well and embrace our efforts more than perfection?

"The baby's fundamental need—precisely because he is a human being—is to be loved. But it takes a mature person to love a baby, because love takes time, love takes patience, love takes fortitude, love even requires a certain kind of humility: to love another better than one's self. The baby needs time to be understood: he needs time in everything he does."

—Taken from a speech given by Dr. Herbert Ratner, editor of *Child and Family*, to the American Montessori Society in 1963

WORKING
TOGETHER

9

WE DON'T WALK ALONE

Parenting can be filled with connection. And at times it can be filled with enormous isolation. We might realize that old friends have different priorities and perspectives, that our family helps too much or too little, or we feel the loss of special family members who will never get to know our baby. Also, the wonders of the internet can make us feel guilty that our lives aren't picture-perfect, like everyone else's seem to be. (You know, having casual picnics on the beach with a large group of easy-going friends with babies in arms, children running wild and free as the sun sets.)

It's time for us to build a village for our families. Because our children can learn so much from the vast array of people who make up the fabric of the world. And they will learn to trust the caregivers we choose for them.

Here are some people that can be part of our village:
- Our partner (if we have one)—we can work toward maintaining the connection, we can spend time together one-on-one, we can spend time together as a family, and we can allow each other alone time while the other bonds with the baby.
- Family (nearby)—they can have a special time in the week to come and be with the baby while we take time to be a version of ourselves before "mother" or "father" took over.
- Family (far away)—we can regularly connect over a video chat, read books together despite the miles apart, and sing sweet songs or play music; maybe they can visit us from time to time to help ground the online connection with real-life connection.
- Friends who parent in the same way—it's never been easier to find like-minded families either online and, even better, in person. These can be some of the fastest connections. Parents who meet at Simone's Montessori playgroup often have long-lasting friendships.
- Friends with whom we don't have to talk about parenting—conversation and connection with these friends can feed our soul and give us new inspiration, helping us be a better parent.
- A well-selected babysitter, nanny, au pair, or a day care—to give us some extra hands (or we can arrange a babysitting swap with another family).
- A cleaning person—if funds allow for a once-a-month deep clean to really scrub those places we don't always have time for.

- A professional caregiver—an osteopath, doctor, psychologist, chiropractor, massage therapist, or the like; to help care for us when we are caring for everyone else (again, if resources allow.
- People who live on our street or people working in our local stores—these people play a small part in our daily lives but become part of our extended family as the years pass.

It's okay to ask for help

We might ask for help with the baby. We can also ask for help with other things so that we can spend time bonding and building a connection with the baby.

Sometimes we are so tired, even with people offering to help, that we don't know what needs to be done or how to ask for help. Here's one idea: We can hang a list on the fridge of things that need to be done around the home or for the baby. Then anyone visiting can choose one of these things and help with it. How helpful would that be?

Working with our partner

In some families, there will be a primary caretaker and secondary caretaker. In other families, parents may take on a shared role. Whatever the balance, we can work to stay connected with our partner even once the focus shifts to be "all about the baby."

In families where one person's focus is largely on the baby in the early weeks, our partner can find their own unique ways of bonding with the baby. During pregnancy, they can talk, sing, and play music to the baby, rub our belly, form a deep connection, and lay a foundation for the coming months. Once the baby is born, they can hold and talk to them, their voice being a strong point of reference from being heard in the womb. They can bathe the baby, sing to the baby, change diapers, play music for the baby, have moments of silence together, and spend time gazing lovingly into the baby's eyes. They can also feed the baby from a bottle (with expressed milk or formula).

The partner can work on providing protection and support for the family unit during this symbiotic period—taking phone calls, managing family and friends who want to visit, preparing meals, and picking up supplies at the store. If there are other children, the partner can be the one who helps and supports them—taking them to the park or listening if they are having a hard time with the transition to being an older sibling.

The partner can provide emotional support. Mood-altering hormones rage and recede during pregnancy and the months after birth (pretty much a year after birth, to be honest), such that it can be helpful for the partner to check in daily: "How are you today? Can I get you anything?" It may be some time before the mother has the space in her head to be able to return this support as she adjusts to her new role—physically, emotionally, and spiritually.

This kind of daily check-in during pregnancy can continue once the baby is born. How can we stand together? How can we keep the partnership strong—the thing that created this special human in the first place? And how can we keep this partnership going long after birth, childhood, adolescence, and when they leave the nest?

Working with grandparents and other caregivers

Grandparents and others can help in many ways too.

They can help by giving us a break. They can offer to cook a meal or three. They can share their stories with the baby. They can enrich our family with their music, craft, history, and culture. They can run errands for the family. They can pass on news to friends to give us space. They can do some washing, fold some clothes, wipe down some surfaces, sweep a floor.

They can love us. And we can be grateful and receive at this time.

It can take some time to get on the same page as the grandparents and other caregivers. Raising children in a Montessori way can be quite different from the way they may have raised their own children and what worked for them. So grandparents may feel criticized if we reject the way that they parented us (or our partner). For some creative ideas on educating people about Montessori principles and getting them on the same page, see page 228.

Recognizing that grandparents and caregivers are not setting out to upset us will get us a long way. There are so many ways to raise children, and they are offering their best with their experience and knowledge.

That is the blessing of living in the world with other humans. Understanding that we are all trying to do our best. And how we might all be acknowledged, seen, and have our needs met.

BEING A SINGLE PARENT
OR CO-PARENT

There are so many different family constellations. We may not have a partner, or we might be a co-parent. Every type of family constellation is perfect for our child.

We may worry that our baby is growing up without two parents in the home. That they will be missing out. If we are a single parent, we can find other role models that we want our baby to grow up around. If we have a co-parent, then the baby does have two parents; they live in separate homes and the baby gets to have two houses to grow up in.

When we own our situation, we find that people accept it and don't judge us for our choices. Accept what we can't change, and change what we can. It is far healthier for people to be happy than to stay living together in an unhappy (or potentially dangerous) situation. And sometimes we didn't choose to be a single parent, but we will own it and be the best parent we can be to our baby. That is what we do have control over.

As a co-parent, we aim to be kind about the other parent when in front of our baby and as they grow. If we are having a hard time with the co-parent, find a safe place to discuss this (with a friend or therapist or the co-parent) when the baby is not around. We may not still be together with our partner, but with a baby we will always be family. As much as possible, it's important for the baby to spend time with both parents (unless the baby's safety is at stake). There is good research to support these points, and, in some ways, we need to get along even better when separated to make arrangements to care for the baby in a loving way.

GETTING ON THE SAME PAGE

Sometimes when we feel strongly about the ways in which we want to raise our baby, it can be frustrating when people in our life and our family aren't on the same page. Imagine the following scenarios (probably common for many of us):

- People in our life have a lot of wisdom and want to share it with us, where we may want to discover these things for ourselves.
- People might show love by bringing us gifts, where we prefer less in the way of material offerings.
- Family and friends we were hoping would support us may not have time to come to see us, call us, or offer to help with the baby.
- Our partner or our family may not support our decision, say, to try a floor bed.

Educate by dripping information

We may be lucky enough to have others in our lives who will sit down and read this book with us.

For most of us, we can operate more stealthily—not in a manipulative way, but slowly over time, sharing different information, in different formats, depending on how others take in information. In this way we aim to educate others about the Montessori approach, and while their views may not shift immediately, they will merge with ours over time.

Look for ways that they like to receive information—a video, a blog post, a newsletter, an article, a research paper, a podcast episode. Share stories of what has worked for other people applying the Montessori method. Talk to them about what we are trying and how things are going.

There are now so many different ways of sharing information, so find one in a format that might resonate for them.

Choose our battles

We may not get agreement on all sides about all matters. So we can decide what is the most important to us and make that the priority, the one thing that we will be firm on.

We can be kind and clear, not aggressive. We could say, for example, to our partner, "I love you. I want to show you something that is important to me. I know you don't care about this stuff, but you care about me, so will you work on this with me/listen to me/hear about it? I will lead the way, but I would love your support. Could we make a time to look at it together? When would work for you?"

We love the phrase "It's important to me." Use it in moderation. But use it. It's a way of expressing something without blaming another and requires us to be enormously vulnerable, sharing something we might otherwise choose to avoid discussing.

Communicate in a way that we will (more likely) be heard

When someone feels judged, there is little connection. We close the door to conversation and possibility.

When we correct someone, they can get defensive. They cannot hear what is important to us, and they get lost in justifying themselves.

When we think there is only one way, they might feel like they have no choice. We can look for ways to make requests rather than demands.

What should we to do instead then?

Everyone has thoughts, feelings, and needs, and we need to be creative to find ways that everyone can have their needs met. No one is right. No one is wrong. We find ways to make it work.

The following incorporates some ideas from *Nonviolent Communication* by Marshall Rosenberg for communicating in a way that will make it more likely that we will be heard by the other person. And it opens up a conversation for creativity rather than conflict.

How does it work?

When we have judgment or a thought, we must first look at our feelings. For example, say we are watching a grandparent hover nervously over our baby. We may think, for example, "Why are they always so overprotective of the baby? Why don't they let them explore?" This might make us feel frustrated, maybe even angry, as this is something we've already discussed with the grandparent.

Before we jump in to critcize, first we must ask ourselves why we are feeling this way.

What need of ours might not be being met? It might be that freedom is important to us (leaving the baby to explore freely). It might be respect, that we want others to accept the way we are choosing to raise our baby.

Only when we have explored this for ourselves and are no longer raging can we let the other person know we'd like to talk about it.

How do we communicate our feelings?

- Agree upon a good time for a conversation (not a lecture). Touch on what it might be about and that we are wanting to come up with an acceptable solution for everyone.
- Meet at the agreed-upon time.
- Make an objective statement and use neutral words: "When the baby was playing with the ball near the small step, they were trying hard to make it move and you picked them up saying 'Be careful.'"
- State how that makes us feel and express our need: "I feel upset when I see that. It's important to me that they learn to move freely and learn the limits of their body."
- Seek to understand their perspective: "Is it that you were worried about them being safe?"
- Make a request, not a demand: "Is there a way that we can let the baby explore and you won't need to worry about them being safe?"
- Look for possibilities together. Be open to creativity. It's not always a compromise— many times there is an even better outcome than we could have imagined. "Maybe you could choose to sit between the baby and the step if you are worried?" Or they might offer, "Would it be okay if I took them outside to the park instead?"

An area of conflict can end up leading to connection with people important to us despite our differences. It sounds formulaic at first, but with practice it will become more natural, we will find our own words to express ourselves, and our intentions behind the conversation will be clear—we really want to find a way to have everyone's needs met.

Tip: If someone asks us to talk about something and we are not ready to talk about it (like feeling triggered, tired, emotional, or distracted), we can say, "I'd really like to explore that with you. I'm noticing that I'm not feeling up to it right now. Could we come back to it at eight o'clock, once I've had time to process my feelings and thoughts a little more?" Make it a specific time. And stick to it.

Come from a place of shared values

If we are able to have a conversation, we can find that we have some common values, for example, that we all want the baby to grow up to feel secure, confident, and loved. Coming from this place, we can come up with creative ways to work with each other instead of resenting each other.

The objective is to share our vision and parenting ideas, or at least to find a middle ground.

We can stay calm without getting upset. We can remember not to take it personally.

The important thing is to maintain our relationships. And see that others are coming from their own experience.

What is beautiful is that often we find ways that grandparents and other caregivers can incorporate Montessori with our baby, for example, by sharing their gifts with them, like their love of gardening, hiking, crafting, or baking.

Schedule a regular parenting chat—with partner or caregivers

It can be super tiring to have parenting conversations all week long. Or there can never be a good time to talk about these things. The best partnerships we know have one time in the week (say, a Wednesday evening) where they can really listen to each other, touch base, check in with how they are both doing, and come up with a plan for the week ahead.

We can keep a list on the fridge where we can write down things that come up during the week. We can look at the calendars to see what is coming up and who will cook, pick up groceries, care for the baby, etc. We can discuss things that are coming up for us and find some creative solutions.

And the following week we can check in about how it went, what went right, and what we might need to tweak in the following week.

Make it fun—add some wine, or tea, or candles, or music. Make a plate of snacks to enjoy. And follow up with watching a movie on the couch, playing a board game, or singing along to the guitar. People on Instagram seem to do that, so it must be a thing.

If we have a grandparent or other regular caregiver, we can also schedule a regular chat at least once a month to see if we are on the same page for the care we offer the baby. Or at least on the most important things.

Seek to understand others

Be curious and understanding about the other adults too, just as we are with our children, rather than correcting them. Sometimes we criticize another parent or grandparent or teacher or carer and speak to them in a way that we would not speak to our children.

Our children pick up how we treat others, so we can keep modeling this respectful approach with everyone in our lives.

"When you shouted at them earlier about _____ , it sounded like it was important to you. Can you tell me more about it?"

Express appreciation and have fun

We can remember not to take things too seriously. At its best, raising a child can be full of joy. So let's laugh. We know they will grow out of their tricky phase (and into a new one). And we are all doing our best.

So let's give appreciation to those working with us to look after our baby. It may not be in the exact way that we would do it, but we can find something to appreciate.
The way they left us some extra food, folded the baby's clothes, danced with the baby, kept them company.

Say thank you and mean it. And we know who will be watching: our baby.

Our baby will learn that we are all different

We are not always going to get everyone to agree with the way we would like to raise our baby. We all come with our own history, and what we learned was right and wrong, and we know how hard it is to change years of ingrained behavior. And who says we are right in any case? Everyone sees the world from their own perspective.

Aim as much as possible to agree on the big picture. And then accept that our baby will learn that different caregivers will respond in different ways—one may be more organized, another more playful. And, as they grow, they will also learn who to go to in order to have their needs met.

WHAT TO LOOK FOR IN A DAY CARE OR CAREGIVER

When parents need or want to return to work, we want to find someone who is able to care for our baby in the same caring way we are choosing to raise our child.

It can be ideal to find someone who can look after our baby one-on-one: a grandparent, nanny, au pair, or similar person. Then our baby will have a rich language environment, one point of connection, and sick days will be less of a problem.

However, we recognize this is not always available to everyone.

A Montessori program for babies up to around 16 months is called a *nido* (Italian for "nest"). Then the child moves into an infant community around 16 months until 3 years.

The *nido* is beautifully prepared following the Montessori principles: well-selected materials arranged for the babies to explore, laid out to be calm and attractive.

In a *nido*, the importance of the staff/caregivers is fundamental. Each one is a unique and special person who:

- is loving, but does not need to be loved by the baby
- has a lot of patience
- can use slow movements
- offers rich language to the baby
- does not get upset when the baby is crying but is able to respond to, and prioritize, crying babies
- understands parents and supports, listens, and provides advice when needed

Ideally the baby has a few dedicated caregivers—their points of reference—who feed them, change them, and with whom they can establish a secure attachment. Research shows that what is important is that the caregivers show sensitivity to the child, understand the child's signals, and that there is consistency (little turnover). So it's also ideal if the child has the same caregivers for the first 3 years (with 8–24 months being a particularly sensitive period for this consistency).

While it would be lovely to have every child in a Montessori *nido*, with a loving carer, a *nido* may not be located near where we live or fall within our budget. So here are some things we can look for when looking for a day care or caregiver:

- The caregiver holds the baby and make eye contact during feeding (as opposed to propping the baby with a bottle or being on their phone).
- The environment is relaxing and attractive for the baby.
- There are age-appropriate materials for the baby to explore—made from natural materials if possible.
- The sleeping area has floor mattresses for the baby to be able to get up from when they wake up.
- Once the baby is eating solid foods, they have access to nutritious food. The baby can feed themselves and sit at a low table or chair to eat (rather than a high chair).
- The caregiver understands the importance of making time for conversation, using gentle hands when handling them, and asking their permission before handling.
- They have an established ratio of one adult to three babies. Babies do not need large social groups. They are still bonding with just a few people as their primary caregivers.
- Absence of televisions

Even these things may be hard to find in a day care or caregiver. Then we do our best to find a cozy place—a place our baby will feel secure, where there is loving staff to care for them.

What if the day care has different values than at home?

This is one of the most difficult questions we get asked. We recognize that we do not live in a utopia and we are asking a lot from these caregivers.

The most important thing is to select a nursery where we feel comfortable leaving our baby. If nothing changes, will we be okay with how it is right now? Sometimes we think that they'll come around to our way of thinking. Many day cares have been around for many years, and these things take time to change, if they ever do.

Look at what they do offer. An outside space, other babies, warm meals, or someone who enjoys laughing and being with babies.

Some caregivers will be stricter than others. Even the Montessori principles can be applied in different ways. Again, it comes back to whether we feel that all the other things outweigh this, for example, beautiful activities to absorb and a cozy space—or if we would rather be in a non-Montessori nursery where the care is warmer.

Once we have a warm relationship with the day care, they may be open to reading some articles on the Montessori approach or pages from this book, or arranging a positive-discipline workshop for the caregivers and/or parents. See the tips for getting on the same page earlier in this chapter.

And if we still don't feel comfortable, then it may be best to take them out of the day care and look for another one that fits our family better. Or come up with a creative solution like changing our working hours, looking after another family's baby one day while they look after ours another, or finding a small group of likeminded families who could share a caregiver.

SAYING GOODBYE TO OUR BABY

When we have someone else to help care for our baby, we will need to practice being confident in saying goodbye. Because remember that they are sensitive too, and pick up how to feel from us.

The first step to saying goodbye to our baby is to make sure we are happy with the care we have chosen. We need to be able to give our baby the message that this is a safe person whom we trust with their care.

Also, babies like predictability, so we can say goodbye in the same way every day. Trina from DIY Corporate Mom told us that she would always tell her baby that she would be home by the time the sun went down. Then she would read a book about goldfish. She would say goodbye. And the caregiver and baby would go to feed the fish. Finding such a connecting activity can be a great idea.

We can also practice hugging for as long as our baby needs to when we say goodbye. We can hug our baby until we feel them release their hold. Trusting this will happen is harder. And so is allowing enough time for it. Some days we may need to tell our baby that we understand they might be feeling sad and we need to leave. And we pass them carefully to their grandparent or caregiver. But most days, if we can allow the time, it will get easier. Maybe even record how many minutes they are upset each time we say goodbye so we can see how they are progressing.

(continued on page 238)

NOTES FOR OUR VISITORS FROM OUR BABY

Dear grandparents, friends, caregivers:

Thank you for visiting me. You are special to me.

Please handle me gently. Ask me if I'm ready before you pick me up, and wait until I respond. Check with me if I'd like a hug or a kiss. And you can tell that I need a little more time if I arch my back, turn away, or cry. Don't take it personally. Sometimes I need more time to warm up.

When changing my diaper, feeding me, or bathing me, talk to me and tell me what you are doing. Touch my body as if it was the first time you had been touched. This is still very new for me. And there is no rush. I love these moments for connection.

Talk to me—if I make a sound, you can copy me. Tell me about all the things around me—the names of those trees, flowers, and vegetables. I want to know everything. I like a bit of a sing-song voice, but it doesn't have to be over-exaggerated and you don't have to use nonsense words like "goo, ga, ga, ga"—copy my sounds, but otherwise talk to me as if I understand everything. Because I am taking it all in.

I know I said talk to me, but I also like quiet when I'm concentrating on something. Let me finish exploring my hands or toes, that leaf, that rattle, that mobile, that ball. My concentration is just as important as yours when you are focused on your favorite thing, so please don't interrupt.

If I fall down and cry, wait a moment before rushing to pick me up. Let me feel it. I am discovering how things work. Sometimes I'll be okay and get back up as if nothing happened. If I do need some comfort, you can check if I'd like a hug. Don't tell me not to worry or not to cry or try to distract me. I want people to allow me to process these feelings. Maybe just ask me if it was a shock.

When I am crying, I am trying to communicate something. Please don't ignore me. I don't just cry because I am hungry. I cry when I am having trouble falling asleep (a comforting hand is sometimes enough). I cry when I'm overstimulated from our day (soothing me and removing stimulation helps). I cry when I want to try something new (perhaps we could try a different space or a different activity). I cry when my stomach hurts (I'm pulling up my legs; please check the section on reflux and colic on page 196 to make some notes). I cry when I have wet or soiled my diaper (it feels so strange against my body). I cry when I'm wearing some clothing that is scratching me (please use soft clothing with few seams or tags that can irritate me), or when there is a crease in the blanket I am lying on (I know it seems small, but it feels like I'm lying on a scratchy log right now). I cry when there is a lot of movement in the house (I love my siblings but can we find a quiet place right now?). I cry when there is little movement in the house (I'd love to lie under the trees and watch the leaves move). I cry when I have drunk too much milk (and my stomach needs time to digest that last feed). And some days I just feel cranky for no apparent reason and I'd like you to love me anyway.

Help me as little as possible and as much as necessary—if you help me too much, I'll never be able to make these wonderful discoveries for myself; but if you don't help me at all, I may give up on the world around me. I know you'll find the right balance.

Let me be close to you.

And let me down on the ground to explore.

Or take me outside. Nature is the best present.

Please share your personal gifts and talents with me. Sing to me, play an instrument, take me out in the garden as you plant the bulbs, show me how you knit or carve wood, teach me your favorite sport or card game, tell me about the old days.

I don't need a lot of physical gifts. I prefer simple toys that don't flash or sing noisy songs. I like ones where I need to think and interact with them. There are lots of ideas in chapter 6 of this book. And they are often not what you find in toy and baby stores. I don't like those screens—the light makes it hard for me to sleep. And I'd rather be able to touch real objects and put them in my mouth.

And speaking of my mouth, that is how I observe the world right now. So let me put things in my mouth, and remove things that won't be safe for me.

Smile at me, laugh with me, look deep into my eyes.

Love me. I love you right back.

So, as hard as it is, this means not sneaking out so that they don't notice us leaving. We are building trust—the baby should know what is happening, where we are going, and when we'll be back. And we do our best to be back at the time we tell them.

We may also need to discuss with the caregiver how to deal with the crying after we leave. It is a lot to take if a baby cries uncontrollably when the parent leaves. We can try to help the caregiver find ways to stay calm when the baby's crying gets too much for them.

Studies show that babies take their emotional cues from the people around them. So if they see we like and trust a caregiver, they will too. It can be ideal for a caregiver to come and spend time looking after the baby in the house when the parent is also there. When our baby sees the caregiver in their home, they will learn that this is someone our family trusts. Similarly, if we are settling them into a day care, we may be able to sit off to the side and allow them to watch us for as long as it takes for them to lose interest and crawl away.

TO PRACTICE

- Can we be creative in finding ways to build our (small) village? There is a lot our baby can learn from others.
- Can we find ways to work with our partner or others so we can all have our needs met?
- Can we practice communication, which fosters connection rather than conflict?
- Can we communicate what is important to us in a way that will (more likely) be heard?

WHAT'S NEXT?

10

THE TODDLER YEARS

As we will quickly notice, just as we are starting to get used to one stage, the baby changes again and we are left catching up. So as our baby approaches the toddler years (from 1 to 3 years), here are a few things to know about toddlers to make this transition a little easier.

Toddlers develop a strong sense of order. Toddlers start to get quite particular about the way things happen. They like things to be done in the same way every day with the same rhythm. The same order getting dressed; the same routine at bedtime. Perhaps even the same spoon every time they eat. They are not trying to make our life difficult. This is important to them. They like to know where things belong and thrive on having a place for everything and everything in its place. Once we know this, instead of battling them, we can work to give them a sense of order and consistency. Research shows that children who grow up in homes with rituals and routines will be the most adaptable in the long run (that goes against the idea some hold that variety will make them more adaptable).

Toddlers do not share easily. Toddlers are busy with mastery. While babies share things easily, most toddlers are so focused on the task at hand that they don't like to give anything up until they are finished with it. Knowing this, we can help them by showing them how to take turns. If they are having a hard time waiting for their turn, we can tell them, "It will be available soon." And, when it is their turn, once they have repeated and repeated until they are finished, another child can have a turn.

Toddlers say "no." As a young toddler, our once easy and accommodating baby will start to show strong preferences. This is an important stage of their development. As they practice being physically independent from us—maybe they start to say a few words or begin to walk or feed themselves—they are asserting themselves as their own person and beginning to use the word "I." Once we know this, we will understand why they are saying "no" and not take it personally. And we will try to find ways to work with them to cultivate cooperation together in a respectful way.

Toddlers need freedom. Toddlers need limits. If there are too many rules, a toddler will fight us at every step. And without any rules, they feel lost; they need some boundaries for security, to feel that someone loves them and will keep them safe. Knowing this, we can decide what limits are important to us and set them with kindness and clarity, maintaining connection with our toddler. Instead of using time-outs or bribes, we will be clear with our expectations: "I won't let you keep hitting me. I'm going over here to calm down, and I'll be right back when I'm ready to talk."

Toddlers can master more steps in a sequence and need increasing challenges. If we don't challenge them, they will challenge us. So we can continue to observe our toddler to see what they are working to master and offer more challenging activities. As they gain mastery, we can also add more steps to add more difficulty, for example, getting an apron first before washing an apple or finding more vases so they can keep arranging flowers.

Toddlers need our help to process a lot of emotions (and yes, they need tantrums too). Toddlers don't hold in their feelings. They need to get them out, otherwise we'll find them bubbling up again and again during the day. Our first response is not, "Don't be silly," but instead, "Oh. Tell me about it," or "Really? Come show me how angry you feel on this pillow," or "Do you wish you could stay at the park and we are leaving now?" Once they've calmed down, then we are ready to leave the park or we can help them to make amends if they've hurt someone or made a mess. They feel safe to let out everything with us and know that we love them at their worst.

Toddlers want to try to do things for themselves. Our toddler's cry of "Me do it" is equally exciting (our toddler wants to learn more) and frustrating (things seem to take four times longer than they should when we are in a hurry). We can set up even more parts of our home so they can manage more and more themselves, for example, so they can help set the table, prepare their own snack, clear the table, and maybe even wash the dishes (the last is a favorite at around 2½ years old). We take time to give them as little help as possible and as much as necessary when they are learning to dress and feed themselves, and all throughout the day. And they are so delighted to manage more and more for themselves over time.

Toddlers are enormously capable. They pick things up easily (the absorbent mind continues). They will make more and more connections in the world around them. They take in everything seemingly without effort. They will start to express themselves and start to move with more and more refinement and coordination.

Toddlers go slowly. They need time to master skills. They need time to process what we say (we can count quietly to ten in our heads to give them time before repeating ourselves). And we need to—as much as possible—slow down to their pace. Rather than rushing them every morning to leave the house, we mostly go slowly and reserve rushing for days when we can't miss the train or we have an important appointment and time has slipped away.

Last, yet most important, toddlers are brilliant. They live in the present moment and are not worried about the past or future. They say exactly what they mean (not trying to be nice or polite), so there's no guessing what they are trying to tell us. They can already do so much for themselves and want to be part of our daily life. They want to help us cook, sweep the floor (really!), and wash the windows with a spray bottle again and again. They hug us and love us like no other.

THE COMING YEARS

Dr. Montessori's theory of childhood is nothing short of remarkable when we see that her overview of childhood development from the ages of 0 to 24 years is now being backed up by research about the brain. Who would have ever conceived in the early 1900s that childhood continues up to the age of 24 years old? Yet now research confirms that the prefrontal cortex (the decision-making center of the brain) is still developing into our early twenties.

She also identified *four planes of development* within this period, each 6 years in length, where there were similar characteristics being shown.

The child from 0 to 6 years

Infancy (0 to 1 year), the toddler years (1 to 3 years), and the preschool years (3 to 6 years) are what Dr. Montessori referred to as the *first plane of development.*

In this plane of development, the child is becoming physically independent—they go from a baby who is completely dependent on the adult to a child who can walk, talk, and do a great deal for themselves.

It is a volatile period with ample change. Never does so much development take place in one plane. So the child will be more emotional as they experience reams of physical, emotional, and social growth in these years.

The child has an absorbent mind across this whole plane, taking in everything in their environment effortlessly.

Where we saw that a baby and then a toddler had an *unconscious absorbent mind,* taking in everything without deliberate effort, a preschooler becomes a curious participant in the process and starts to want to understand more consciously everything they see around them. We call this the *conscious absorbent mind.*

The child begins to ask "What?" and "Why?" and from 3 to 6 years they seek to crystallize everything they absorbed from 0 to 3 years. Around 3, children start to see that symbols can be representations, sometimes showing interest in letters and numbers at this age.

The child from 6 to 12 years

The elementary child becomes a citizen of the world. This is the *second plane of development*. Their curiosity begins to reach beyond the world in front of them, and they want to know more about distant places, ancient civilizations, and the universe and beyond.

Rather than simply accepting and absorbing things as true, the 6- to 12-year-old child will ask questions about the gray areas. They might ask why our family approaches things differently than another family, for example, our religion or our family constellation. They are busy with concepts like right and wrong, good and bad, fair and unfair, and other moral questions.

They also have more complex thinking and can make amazing discoveries for themselves, if we allow them. As their parent or teacher, we can stimulate an interest just enough to draw them in, then leave them to make connections, develop theories, and sometimes explore questions that one might generally discuss in high school, at university, and beyond. It is limitless.

Parents may also be reassured to know that these years are less volatile than other years. With less explosive growth and fewer changes, the child is in a more stable period.

The child from 12 to 18 years

Teenagers have been largely misunderstood. We think that they want to rebel, they don't listen, and are characterized as being moody and grumpy. We can assure you that teenagers are lovely humans to be around. Yes, they have enormous changes going on in their bodies and hormones that can lead to a lot of emotional volatility. Yet they are not so dissimilar from toddlers—they need our support when they are having a hard time. And they need to pass through an important development stage of increasing *social independence*, moving socially away from their family and closer to friends.

This is the *third plane of development*. It's a time of big feelings. But it's also a time when children start to use their imaginations to solve social problems (from climate change, to poverty, to the availability of food, and more). They'll mostly want to spend time with friends, but they also need the security of a solid home base where they can return when they need our support.

FOUR PLANES OF DEVELOPMENT

FIRST PLANE	SECOND PLANE	THIRD PLANE	FOURTH PLANE
0–6 years	**6–12 years**	**12–18 years**	**18–24 years**
We are planting the seeds.	The stem is growing tall and strong.	Leaves and blossoms unfurl, nearing maturity.	The plant is fully grown.
• physical and biological independence	• mental independence	• social independence	• spiritual and moral independence
• absorbent mind	• developing moral sense (right and wrong) and exploring how things work and connect	• developing social policy (how they would change the world)	• giving back to society
• concrete understanding of the world	• movement from concrete to abstract learning	• sharing ideas and ideals with others	• reasoning, logical mind
• sensorial learner	• mode of learning through imagination	• enormous physical and psychological changes (similar to the first plane)	• more stable period (similar to the second plane)
• working in parallel with small amounts of collaboration	• collaboration in small groups		
• rapid growth and change	• less growth, more stable period		

The child from 18 to 24 years

In the *fourth plane of development*, the child is between childhood and adulthood. They are curious about what is ahead but do not feel like an adult quite yet.

They are finding their place in society. It may be that they go on to further study. They may join the Peace Corps. It is often a time of volunteering. And it is a time of enormous freedom.

Dr. Montessori said that if everything in the first three planes of development has been done, the final plane of development takes care of itself.

And now it's time to let our children go. They will always keep the roots we have given them; now they can spread their wings wider and farther.

TO PRACTICE

- What can we prepare for the coming toddler years? How can we adjust our home to meet their changing needs?
- Can we recognize the stages of the four planes of development from our own childhood?
- How can we apply the principles of love, understanding, and respect we learned in this book to others in our lives? Our partner? Other children in our family? Our parents? Neighbors? Siblings? And those who think differently?

THE PATH TO PEACE

Back in the first chapter, we referred to our baby as a hope for the future. Yet we are not waiting for them to solve the problems that we have helped create.

It is together, with our baby, our child, our teenager, our young adult, that we can create a better world.

If we can raise them with this love, respect, and gentle hands, this is how they will learn to treat others. They will love, not hate; they will build bridges, not walls; they will work with nature, not use it up or destroy it.

Let's walk together with our family, with the next family, with our neighbor, with someone who thinks differently. Let's see and accept each other. Let's find ways to work together to meet all our needs.

Let's join Dr. Montessori in her wish for peace in all humankind.

> "I beg the dear all-powerful children to unite with me for the building of peace in Man and in the World."
>
> —inscription on Dr. Maria Montessori's grave in Noordwijk aan Zee,
> the Netherlands

BONUS
REAL STORIES

We are delighted to share some stories from families around the globe who are incorporating Montessori principles with their babies. Enjoy!

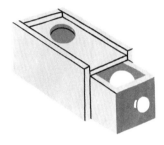

INDIA/UGANDA
(LIVING IN NEW ZEALAND)

Jaya, Nikul, and Anika
Forest Montessori

"I absolutely loved the 'symbiotic period.'
We kept visitors to a minimum and just
bonded one-on-one at home with Anika.
This was our most special time together.

"I was amazed that a baby could concentrate
for so long. [The] dancer's mobile, Gobbi
mobile, and the wooden bell chimes mobile
were her absolute favorites. She also loved
grasping her rattles and play silks; she
danced with joy every time she could see
trees or rain; she loved seeing high-contrast
pictures during the first few months; and we
read lots of books from birth.

"Long days and nights pass by fast, but
the trust they receive from you in the first
year will lay the foundation for their secure
attachment and their personality. You will
reap the fruits of your endless love and hard
work in the first year, for the rest of your and
their life.

"Routines are very important for a baby—they
like to know what to expect. We had a well-
defined, but still flexible, rhythm to our day,
and Anika thrived knowing what to expect
next. I even made us a weekly calendar with
pictures, and I would show Anika exactly
where we were going before heading out in
the car each day. This made car rides much
more bearable for her."

UK

Charlie, Maria, and Lukas
Montessori Chapters

"I loved observing the new things he was learning constantly. From noticing the first time he started to focus on an object (our window shutters fascinated him!), to seeing his determination to wriggle himself to get somewhere, before he could crawl, to the first time that he rolled over on his own—they were all such exciting moments to see as a parent!

"We spoke to him as a real person from the moment he was born, letting him know what was happening when we were changing and feeding him and also what we were doing in our day-to-day lives, so he could learn to understand.

"Lukas has loved having the freedom to move around, and we have tried to offer this to him as much as possible—in the house and outside in nature. The day that he learnt to roll, we decided to move our sofa to open up our lounge space in order to give him the opportunity to move around as much as he could with minimal obstacles in the middle of the room.

"I think so much of Montessori is about the mindset, and you can learn lots as you go. Accepting that it is, and always will be, an ongoing process and not putting any pressure on yourself—enjoying it as much as possible.

"I mainly looked out for light cotton clothing that allowed his hands and feet to be uncovered so that Lukas had the opportunity to experience all of the textures around him. We looked for loose, stretchy trousers and tops that enabled him to move easily and as much as he wanted to. We kept the main rooms in the house warm so that he could have fewer layers on, and, whenever possible, we would go outside so that he could feel grass and leaves, roll around, and explore being in nature."

USA

Theresa, Chris, D, and S
Montessori in Real Life

"Montessori has allowed me to give my baby the space and tools to discover, communicate, and realize his own capabilities. It has also helped me to see him as a beautiful and unique individual, with different interests, strengths, and challenges than his sister.

"My favorite moments were the quiet and calm minutes spent nursing, when we'd simply gaze at each other. There was nowhere we needed to be but right there. I still can't get enough of that look of contentment right after nursing, when he stretches his arms and beams up at me.

"Both of my children were captivated by the butterfly mobile between two and three months of age. Once they began to grasp, they adored hanging tactile mobiles, such as ribbons, bells, and teething rings. A long-time favorite in the second half of the first year has been household objects of any kind, boxes that open and close, and simple DIY shakers!

"Our home has played a role in allowing for freedom of movement and natural gross-motor development. Since birth, we have placed our infant on a soft mat or rug on the floor to allow him to stretch and move without constraints. With a low mirror, he has also been able to see his own movements as he learns to move and work in new ways, connecting the mind and body."

TOGO (LIVING IN JAPAN)

Ahoefa, Gabin, Yannis, and Kenzo
Raising Yannis

"Montessori has allowed me to be intentional with my children. It was the guide we needed as first-time parents who were looking for a different parenting style.

"With the newborns, the talking stage was my favorite. My boys are very vocal. It started with the baby talk, so we followed their lead and continued the conversation.

"I wished I'd taken the time to embrace our Montessori journey at home. During our first year, I was very focused on making our home identical to a Montessori classroom. This caused a lot of confusion and difficulty for us and my child, until we decided to embrace this journey from our home. Montessori at home is amazing and very flexible.

"Montessori is a lifestyle; if used properly, it can help establish a healthy bond. My advice to new parents would be to live what you want your children to learn."

SPAIN (LIVING IN USA)

Neus, John, and Julia
Montessorian By Heart

"I observed the magic of Montessori for babies, and it keeps amazing me every day. The freedom of movement helped my daughter love to play and explore independently. She is a baby eager to engage with the world by moving, batting, rolling, grasping, and using all her senses. The Montessori-prepared environment for feeding, changing, and sleeping also helped her feel calm and safe and look forward to new and exciting adventures.

"A quiet, calm, and safe home environment is key to help a baby settle and start engaging with the world around them. We set up designated spaces for sleep, eating, and play, and that helped her anticipate these routines and give her a sense of security.

"I stressed too much in following the presentation timeline of Montessori materials instead of focusing more on my own daughter and her own development. That hit me when I was setting up the Gobbi mobile, and I observed in her facial expression that it was not what she was interested in at that moment. This observation allowed me to pause my mom self and go back to my Montessori self and follow her lead."

NIGERIA

Junnifa, Uzo, Solu, Metu, and Biendu
Nduoma Montessori and
Fruitful Orchard Montessori School

"Montessori helps me to notice and celebrate the effort my children have made, no matter how small. It could be trying to turn over or figuring out how to get a ball into a hole. I never cease to be amazed by how persistent and resilient they can be. Observing them is my favorite thing to do, and it is what allows me to notice. I don't celebrate it in an external way, but I allow it, and give time and space for it. This is a celebration for me, and these little moments add joy to my parenting.

"One of my favorite stages was when they'd wake up from their floor bed and without waking up crying, they'd quietly crawl over to my room, pull up on the side of our bed, and wake me up by rubbing my face with their hand or making small sounds. It happened many times with all three of my babies, and I still smile at the memories. I loved this stage when they were mobile and starting to independently explore. Using a Montessori floor bed definitely contributed to their independence in this regard.

"Having a baby with older siblings comes with its own challenges but is also beautiful to watch. I was lucky to discover Montessori before my first child, and all the work I put in him flowed over to my next child and again from both of them to my third child. They do have times when they disagree or when one interferes with the other's work, but even these moments are opportunities to learn how to express themselves kindly and how to resolve conflict.

THE NETHERLANDS

**Simone's parent–baby classes
Jacaranda Tree Montessori and
The Montessori Notebook**

"The wonder in a baby's eyes when they
realize they made something happen—
the way the ball rolled, the sound of a
bell when they shake a rattle, or reaching
their toes for the first time. These are
the simple moments of discovery that
will lay the foundation for their love of
learning and the belief that they can have
an effect on the world.

"I love to see the babies exploring the
space in their unique way. One baby will
be busy practicing crawling, another sitting
to repeatedly drop a ball into a hole, and
another lying on their belly to watch another
baby in the class.

"The parents can do less than they think. If
their baby is concentrating, they can sit to
observe. And respond when the baby calls
out to them. It's actually a more relaxing
way to parent than feeling like we need to
entertain the baby all day."

APPENDICES

MONTH-BY-MONTH MILESTONES AND PREPARATION

DURING PREGNANCY

The baby in utero is already absorbing everything.

IMPORTANT IDEAS IN THIS PERIOD

We have 9 months to prepare ourselves to become parents. This gives us time to fully comprehend that we are growing a special human with whom we can already connect. For those of us who are not carrying our baby, there are ways we can prepare to connect (see page 209). We prepare our space so that when they arrive, they will know we have been waiting for them. We communicate that they are loved, accepted, and wanted.

BOND WITH OUR BABY

- Massage the belly.
- Talk to the baby in the belly.
- Our partner (if we have one) can also talk to the baby in the belly and rub the belly.
- Communicate to the baby that they are wanted.
- We are creating points of reference for the baby to help them transition from the womb after birth.
- For adoptive or non-gestating parents, see page 209.

PREPARATION OF PARENT(S)

- Good nutrition
- Emotional/spiritual preparation
  - Make space for a baby in our lives.
  - Speak to others about being a parent.
  - Find like-minded families.
- Keep the emotional environment as stable as possible.
- If we have a partner, create a ritual of being together and checking in with each other that can continue after birth (e.g., having a cup of tea/glass of wine at the end of the day or spending some time in the morning sitting outside together).
- Look into birth options.

PREPARE CLOTHING FOR OUR BABY

- Soft clothing without seams and labels
- Made of natural materials, if possible
- Kimono-style tops or buttons at neck to make it easy to go over the baby's head
- Cloth diapers, if available

PHYSICAL PREPARATION OF OUR SPACE

- Keep the baby's space attractive and simple, with essentials at the ready.
- Cestina (Moses-style basket) and floor mattress for sleep
- Movement area with horizontal mirror
- Adult chair for feeding (if space allows)
- Changing pad
- Baby carrier and stroller
- Topponcino (thin, quilted pillow) to hold the baby during the first weeks
- Baby bath
- See chapter 4 for more details.

MONTHS 1 TO 2

The symbiotic period

IMPORTANT IDEAS IN THIS PERIOD:

1. **SECURITY.** We are building trust with our baby during the first hours, days, and weeks; we respond to their cries; we cradle them with gentle hands; we address them before picking them up.
2. **ADAPTATION.** During this period, the baby is adjusting to life outside of the womb and getting to know us, and we are getting to know them. We can make this transition as smooth as possible by keeping things simple.
3. **ORIENTATION/POINTS OF REFERENCE.** The baby learns to orient to us; we can help them with this by having a limited number of caregivers at this time and by providing consistent areas for feeding, sleeping, playing, and changing/dressing.
4. **ATTACHMENT/SEPARATION.** These early weeks are critical for the baby's attachment. We begin laying the foundation for strong attachment in the first months (with attachment happening around 8 months).
5. **TOUCH.** We use gentle, respectful touch when handling the baby. Confident, efficient movements give the baby a feeling of security and prevent us from startling the baby with unexpected movements.
6. **PHYSICAL CARE.** A lot of time will be spent feeding, changing diapers, establishing sleep patterns, and bathing the baby. We can use this time mindfully as moments of connection with the baby.

BOND WITH OUR BABY

- Hold the baby, looking into their eyes.
- Have simple conversations.
  - While nursing
  - While bathing the baby
  - During diaper changes
  - Through gentle baby massage
- Sing/dance/play music
- Skin-to-skin

PREPARATION OF PARENT(S)

- Partner can provide "protection" for family unit.
- Ask for help from partner, grandparent, caregiver, cleaner, or friend with cooking, cleaning, picking up groceries, looking after older siblings.
- Get as much sleep as possible; rest when the baby rests.
- Observation: Learn to understand our baby's needs, their ways of communication, and their unique development.

DAILY RHYTHM AND CARE

- The baby will wake to feed, then take some brief time to play/get changed/be held/have conversation, and then go back to sleep.
- Follow the baby's natural rhythm.
- Feeding on demand and many naps
- Choose clothing for free movement that is gentle on skin and easy to put over the baby's head or kimono-style.
- Ask permission from the baby before handling them—always with gentle hands.
- Keep the baby's hands free—a point of reference from the womb.

PHYSICAL PREPARATION OF OUR SPACE

- Keep space a little warmer and dimmer in the first days to help the baby adjust from the womb.
- Feeding area—try to keep consistent; at night, sit in a chair in the bedroom if space allows.
- Sleeping area—a cestina on floor bed
- Changing area—a changing pad used in the same place every time
- Movement area—a floor mat where the baby can stretch and see themselves in a mirror
- Topponcino to use as a point of reference and to remove overstimulation when the baby is being held

ACTIVITIES FOR OUR BABY

- Visual development—the baby can focus around 12 inches (30 cm); make eye contact; follow shadows from trees; interact with Montessori mobiles (Munari, octahedron, Gobbi); track older siblings
- Physical development—movement mat; let the baby stretch and learn about their body, studying their hands and feet
- Language—conversation (give them time to respond); read simple books to them; and from birth, speak to the baby in multiple languages if you have a multilingual family
- Aural development—our voices, bells, wind chimes, gentle music (especially the same music played while the baby was in the womb)

MONTHS 3 TO 4

More wakeful and alert, and trying new skills

IMPORTANT IDEAS IN THIS PERIOD:

We continue to lay the foundation for security, adaptation, orientation, attachment, touch, and physical care from the first two months. The baby is more wakeful and alert and seeks more information from their "environment"—the people, activities, and our spaces. We can see them respond to sounds and track with their eyes and reach out to the world—sensorial explorers. They are working on visual development, aural development, coordination of their limbs (to bat something with their hands or feet), and can perhaps hold something in their grasp.

BOND WITH OUR BABY

- Moments of physical care don't have to be rushed through—they can be moments of connection with the baby.
- Time for singing, playing music, moments of silence, making eye contact
- Gentle massage
- Interest in faces and watching our mouth
- Involve them in daily life around the home (and take them on simple outings).

PREPARATION OF PARENT(S)

- Take time to rest when the baby sleeps.
- Observe our baby's unique development— what is our baby like? What are they interested in? How can we support their development right now?
- Find ways to continue to connect with our partner (if we have one)—e.g., having a morning cup of tea, foot massages in the evening, lying together in bed.
- Separating: Some parents may be returning to work at this time and this is also a time to take little breaks away to refresh one's self. Always tell the baby where you are going and when you'll be back.

DAILY RHYTHM AND CARE

- Clothing—ensure free movement; uncover head, feet, and hands whenever possible
- Pacifiers— generally not used in Montessori, limit to sleep time if used
- Limit time in "buckets," meaning containers like car seats or bouncers, and allow free movement.
- Continue to ask permission to handle the baby.

PHYSICAL PREPARATION OF OUR SPACE

- Most areas will be the same as months 1 to 2.
- Once the baby is too big for the cestina, they can sleep on the floor bed or in our bed if co-sleeping.
- Play area—includes movement mat, mirror, and a low shelf with simple grasping toys

ACTIVITIES FOR OUR BABY

- Visual development—the baby can continue to use mobiles, make eye contact, and track movement in the space
- Gross-motor development—with time to explore, the baby may try rolling and will show interest in their hands and feet
- Fine-motor development—they may start to bat at the mobiles, so we can then add grasping toys for them to pull on and kick; provide interesting things for them to touch
- Language—increased vocalizations; continue to provide rich language, books, and conversation with the baby; they may practice bubble-blowing with their lips
- Aural development—think of sounds for the baby to explore

MONTHS 5 TO 6

Increasing awake time, movement, and vocalizations

IMPORTANT IDEAS IN THIS PERIOD:

The baby may wake without being immediately hungry. They can play for increasing periods of time, and they become interested in things that move, roll, and can be manipulated. Order remains important in their physical space and with their caregivers and the rhythm of their day. When they begin to eat solids, they are beginning to move from collaboration to independence as they bring food to their mouth by themselves, for example, pieces of bread or well-cooked vegetables. They may express preferences.

DAILY RHYTHM AND CARE

- 3 to 4 naps a day
- Allow time to play/explore without interrupting
- Introduction of first solid foods at 6 months

PREPARATION OF PARENT(S)

- Give as little help as needed and as much as necessary when the baby is playing—a little frustration can lead to a positive sense of mastery.

ACTIVITIES FOR OUR BABY

- Grasping toys—made of beautiful natural materials, items that fit in their hand, can include a bell/small beads inside to give aural feedback
- Treasure or discovery baskets to explore
- Language—babbling and practicing sounds

PHYSICAL PREPARATION OF OUR SPACE

- Largely the same as previous months
- Weaning table and chair

MONTHS 7 TO 9

World opening up, food exploration begins, and baby starts to seek some independence

IMPORTANT IDEAS IN THIS PERIOD:

The baby often begins to crawl and pull up to stand in this period. There is an increasing interest in food and feeding themselves. They seek independence (and then return to us). The baby begins to explore further in an expanded area beyond "their room." We can leave their door open while they nap or play (as long as it's safe). When they wake or are done playing, they find us by following our voice or sounds. When we are together, they may crawl farther and farther away from us, check to see that we are still there, and continue exploring. We can help these explorations by keeping our home environment consistent and predictable. In those moments when we notice them exploring farther than usual, we can remain where we are, a point of reference and refuge that they can come back to as necessary. Separation anxiety can begin around this time. We can tell the baby where we are going when we leave them and reassure them on our return.

DAILY RHYTHM AND CARE

- Introduction of solids continues to three meals a day
- Breastfeeding/bottle-feeding
- Two or three naps during the day

PREPARATION OF PARENT(S)

- Ensure safe spaces to explore.
- How to handle difficult behavior, for example, during diaper changes or when put in a car seat. When we view these processes as collaborative ones and involve the baby, we find that it becomes less difficult. We notify them, "I am going to change your diaper/put you in the car seat. Please lift your leg/put in your arm or I am going to help you lift your leg/put in your arm." We follow a consistent process, and our baby knows the process and feels like part of it.

ACTIVITIES FOR OUR BABY

- Grasping toys—made of beautiful natural materials
- Opening and closing
- Posting objects like balls
- Threading bangles/rings onto a stick
- Language—can begin introducing a few signs if doing sign language
- Basket of balls—to crawl after, roll between us, encourage movement

PHYSICAL PREPARATION OF OUR SPACE

- To allow more space to move, remove movement mat when the baby starts crawling.
- Provide places to pull up on—low, heavy furniture like ottomans or a bar in front of a mirror.

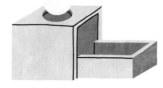

MONTHS 10 TO 12

Our explorer

IMPORTANT IDEAS IN THIS PERIOD:

The baby is often pulling themselves up to stand during this period—their world is opening up. Fine-motor skills are developing, including full-hand grasping, grasping between thumb and fingers, and the pincer grip. The baby's independence is increasing—moving away from the parents to explore the world around them. Baby is moving faster and farther, and then coming back to check in. There is more independent play. Language efforts begin to increase—babbling as if speaking in sentences, possibly repeating words or sounds, and making sounds of animals and single words can start at around 12 months. It takes so much neurological effort to learn to walk and talk that we often find that one will plateau as the other takes off; we may see a child walk before talking or vice versa. There is an increasing trust in self.

DAILY RHYTHM AND CARE

- Take time to explore the world around us—outdoors, supermarket, library, the beach or forest; show them our daily life.
- Around two naps a day
- Breakfast, lunch, and dinner—solid food they feed themselves
- Breast milk/bottle—morning and night
- Toileting—we can introduce some of the skills that will be required for toileting. We can introduce a potty, the baby can spend time in training pants instead of diapers, and we can observe and note their toilet patterns.
- Dressing—moving from collaboration to some independence

PREPARATION OF PARENT(S)

- Offer a firm foundation as their secure place, while giving them the emotional message that it's okay to explore places farther from us.
- Continued observation to see where they are developing
- Acceptance of their uniqueness and particular timeline of development
- The baby can be worn in a baby carrier while also allowing a lot of time out of the carrier for free movement. Once the baby is walking, we can let the baby walk when going out (at first small distances, then gradually increasing).

ACTIVITIES FOR OUR BABY

- Post a ball into a hole—the ball comes straight out; put a ball into a hole—open a drawer to find it again; ball hammering
- First puzzles—putting a wooden egg into an egg cup; a pop-up toy; nesting cups; simple one- to two-piece puzzles with large knobs
- Basket of balls—to crawl after, roll between us, encourage movement
- A wagon to push—once they can pull themselves up
- Rich language—books, conversations and naming *everything*
- When the baby takes their first steps, their hands become free to carry things and they see the world again from this higher perspective—try to avoid being tempted to hold both their hands to allow them to walk before they are ready.
- Allow time and space for climbing, and show them how to climb down backward, e.g., using stairs in the home.

PHYSICAL PREPARATION OF OUR SPACE

- Create a "yes" space for them to explore freely.
- Avoid playpens at any age but particularly now that they are on the move.
- Have low furniture for them to pull themselves up on and cruise—an ottoman, a bar on the wall, low shelves, the couch.
- Low shelf with simple activities that challenge their growing abilities
- Low table and chair—for eating and to bring an activity to
- Potty

ACTIVITIES LIST FOR BABIES

Ages listed below are to be used as guidelines only. Activities should be chosen based on the baby's individual interests and what skills they are currently developing. Follow your child. See which activities keep their attention, and remove those that are too hard or too easy.

BABIES UP TO 6 MONTHS

AGE	ACTIVITY NAME	DESCRIPTION	AREA OF DEVELOPMENT
All ages	Music/dance/ movement/ singing	• Play musical instruments • Listen to beautiful music (preferable to listen actively, not just as background music). • Dance with the baby • Movement—starting from birth, and on a mat with a mirror hanging lengthwise on the wall; time to move, stretch, and explore the body • Sing—starting from birth	• Music and movement
All ages	Books	• A collection of realistic books that are of interest to a young child; should relate to the life a young child is living • Begin with books that have one picture on one page, then move on to a picture with one word, next a picture with a simple sentence, building to simple stories and finally, more complex stories. • Arranged so that children can see their fronts and access them easily, perhaps in a small basket for a few books or on a small bookshelf • Start with board books and move on to hardcover and paperback.	• Language
All ages	Rhythmic language	• Simple, short poetry; songs; rhyming ditties • If it is too long, it is overwhelming for the child. • Be fairly realistic. • Finger and body movements that go along with the stories, songs, or rhymes or create your own • Examples: action rhymes, finger rhymes, haiku, patty-cake	• Language

AGE	ACTIVITY NAME	DESCRIPTION	AREA OF DEVELOPMENT
From shortly after birth	Self-expression	• In moments of care during the day—diapering, dressing, eating—we can allow the baby to respond to our conversation. • When the baby is non-verbal, conversation can be sounds, facial expressions, or poking out their tongue. • As the baby becomes verbal, they will use first words, then later phrases and sentences. • The adult gets down to the baby's eye level, maintains eye contact (if culturally appropriate), and is present. • The adult transmits that they are very interested in what the baby is sharing; for example, through body language, like nodding, or through affirming language, using words like "Really?," "Yes!," "Is that so?" "Sounds interesting."	• Language
Newborn	Munari mobile	• A black-and-white mobile • Hang it at the baby's focusing distance, no more than 12 inches (30 cm) away (generally newborns can focus the distance to their parent's face when held).	• Visual development
From 2 to 3+ weeks old	Music box	• A hanging music box with a string that the adult or child pulls to activate (or with a crank suitable for an older child) that plays a classical piece of music • Initially, the adult starts the music box for the baby. Once the child is sitting, the music box can be attached to a wall and the child can be shown how to pull cord to make it play. • Can also become a postnatal point of reference if used as part of a routine, e.g., diaper changing	• Auditory development
Around 2+ months	Octahedron mobile	• Has three different colors; light reflects on reflective paper • Introduces primary colors • Hang at a height the baby can focus on; this may now be a little higher than at birth.	• Visual development
Around 2+ months	Interlocking circles	• One full circle and one with a slot card that is half the diameter of the circle • Initially, place it in the baby's hand so they can use their reflexive grasp. • As reflexive grasp changes to intentional grasp, the baby will reach and grasp with their whole hand, a finger, etc. • An older baby will do hand-to-hand transfer, roll along the ground, etc.	• Grasping materials

AGE	ACTIVITY NAME	DESCRIPTION	AREA OF DEVELOPMENT
Around 2 to 3 months	Gobbi mobile (see page 135)	• A single color gradation of five to seven balls • Arranged from lightest to darkest in increasing lengths of cotton or coming to the lowest point in the middle • The thread used to hang each ball is the same color as the ball.	• Visual development
Around 3+ months	Mobile with stylized paper figures, e.g., reflective paper dancers (see page 136)	• Figures made of reflective paper which would realistically move, e.g., dancers, fish, pinwheels	• Visual development
Around 3+ months	Other mobiles	• Make mobiles by hanging small objects from an embroidery hoop, then hanging the hoop parallel to the ground. • Examples: pictures of faces, reflective paper, or leaves	• Visual development
Around 3+ months	Mobile with stylized wooden figures	• Three to seven different wooden figures that can move realistically, e.g., dolphins, birds, waves • Eye-catching colors to attract attention	• Visual development • Stimulus for reaching, grasping, and batting
Around 3+ months	Rubber ball with protrusions	• A nontoxic rubber, vinyl, or plastic sphere with raised protrusions • Initially hold the ball near the baby's hands; easy for the child to grasp, manipulate, and suck on. An older child will do hand-to-hand transfer, bang on surfaces with the ball, and explore other movements.	• Grasping materials
Around 3 to 3.5+ months	Three colored spheres	• Three colored balls suspended at an angle or in a triangle, with the longest thread in the middle • Red, blue, and yellow are a good start, or else another color combination, with the darkest color on the longest thread. • Balls should fit in the baby's hand but not be too small (which would be a possible choking hazard) (see page 107).	• Visual development • Stimulus for reaching and grasping and batting
Between 3 and 4+ months	Grasping beads	• Five wooden beads threaded and knotted onto leather cord or rope or sturdy cotton cord • The baby holds, manipulates, and mouths the beads.	• Grasping materials

AGE	ACTIVITY NAME	DESCRIPTION	AREA OF DEVELOPMENT
Around 4+ months	Bell on a ribbon	• A bell threaded onto a ribbon that hangs from elastic, allowing the baby to pull the bell toward themselves	• Auditory development • Visual development • Stimulus for reaching and grasping and batting
Around 4+ months	Ring/bangle on a ribbon	• A ring/bangle made from bamboo, metal, or wood and suspended on a ribbon with elastic at the top • The ring should be big enough for the baby's hand to fit through and grasp.	• Visual development • Stimulus for reaching and grasping and batting
Around 4+ months	Interlocking rings	• Three or four rings that interlock • Made of metal or wood—different materials produce a different sound • Place close enough to the baby for reaching, grasping, and manipulating.	• Grasping materials

Around 4+ months	Home objects	• Examples include:
		  ◦ Honey dipper (with the handle cut short and sanded)
		  ◦ Doll made from a wooden clothes pin
		  ◦ Spoon
		  ◦ Belt buckle
		  ◦ Bangle bracelets
		  ◦ Keys on a keyring
		• Provide grasping and manipulating experiences for the child to explore using their hands.
		• Check for safety, e.g., choking hazards or sharp edges.
			• Grasping materials

Around 4+ months	Bamboo cylinder rattle	• Rice, tiny pebbles, or grains placed inside a piece of bamboo, with the ends plugged with non-toxic wood putty • The baby holds it, shakes it, and experiences the sound it makes.	• Auditory development • Tactile experiences
Around 4+ months (or earlier when baby has reflexive grasp)	Cylinder rattle with bells	• A piece of doweling sanded smooth with a bell safely attached to each end or hollow with a wire inside to hold a bell at each end • Check for sharp bits that could cut the baby. • The baby holds it, shakes it, and experiences the sound it makes.	• Auditory development • Tactile experiences
Around 4+ months (or earlier, with reflexive grasp)	Commercial rattles	• Look for rattles that are wooden or made of natural materials. • Should be ones that are easily grasped and not too big, so the baby can hold it to make a sound • For shaking and experiencing sound	• Auditory development • Tactile experiences

AGE	ACTIVITY NAME	DESCRIPTION	AREA OF DEVELOPMENT
Around 4+ months	Cube with bell	• A hollow cube with rounded corners and a bell inside • For shaking and experiencing sound	• Auditory development • Tactile experiences
Around 4+ months (or earlier, with reflexive grasp)	Bells on leather strap	• Three bells attached to a leather strap • The baby can grasp and manipulate it.	• Auditory materials • Tactile experiences
Around 4+ months (or earlier, with reflexive grasp)	Silver rattle	• A lightweight silver rattle • The baby can grasp and manipulate it.	• Auditory development • Tactile experiences
Around 5+ months	Other sound objects	• Simple musical instruments like maracas • Gourds filled with beans, rice, etc. • For shaking and experiencing sound	• Auditory development • Tactile experiences
Around 5+ months or once sitting	Toy on a suction-cup base	• An object that will rock when it is hit but stay attached to surface • For example, a clear ball filled with lots of tiny balls on a rubber suction stand • The child bats, reaches, and attempts intentional grasping without material moving away.	• Activities for eye-hand coordination
5 or 6+ months	Basket with known objects	• Place two or three of the child's most frequently used toys in a small soft basket • The adult can change the objects as their favorite ones change. • The baby lies or sits and chooses one of the objects.	• Activities for eye-hand coordination
5 to 7+ months	Knitted or crocheted ball	• A pliable, soft knitted or crocheted ball • When the child grabs it, they can get a good hold on it with their fingers. • Placed near the baby to encourage movement	• Activities for gross-motor movement
Around 6 to 8+ months	Cylinder with bell	• This is a wooden rattle that rolls with a bell inside. • Placed near the baby to encourage movement	• Activities for gross-motor movement • Auditory stimulus as a movement incentive
Once baby starts to pull up, from 7+ months	Ottoman	• A heavy, stable ottoman that does not tip when the baby pulls to standing • The height of the ottoman should be at stomach height for the baby.	• Activities for gross-motor movement • Offers the baby an independent means for pulling to standing and cruising

AGE	ACTIVITY NAME	DESCRIPTION	AREA OF DEVELOPMENT
Once the baby starts to pull up, from 7+ months	Bar on wall	• A bar secured safely to the wall to enable the baby to pull up and cruise • About one inch (3 cm) away from the wall to allow the hand to wrap around the bar • Should be at chest height for the child • Could put a mirror behind the bar	• Activities for gross-motor movement • Offers the baby an independent means for pulling to standing and cruising
Between 7 and 9+ months	Egg in an egg cup/cup with ball	• A wooden egg cup with a wooden egg inside, or a large ball in a cup • To practice removing and releasing an object into a container	• Activities for eye-hand coordination
Between 7 and 9+ months	Box with cube	• A wooden cube that fits into a handmade box • To practice removing and releasing an object into a container	• Activities for eye-hand coordination
Around 8+ months	Box with tray and ball (object permanence box)	• A rectangular box with a tray attached with a hole in the top of the box for posting the ball (see workman.com/montessori for a tutorial on making this) • The ball should have a nice sound to it, like a wooden ball or table tennis ball. • To practice posting and intentionally releasing an object • To help the child understand object permanence • You can observe the child's different grasps on the ball, such as a whole-hand grasp, four-finger grasp, or two-finger grasp.	• Activities for eye-hand coordination
Once child is creeping, around 8 or 9 months	Basket of balls	• A collection of balls that are different sizes and textures • Examples: rattan ball, ball with protrusions, mini football • The baby can kick, roll, chase, manipulate, and feel the balls with their hands.	• Activities for gross-motor movement
From creeping until walking well, around 8 or 9 months	Stair	• Three stairs with a railing to hold on to on either end of a bridge • The stairs are wide but not very high.	• Activities for gross-motor movement
From creeping, around 8 to 10+ months	Ball tracker	• A series of ramps in a frame with a small ball • A hole at top left for dropping in the ball and another hole at the end of each ramp for the ball to drop onto the next ramp (instructions online at workman.com/montessori)	• Activities for gross-motor movement • Visual tracking • Auditory tracking from the sound of the ball in the tracker

AGE	ACTIVITY NAME	DESCRIPTION	AREA OF DEVELOPMENT
When the child pulls to standing, around 8 to 10+ months	Low, heavy table	• A low table made of very heavy wood for the baby to grasp and pull up on	• Activities for gross-motor movement
Once the child is able to sit stably, around 8 to 11 months	Rings and peg on rocking base	• This can be the classic Fisher-Price toy or a smaller five-ring model, with rocking base. • Initially, use it with the largest ring only. • A rocking base is used so it won't fall over.	• Activities for eye-hand coordination
8 to 12 months (depends on skill level of previous activity)	Rings/peg on stable base	• A wooden base with a peg and a ring • Initially, the ring should have a very large opening.	• Activities for eye-hand coordination
Around 8 to 12+ months	Spinning top	• A traditional tin spinning top with a handle to pump to make it spin • Babies enjoy moving after it and eventually will be able to make it spin.	• Activities for gross motor movement
Between 9 and 11+ months	Box with drawer and ball	• A box with a hole in the top for posting and a drawer that pulls out • To practice posting and intentionally releasing an object • To help the child understand object permanence	• Activities for eye-hand coordination
Between 9 to 12+ months	Box with knitted ball	• A square box with a hole in the top slightly smaller than the knitted ball and a drawer • To practice posting and intentionally releasing an object • To help the child understand object permanence	• Activities for eye-hand coordination
Around 10+ months	Box with balls to push	• A rectangular box with three holes and balls on top • To practice posting and intentionally releasing an object • To help the child understand object permanence	• Activities for eye-hand coordination
From 10+ months	Furniture with keys	• Any piece of furniture with a lock and key that the child could work to open • Attach the key to the furniture with string.	• Activities for eye-hand coordination
10 to 12+ months	Wagon	• A wagon that is heavy enough so it does not tip as the child pulls up on it; a sandbag can be used to weigh it down	• Activities for gross-motor movement

AGE	ACTIVITY NAME	DESCRIPTION	AREA OF DEVELOPMENT
10 to 12+ months	Cabinet doors and drawers	• Cabinet doors and drawers, vanity cupboards • The adult places room-appropriate items for the child to find, for example, plastic pots and pans in a kitchen cupboard or items such as hairbrushes or clips in a bathroom drawer.	• Activities for gross-motor movement
10 to 12+ months	Basket with rings and peg	• Two or three rings in a basket and a base with a peg • The thickness of the rings can be the same or varied for an additional challenge.	• Activities for eye-hand coordination
11 to 12+ months	Spindle with napkin rings	• A spindle with two or three round metal or wooden napkin rings of identical size • On a shelf, with the rings sitting on the spindle, OR it could be on a tray with a basket for the rings	• Activities for eye-hand coordination
12+ months	Using chalk, crayon, or pencil	• A block crayon or chunky pencil (like a Stabilo woody 3 in 1 pencil) • Paper in a variety of shapes, colors, and textures • Use an underlay to protect the table.	• Art/self-expression

12+ months	Easel with chalk	• A chalkboard that is any of the following:
		  ◦ On the other side of a painting easel
		  ◦ A very large piece of plywood mounted low on the wall covered with chalkboard paint
		  ◦ A small chalkboard that sits on a shelf
		• For chalk, start with white and gradually introduce colors and different types.
		• A small eraser
			• Art/self-expression

Able to stand unaided	Easel with paint	• An easel • Paper cut to completely cover the surface of the easel • Start with one color of (very thick) paint in a paint pot. Gradually introduce other colors one by one. Can use two or more pots for an older child. • A chunky paintbrush with a short handle for small hands to hold easily • A painting smock/apron • A cup hook to hang the smock/apron • Extra paper placed in a bin • A wet cloth to wipe up spills	• Art/self-expression
12+ months	Base with rings of dimensional gradation	• A base with spindle and four or five rings of varying gradation, ideally alternating colors • The bottom ring should not be bigger than the child's hand span.	• Activities for eye-hand coordination

AGE	ACTIVITY NAME	DESCRIPTION	AREA OF DEVELOPMENT
12+ months	Nuts and bolts	• One or two large bolts with a corresponding nut; start with the nut on the bolt.	• Activities for eye-hand coordination
12+ months	Opening and closing	• A basket with two or three common household objects for opening and closing, e.g., a decorative box, tin, purse with snap fastener, makeup container (such as a powder compact or lipstick case), toothbrush holder	• Activities for eye-hand coordination
12+ months	Vocabulary objects	• Classify real or replica objects; three to six objects • Examples: fruits, vegetables, clothing, zoo animals, farm animals, pets, insects, mammals, birds, vertebrates, invertebrates	• Language development • Expands vocabulary
12+ months	Peg box	• A wooden box with six holes and an inset tray area for placing pegs removed from the holes	• Refinement of eye-hand coordination and grasp
12+ months	Cubes on a vertical dowel	• A base with three cubes on one dowel; cubes stored in the basket or on the dowel • Preparation for bead stringing	• Refinement of eye-hand coordination and grasp
12+ months	Puzzles	• A collection of puzzles starting with one-piece knobbed puzzles and progressing to greater and greater difficulty • The kinds of subject matter depicted on puzzles need to be realistic and appealing, e.g., animals, construction vehicles.	• Refinement of eye-hand coordination and pincer grasp • Develops the ability to recognize a background shape
Around 13+ months	Locks and keys	• A lock and key placed in a basket	• Activities for eye-hand coordination
Around 13+ months	Slotted box with chips	• A box with a slot cut into it • A latch on the box adds a challenge for the fingers. • Examples of posting items include large coins, small letters (laminated), and poker chips. • Use a tray to hold both the box and the basket of posting items.	• Refinement of eye-hand coordination and grasp
Once a child can walk	Table wiping	• A tray or basket with a sponge/drying mitt • A supply of replacement drying mitts	• Care of environment

PRIMITIVE REFLEXES

MORO: involuntary startle reflex

BAPKIN: movement of the mouth and tongue when the palms of hands are stimulated

ROOTING: when the cheek or lip is touched, baby faces toward the stimulus and makes sucking motions with the mouth

TONIC NECK, ALSO KNOWN AS FENCER: baby's head is turned to one side and the arm on that side stretches out; the opposite arm bends up at the elbow

BABINSINKY: when the sole of the foot is firmly stroked, big toe moves upward and other toes fan out

AGE	REFLEX
BIRTH	Moro Sucking Bapkin Grasping Rooting Tonic neck Walking Babinsky
2 MONTHS	Moro Grasping Rooting Tonic neck Babinsky
4 MONTHS	Moro Tonic neck
6 MONTHS	Moro Tonic neck
8 MONTHS	Moro Tonic neck
10 MONTHS	Moro Tonic neck
12 MONTHS	Moro Tonic neck

FURTHER READING

BOOKS BY DR. MARIA MONTESSORI

The Absorbent Mind: A Classic in Education and Child Development for Educators and Parents, Holt Paperbacks, 1995

The Child in the Family, ABC-CLIO, 1989 version

Maria Montessori Speaks to Parents: A Selection of Articles, Montessori-Pierson, 2017

BOOKS ABOUT THE MONTESSORI APPROACH

The Joyful Child: Montessori, Global Wisdom for Birth to Three, Susan Mayclin Stephenson, Michael Olaf Montessori Company, 2013

The Montessori Toddler, Simone Davies, Workman Publishing, 2019

Montessori from the Start: The Child at Home, from Birth to Age Three (1st Edition), Paula Polk Lillard and Lynn Lillard Jessen, Schocken, 2003

Understanding the Human Being: The Importance of the First Three Years of Life (The Clio Montessori Series), Silvana Quattrocchi Montanaro, ABC-CLIO, 1991

Montessori: The Science Behind the Genius, Angeline Stoll Lillard, Oxford University Press, 2008

BOOKS ABOUT BIRTHING

Birth Without Fear: The Judgment-Free Guide to Taking Charge of Your Pregnancy, Birth, and Postpartum, January Harshe, Hachette Books, 2019

Ina May's Guide to Childbirth, Ina May Gaskin, Bantam, 2003

Spiritual Midwifery, Ina May Gaskin, Book Publishing Company (TN), 2002

BOOKS ABOUT BABIES

Baby's First Year Milestones: Promote and Celebrate Your Baby's Development with Monthly Games and Activities, Aubrey Hargis, Rockridge Press, 2018

Dear Parent: Caring for Infants with Respect (2nd Edition), Magda Gerber, Resources for Infant Educarers (RIE), 2003

Your Self-Confident Baby: How to Encourage Your Child's Natural Abilities—From the Very Start, Magda Gerber and Allison Johnson, John Wiley & Sons, Inc., 2012

Elevating Child Care: A Guide to Respectful Parenting, Janet Lansbury, CreateSpace Independent Publishing Platform, 2014

60 activités Montessori pour mon bébé (365 activités), Marie-Hélène Place, Nathan, 2016

POSITIVE PARENTING

Positive Discipline: The First Three Years, Revised and Updated Edition: From Infant to Toddler— Laying the Foundation for Raising a Capable, Confident Child, Jane Nelsen, Ed D, Cheryl Irwin, MA, and Rosyln Ann Duffy, Harmony, 2007

How to Talk So Little Kids Will Listen: A Survival Guide to Life with Children Ages 2-7, Joanna Faber and Julie King, Scribner, 2017

Nonviolent Communication: A Language of Life, Marshall B. Rosenberg, PhD, Puddledancer Press, 2015

GRATITUDE AND APPRECIATION FOR. . .

EACH OTHER—This book could not have been written without the magic of having each other as writing partners. To be able to collaborate on this book was a dream. We are so grateful for the opportunity to birth this book together with ease and grace.

OUR DESIGNERS—Our enormous thanks to Sanny van Loon for her beautiful illustrations that bring the book to life. Sanny has been so patient with our requests to ensure everything is accurate and clear, and she delivered such delightful artwork, which we adore. To Galen Smith for your genius in laying out the book and making it easy to read, and also for putting up with all our requests. And we are so happy to use the book design of Hiyoko Imai who designed Simone's first book, *The Montessori Toddler.*

THE PUBLISHER—To the Workman Publishing team for jumping on board with a resounding YES! at the idea for this book. Thanks to Maisie for the always thoughtful feedback and questions; to Sun for your help editing; to Kate for your careful eye; and to Moira, Chloe, Rebecca, Cindy, and the team for getting this book into readers' hands. A small but mighty team.

OUR CONTRIBUTORS—Thank you so much for being part of this project. Your contributions make this book even richer. Big thanks to Nicole, Ahoefa, Jaya, Maria, Neus, Theresa, Pilar, Amy, and Pamela for sharing your Montessori experiences with us. And to Karin for being the voice of the newborn—your work is so important.

OUR SUPPORTERS—We'd love to thank our sisters and friends who supported us through this writing process, read through and shared feedback. Thank you Florish Echefu, Rahma Yelwa, Zoe Paul, and Sophia Ohuabunwa. And to Jackie and Tania and also to early readers Julia, Mila, Meghan, and Chloe for all the valuable insights and encouragement. Thank you so much to Angeline Stoll Lillard. Your kindness in offering to read the book, your support—and like an added gift, your meticulous comments—are all so appreciated.

OUR MONTESSORI FAMILY—we both receive so much support and love from the Montessori community. You truly fuel us. Judi Orion helped Simone see the world through the eyes of the infant; Ferne van Zyl;

An Morison and Annabel Needs were responsible for Simone falling in love with the Montessori approach; Heidi Phillipart-Alcock introduced Simone to the wonders of Amsterdam as well as being a Montessori mentor over the years; Julia Preziosi and her school Northern Kentucky Montessori Academy introduced Junnifa to Montessori and caused her to immediately fall in love. Pilar Bewley and Jeanne Marie Paynel guided Junnifa to take the AMI 03 training. Patty Wallner's training inspired Junnifa and prepared her to understand and support babies. And to all the Montessori friends who have been such a sounding board from Instagram to Facebook groups and beyond.

FAMILIES AT JACARANDA TREE MONTESSORI and **FRUITFUL ORCHARD MONTESSORI**—Simone feels very grateful to work with the amazing families who come to her classes at Jacaranda Tree Montessori in Amsterdam. She loves learning from these families every day. Junnifa is honored to be entrusted by the families at Fruitful Orchard with their most precious possessions. It is a constant joy to watch the children blossom and see the parents grow and transform along with their children.

OUR FAMILIES—To our own families for being patient with us as we jumped on Zoom calls, edited into the evenings, and discussed colors of illustrations until we were completely satisfied. Your support means so much. Uzo, Oliver, Emma, Solu, Metu, and Biendu—you collectively are our inspiration. To our parents who have never doubted us and always supported us. We love you so much.

ALL THE THINGS—For freedom, for knowledge, for connection, for nature, for cycling through the city and the fields, for cups of tea and sweet treats, for cabins and blankets, for nourishing food and simple pleasures, for museums and photography. The things that feed the spirit for us to do the work we do with such joy. Junnifa would also like to thank God and Jesus Christ, the author and finisher of her faith.

A special mention to Grazia Honegger Fresco who has continued Dr. Montessori's work in Rome and who passed in her sleep on September 30, 2020. Thank you for your unending and rich work for all the children.

INDEX

ONLINE RESOURCES

Visit Workman.com/montessori for DIY Montessori mobile templates and other bonus material.